YOUR SEXUALITY WORKBOOK
Fourth Edition

Mary Ann Watson
Metropolitan State College
of Denver

with student associates
Jessie Briegel
Jason O'Connor
Nadja Tizer

KENDALL/HUNT PUBLISHING COMPANY
4050 Westmark Drive   Dubuque, Iowa 52002

YOUR SEXUALITY WORKBOOK

TABLE OF CONTENTS

From the Author, to You the Student:

How do you learn? I've observed over many years of classroom teaching experience and clinical psychology practice that learning primarily takes place outside the classroom or office. Those few hours that I have direct contact with you the student should be times for inspiration--a jogging of your thought processes, a piquing of your curiosity about a certain subject. Yet most learning will take place outside--in your home, at your work, with your friends, and/or when you apply some of the ideas to your day-to-day life.

This workbook is a learning tool, a way to transition between the classroom and your life. You are (probably) willing to reveal only so much within the classroom setting, particularly on a subject as personal as sexuality. Even the safest and most nonjudgmental of classrooms leave many feelings and issues unexpressed. I hope that this workbook will allow you, and push you, to explore some of these thoughts and feelings. This will provide you, individually, an opportunity to evaluate your own values, beliefs, and behaviors, and come to a greater understanding of your own sexuality.

This workbook consists of research excerpts, worksheets, case studies, activities, and other materials organized around three components of your sexual life--**the personal, the relational, and the cultural**. The first five chapters--**the personal**--focus on self-assessment. You will have an opportunity to assess your own values and beliefs, conduct your own sex history, and trace your own sex education. The values and behavior assessment devices will be repeated in Chapter 21 so that you can compare your before-course and after-course beliefs and behaviors.

Chapters 6 through 14 look at your **relational** sexuality. Why do you like and love certain people? What sorts of communication do you have with friends and partners? What are the similarities and differences among persons in what they find arousing? Is your point of view the only acceptable point of view? If you were to have a sexual problem or your partner had a sexual problem, what would you do?

The final chapters--15 through 21--include exercises related to the **culture** in which you live. How is sex presented in the media? How have these images affected you? What are the laws about sex in your state? How do laws differ from state to state? How do different cultures think about sex?

This workbook also includes additional features:

(1)   A brief bibliography for each chapter at the end of the book with a few well-known primary source studies or books that might be of interest if you wish to pursue the subject;

(2)   A glossary of words appearing in this textual material that may not be familiar to you;

(3)   A brief resource list of national addresses, phone numbers, and websites for organizations that could be contacted for more information.

As you can see from the back cover of the book, I did not work alone on this project. I've had the able assistance of three students: Jessie Briegel, who served as a teaching assistant in my human sexuality course at Metropolitan State College of Denver and is presently an educator at Planned Parenthood of Colorado, and Jason O'Connor and Nadja Tizer, outstanding undergraduate students in my sexuality courses who are planning to complete graduate work in this field of study. They tempered my tendency to become too academic. They provided the necessary balance to keep this a workbook of challenging and fun exercises for sexual self-assessment.

Enjoy! Hopefully this workbook will be an exciting adventure into your personal sexual world.

M.A. Watson

CHAPTER 1

WHY STUDY SEXUALITY?

"Being sexual is an essential part of being human."

Strong, DeVault, Sayad, and Yarber,
Human Sexuality, 2002

Sex is central to your existence. It is a subject that is thought of frequently and yet rarely discussed. What are your sexual values? What are your sexual behaviors? Do you believe that your behaviors or values will change as a result of taking a course in human sexuality? Evaluate this by completing the two short tests in this chapter ("A Look At Your Sexual Values" and "A Look At Your Sexual Behaviors") and then by comparing the results with your answers on the same tests taken at the end of the semester (Chapter 21). These exercises will aid you in assessing your sexual world.

Chapter 1 Contents:

A. **Are You a Sexpert?**
B. **A Look At Your Sexual Values**
C. **A Look At Your Sexual Behaviors**
D. **Research Excerpt: "Effects of a University Subject on Attitudes Toward Human Sexuality" and Reaction Questions**
E. **Activities**
    1. **Newspaper Article**
    2. **Magazine Sex Survey**
    3. **Volunteer Bias**

Are You a Sexpert?

Complete this pre-test before you start reading your sexuality textbook to evaluate your basic knowledge of human sexuality. Answer the questions and then check the correct responses on the following pages.

Mark **T** or **F** on the line before the question.

F   1. The average American first has intercourse at 13 or 14.

F   2. A person can get AIDS by having anal intercourse even if neither partner is infected with the AIDS virus.

T   3. Petroleum jelly or Vaseline are not good lubricants to use with a condom or diaphragm.

T   4. More than one of four (25%) American men have had a sexual experience with another male during either their teens or adult years.

T   5. It is difficult to tell whether a person is homosexual just by their appearance and gestures.

F   6. A woman cannot get pregnant if a man withdraws his penis before he ejaculates.

T   7. Teenage boys and men should examine their testicles for lumps just as regularly as women should examine their breasts.

F   8. Menopause causes most women to lose interest in having sex.

T   9. Sixty to eighty percent of women have masturbated either as children or after they have grown up.

F   10. The average length of a man's erect penis is eight to ten inches.

T   11. Women, like men, experience nocturnal (during sleep) orgasms.

F   12. Both women and men ejaculate fluid at orgasm.

F   13. Presence of the hymen is positive evidence a female is a virgin.

T   14. Athletic performance is not affected by sex prior to a game.

F   15. The size of a man's penis can be judged by the size of his hands and feet.

T   16. Semen is fattening.

F   17. Persons of differing racial backgrounds have varying sex drives.

F   18. Alcohol and marijuana inhibit sexual responses.

F   19. Sexual desire and ability decrease markedly after 40 or 50.

T   20. A woman can get pregnant at any time during her monthly cycle.

F   21. Urination after intercourse, or having sex in a standing position, will prevent pregnancy.

F   22. Sexually explicit material provokes persons to commit criminal sex acts.

F   23. Married couples in the US may legally engage in any type of sexual activity they mutually agree upon.

_F_ 24. Physicians are the best trained of all professionals to deal with the sexual problems of their patients.

_F_ 25. A full penile erection is necessary for ejaculation.

_T_ 26. Intercourse can ease the pain of arthritis.

_F_ 27. If you don't feel jealous, you are not in love.

_T_ 28. All males have erections at certain intervals during their sleep.

_F_ 29. A transvestite is someone who wants a surgical gender change.

_F_ 30. The time from testing HIV+ and getting AIDS is at most 5 years.

_T_ 31. The majority of sex crimes against children are committed by adults who are acquaintances or relatives of the victim.

_F_ 32. A female must experience orgasm in order to become pregnant.

_T_ 33. A female can become pregnant the first time she has sexual intercourse.

_T_ 34. Alcohol is a common cause of temporary erectile problems.

_F_ 35. An imbalance of sexual hormones is the most frequent cause of homosexuality.

_T_ 36. A large majority of parents want their children to be given sex education in the schools.

_F_ 37. The age at which puberty starts has stayed constant over the last 200 years.

_T_ 38. The most common sexually transmitted infections on college campuses are gonorrhea and chlamydia.

_T_ 39. A man usually expels more than 200 million sperm in each ejaculation.

_F_ 40. Fertilization of the ovum occurs in the vagina.

_F_ 41. In all countries, AIDS is mainly a disease of male homosexuals.

_T_ 42. For most women, birth control pills have more benefits than negative health effects.

_F_ 43. Teenage girls have easier pregnancies and healthier babies than older women.

_F_ 44. Herpes can be cured.

_T_ 45. RU-486 is a new type of AIDS test.

_T_ 46. Women can get pregnant without penetration of the vagina by the penis.

_T_ 47. The HIV virus can be transmitted via oral sex.

_F_ 48. All females who are HIV+ will pass the virus to their unborn children.

_F_ 49. Masturbation can be harmful if it occurs more than twice per week.

_T_ 50. Infants are capable of erections, vaginal lubrication, and orgasm.

Answers to Pre-test: Are You A Sexpert?

1. **F:** The average American first has intercourse at 16 or 17.
2. **F:** A person cannot contract AIDS unless their partner is HIV+.
3. **T:** These products will tend to break down the material of the condom or diaphragm and make them less effective.
4. **T:** Fewer than 25% of males identify themselves as homosexual, yet 25% have had one or more same-sex sexual experiences.
5. **T:** Most homosexuals do not fit a stereotypical picture of homosexuals.
6. **F:** Cowper's gland fluid containing viable sperm is released prior to the main ejaculation.
7. **T:** Testicular cancer is very dangerous and can be life-threatening. Testicular cancer is found most often in men between the ages of 18-35.
8. **F:** Menopause for some women leads to an increase in sex drive; for most women, sex drive stays the same as before menopause.
9. **T:** Because masturbation is seen as a private activity, many women do not realize how common the activity is.
10. **F:** The average length is five to seven inches.
11. **T:** Women as well as men can have orgasms during REM (Rapid Eye Movement) sleep.
12. **F:** A certain percentage of women have some emission of fluid at orgasm, but no spurting of ejaculate as men do.
13. **F:** Hymens can stretch out of place with a finger, a tampon insertion, or certain types of rigorous exercise. Some women are born without hymens; some may retain them even after intercourse.
14. **T:** Loss of semen does not weaken a male in any way.
15. **F:** There is no correlation between penis and foot or hand size, but there is a correlation between flaccid (non-erect) penis size and body type or shape.
16. **F:** A teaspoon of semen is approximately 36 calories, composed of protein and fat.
17. **F:** There is no evidence to support racial differences in sex drive.
18. **T:** All drug use deadens nerve endings, therefore lessening sexual response. Small amounts, however, lessen inhibitions, and therefore may increase sexual comfort.
19. **F:** Sexual frequency may decrease in long-term relationships but ability and desire do not generally decrease.
20. **T:** There are cases on record of pregnancies at any time during a female cycle.
21. **F:** The urinary tract is separate from the vaginal tract.
22. **F:** Violent, not sexually explicit, material leads to possible increases in aggressive behavior of those already violence-prone.
23. **F:** Each state has separate laws regulating sexual behavior. Many states outlaw even consensual marital acts of a certain nature, e.g. oral sex or anal intercourse.
24. **F:** Some medical schools do provide sexuality training for their students; many, however, do not.
25. **F:** The process of ejaculation and erection are separate physiological processes.
26. **T:** Any exercise can be helpful to ease joint pain.
27. **F:** Jealousy is more a sign of insecurity than love.
28. **T:** Normally, males have erections during REM (Rapid Eye Movement) sleep, at approximately two to three hour intervals.
29. **F:** Many transsexuals want surgical changes in their genitals; transvestites are generally content with their biological sex.
30. **F:** There are many documented cases of persons carrying the virus for over 10 years and not being diagnosed with AIDS.
31. **T:** It is usually heterosexual male family members who commit crimes against children.
32. **F:** Orgasm and pregnancy in women are two separate physiological functions.
33. **T:** Pregnancy is possible any time sexual intercourse occurs, from the first ovulation until menopause.
34. **T:** Alcohol abuse can lead to erectile problems.
35. **F:** We do not know how sexual orientation is determined but hormone levels do not seem to be a primary factor.

36. **T:** Most parents want sex education for their children.
37. **F:** Over time puberty has occurred at a younger and younger age.
38. **T:** The most common college STD's are chlamydia and gonorrhea.
39. **T:** The numbers show how small a sperm cell is.
40. **F:** Fertilization usually takes place in the fallopian tubes.
41. **F:** In many countries the numbers of men and women affected are equal. AIDS is no longer a primarily homosexual disease; the greatest increase in incidence is in heterosexual women.
42. **T:** Most women have more positive than negative effects.
43. **F:** Teens have higher risk pregnancies and more health problems.
44. **F:** A drug can lower the pain and reduce the symptoms of herpes, but the virus stays in the body throughout a person's lifetime.
45. **F:** RU-486 is a drug that terminates pregnancies.
46. **T:** While rare, sperm deposited close to the vagina can cause a pregnancy.
47. **T:** HIV can be transmitted orally when infected semen or vaginal secretions get into open sores or cuts in and around the mouth.
48. **T:** Actually, all babies born to HIV+ women will be born HIV+. Seventy-five percent will seroconvert to HIV-, and twenty-five percent will remain HIV+.
49. **F:** Masturbation does not have harmful effects.
50. **T:** These are responses that happen normally in infants.

Are you a Sexpert? What is your score? Count the number of answers you had correct out of the 50 questions:

      41 - 50......................**SEXPERT**
      31 - 40......................**Almost there**
      25 or lower...............**Listen well this semester!**

A Look At Your Sexual Values

Take a few minutes to complete the following <u>values</u> survey. Circle your response on the 7-point scale below indicating your **intolerance for, neutrality toward, or tolerance for** the behaviors in the column on the left. Your answer does not reflect your personal behaviors, simply your tolerance or intolerance for each specific behavior in general.

Values	Intolerant (disagree with)			Neutral	Tolerant (agree with)		
1. Masturbation	-3	-2	-1	0	+1	+2	(+3)
2. Sex education in schools for adolescents	-3	-2	-1	0	+1	+2	(+3)
3. Condom availability in junior high and high schools	-3	-2	-1	0	+1	+2	(+3)
4. Homosexuality	-3	-2	-1	0	+1	+2	(+3)
5. Bisexuality	-3	-2	-1	0	(+1)	+2	(+3)
6. Teenage sexuality (13-17 years of age)	-3	-2	-1	0	(+1)	+2	+3
7. Sex with someone you do not love	-3	-2	-1	0	(+1)	+2	+3
8. Women initiating sex	-3	-2	-1	0	+1	(+2)	+3
9. Abortions available to anyone who desires to terminate a pregnancy	-3	-2	-1	0	+1	(+2)	+3
10. Prostitution as a legal behavior	-3	-2	(-1)	0	+1	+2	+3
11. Explicit magazines being available in stores	-3	-2	(-1)	0	+1	+2	+3
12. Parents being notified and giving permission for a teen daughter's abortion	-3	-2	-1	(0)	+1	+2	+3
13. All doctors being HIV tested and all patients notified	-3	(-2)	-1	0	+1	+2	+3
14. All patients being HIV tested and all doctors notified	-3	-2	-1	0	+1	(+2)	+3
15. Rights of the biological father to continue an unwanted pregnancy	-3	(-2)	-1	0	+1	+2	+3
16. Oral sex	-3	-2	-1	0	+1	(+2)	+3
17. Premarital sex if in love	-3	-2	-1	0	+1	(+2)	+3
18. Premarital sex if engaged	-3	-2	-1	0	+1	(+2)	+3
19. Extramarital necking or petting	-3	-2	-1	(0)	+1	(+2)	+3
20. Extramarital sex	-3	-2	-1	(0)	+1	+2	+3

A Look At Your Sexual Behaviors

Take a few minutes to complete the following sexual <u>behaviors</u> survey. Mark on a 5-point scale below the frequency with which you have engaged in this behavior.

Behavior	Never	Rarely	Some-times	Frequently	Very Often
1. Oral sex	1	2	(3)	4	5
2. Sex without contraception	1	2	(3)	4	5
3. Sex with contraception	1	2	3	4	(5)
4. Use of different positions in sex	1	2	3	4	(5)
5. Masturbation	1	2	(3)	4	5
6. Masturbation with a partner	1	2	(3)	4	5
7. Talk about sex with friends	1	2	3	(4)	5
8. Talk about sex with partner	1	2	3	(4)	5
9. Talk about sex with family	1	2	(3)	4	5
10. Watch sexually explicit movies	1	2	(3)	4	5
11. Read sexually explicit books or magazines	1	2	(3)	4	5
12. Abortion	1	(2)	3	4	5
13. Use sex toys (i.e., vibrators, food)	1	2	(3)	4	5
14. Sex with more than one partner simultaneously	1	(2)	3	4	5
15. Have safe sex (when sexual)	1	2	3	(4)	5
16. Anal sex	1	(2)	3	4	5
17. Extramarital affairs	1	(2)	3	4	5
18. Premarital sex	1	2	3	(4)	5
19. Sex with a partner of the same sex	1	(2)	3	4	5
20. Using fantasy during sex	1	2	(3)	4	5

Research Excerpt

Question: Do sexual attitudes and behaviors change as a result of taking a sex education class?

Effects of a University Subject on Attitudes Toward Human Sexuality*
Wendy Patton, Ph.D., and Mary Mannison, M.A.

Although previous investigations into the effects of human sexuality by and large support the common-sense notion that learning does have some bearing on attitudes (Alzate, 1974; Dearth & Cassell, 1976; Fischer, 1986; Kilman, Wanlass, Sabalis & Sullivan, 1981; Redfering & Roberts, 1976; Rees & Zimmerman, 1974; Serdahely & Ziemba, 1984; Taylor, 1982; Zuckerman, Tushup & Finner, 1976), there are some anomalies in the findings, including reports that even negate the relationship altogether (Woods & Mandetta, 1975). Inconsistencies in the findings have led to questions about possible bias due to the characteristics of students who elect to enroll in a Human Sexuality subject (Bernard & Schwartz, 1977; Carter & Frankel, 1983; Cerny & Polyson, 1984), the effect of age and gender on the extent of attitude change (Dearth & Cassell, 1976; Rees & Zimmerman, 1974; Taylor, 1982), and about the legitimacy of measuring attitude change over the relatively short time span of one semester (Smith, Flaherty, Webb, & Mumford, 1984; Stevenson, 1990; Story, 1979).

Questions have also been raised as to why some attitudes changed but not others (Bernard & Schwartz, 1977; Carter & Frankel, 1983; Fischer, 1986; Lance, 1975; Taylor, 1982). Some investigators found a change in attitude, but little change in self-reported behavior (Story, 1979; Taylor, 1982; Yarber & Anno, 1981); others distinguished between gaining *information* about a topic and the attitude held towards it, measuring the former with true/ false or multiple-choice questions and the latter with Likert-type scales (Carter & Frankel, 1983; Fischer, 1986; Smith et al., 1984). Differences in the use and meanings of these words complicate comparisons between studies and pose further questions for analysis.

The intent of the subject in the first place may also be relevant to the investigation of the effects of learning on attitudes, particularly when stated aims can vary widely; for example:

The main focus of this course is to increase the substance and accuracy of the students'
sexual knowledge (Godow & LaFave, 1979, p. 164).

…the cirriculum focus is predominantly on attitudes, values and the students' personal
feelings about their own sexuality (Taylor, 1982, p. 125).

In spite of the fact that their emphasis was informative rather than persuasive, the present authors shared, along with other researchers in this area, a "general impression" that the subject made a difference to the lives of the people taking it (Godow & LaFave, 1979; Serdaheley & Ziemba, 1984). Repeated comments at the end of the semester to the effect that "this subject has changed my life" caused the investigators to wonder "how" and "to what extent."

The following questions, formed by the experience and conclusions of the above-mentioned investigators, led to the main features of the present study:

1. Does a semester's study of Human Sexuality bring about a significant change in overall attitudes?
2. Do attitudes towards some aspects of sexuality change, but not others?
3. Is attitude change tied in any significant way to differences in age and gender?

Instrument
Attitudes towards Sexuality Inventory required participants to respond on a 6-point scale (from Agree Very Strongly to Disagree Very Strongly, with no neutral point) to 72 statements representing 10 attitudinal categories. There were 5 to 11 items in each category. The categories were selected to represent the main content areas of the subject and included (1) contraception, (2) masturbation, (3) sexual behavior across the life span, (4) gender role, (5) gay and lesbian lifestyles, (6) abortion, (7) sexually transmitted

diseases, (8) child sexual abuse, (9) rape, and (10) sex education.

Examples of items in each subscale appear below:

(1) *Contraception* (6 items): Difficult access to contraceptives is one way to control adolescent promiscuity.

(2) *Masturbation* (5 items): Understanding your own body through masturbation helps achieve fulfilling sexual expression.

(3) *Sexual Behavior Across the Life Span* (6 items): The idea of sexual intercourse among the elderly is discomforting.

(4) *Gender Role* (9 items): Women who initiate sexual encounters will probably have sex with anybody.

(5) *Gay and Lesbian Lifestyles* (11 items): Female and male homosexuality is a natural expression of sexuality in humans.

(6) *Abortion* (7 items): Abortion should not be an option for women who have unprotected intercourse.

(7) *Sexually Transmitted Diseases* (5 items): People who have AIDS should be allowed to be members of normal classrooms.

(8) *Child Sexual Abuse* (7 items): Child sexual abuse usually occurs as a single, isolated incident.

(9) *Rape* (8 items): Rape is an expression of an uncontrollable desire for sex.

(10) *Sex Education* (8 items): Sex education is solely the parents' responsibility.

DISCUSSION
Pretest Equivalence

The pretest revealed no significant difference in attitudes between experimental and control groups. A number of researchers have found similar pretest equivalence between groups (Bernard & Schwartz, 1977; Davidson & Darling, 1988; Fischer, 1986; Story, 1979), although the control group for the Bernard and Schwartz study consisted of students who had attempted to enroll in the subject but were not admitted because of quota limits. In other studies, pretests revealed existing differences in attitudes between experimental and control groups, with students electing to enroll in a human sexuality subject being more "permissive" or "accepting…egalitarian" in their attitudes, and more experienced in behavior (Allgeier & Allgeier, 1984; Godow & LaFave, 1979; Yarber & Anno, 1981; Zuckerman, Tushup, & Finner, 1976). Similarly, Cerny and Poulson (1984) found that students in their control group (enrolled in Introductory Psychology) held more homonegative attitudes than students who enrolled in a Human Sexuality course. On the same issue, Stevenson (1990) found students interested in taking a sexuality course did *not* differ significantly in their attitudes toward homosexuality from students who were not interested in taking the course.

In any event, the proposition that students who choose to enroll in a Human Sexuality elective may start their study with already better-informed attitudes about sexual issues was *not* supported by pretest results in the present study, suggesting attitude shifts measured at the end of the semester have a genuine relationship to the intervening educational experience.

The posttest revealed a significant shift in attitudes overall for both experimental groups and no such significant shift in the control group, confirming the authors' original impression, based on informal comments made by students, that the subject did "make a difference" to their lives. The results support the findings of other works which have used control groups in their research design and which have shown some change in student sexuality attitudes after subject input (Carter & Frankel, 1983; Bernard & Schwartz, 1983; Cerny & Poulson, 1984; Godow & LaFave, 1979; Fischer, 1986; Story, 1979).

Changes Related to Age and Gender

Subjects in the present study were from a wide age range (20-29 through 50-59); however, statistical analysis indicated no difference between the four age groups at either pretest or posttest.

There is no clear picture with regard to gender effects, with some studies reporting little difference between males and females (Carter & Frankel, 1983; Godow & LaFave, 1979), and others reporting significant differences (Abler & Sedlacek, 1989; Dearth & Cassell, 1976; Yarber & Anno, 1981). Again, the present study had a very small number of males in each group, an element which has been consistent for the seven years the course has been operating. Informal comparisons of data suggest this may be an area that deserves further investigation.

In conclusion, the findings of the present study offer further support to the majority of research in this area. One of the outcomes of sexuality education is a significant change in attitude, even in this case, where the emphasis was on information-giving rather than specific persuasion. The importance of ongoing evaluation of such courses is not only important for course administrators, but also for the continuing development of sex education. Kirby's (1980) review of school sex education programs may increase knowledge and facilitate attitudinal changes. As many of the men and women in the present study may teach human sexuality in schools, the importance of helping them to identify and assess their own attitudes, and evaluating the success of these processes, remains vital.

* Reprinted by permission of the *Journal of Sex Education and Therapy*

Research Excerpt Reaction Questions:

1. Does a semester-length university course in human sexuality bring about a significant change in a student's overall sexual attitudes?

   Yes, any education that directly relates to an individual especially in their everyday lives will impact/benefit/make aware

2. Is attitude change tied in any significant way to differences in age and gender of a student?

   Sometimes older individuals can be harder to convince due to personal experience & sometimes males can be more difficult to influence but its very subjective to the person

3. Do student enrollees in a human sexuality course begin with better informed attitudes about sexual issues than students not interested in taking the course? Explain.

   Yes. College is geared more to the personal interests of people & its a choice whether or not to take the course.

4. Which of the references cited in the text of the article sound most interesting to you? Why?

   "General impression" that the subject made a difference in the lives of people taking it.

   - Why? To examine results in more detail

Activities

1. **Newspaper Article**

   Clip a recent newspaper article on a sexuality issue. Evaluate the article using critical thinking skills. Write a few paragraphs about the article considering the following questions: *"Seniors having more sex than you might think, study says"*

   1. What are the assumptions that the researchers are making?

   2. What is the sample size?

   3. What were the conclusions of the researchers from this material?

   4. Are there any alternative conclusions that have been drawn?

2. **Magazine Sex Survey**

   Look up two previously published sex surveys. (See Chapter One References at the end of the book for examples.) Compare the two surveys for language used, populations studied, dates the surveys were taken, and results of the surveys.

3. **Volunteer Bias**

   Definition: A type of sampling problem in research where there are often specific differences between people who agree to participate in a sex research project and those who do not agree to participate.

   How many of you would volunteer to complete a lengthy questionnaire about your sexual attitudes or behaviors? What differences might there be between those who would volunteer and those who would not? Test these questions by choosing a sexual topic (any topic of hypothetical interest) and asking ten persons if they would be willing to answer a lengthy survey on the topic. If they agree, check a few demographic characteristics (i.e., age, vocation, sex) and compare them with the same demographic characteristics of those who would not agree to participate.

CHAPTER 2

SEX RESEARCH

"Perhaps never before in history has there been such a huge disparity between the open display of eroticism in a society and that society's great reluctance to speak about private sexual practices."

Michael, Gagnon, Laumann,
and Kolata, *Sex in America*, 1994

Why do sex research? There are so many unanswered questions--questions concerning sexual behavior, values, beliefs, cultural differences, what is typical or atypical--that research is often the only way to answer these questions. All research starts with a question, a researcher, and observations of behavior. This workbook includes many excerpts from research material. Maybe you will find yourself asking questions which may result in your detailed observation of your own or others' behavior.

Chapter 2 Contents:

A. Research Excerpt: "Sexual Behavior in the Human Male" and Reaction Questions
B. Tips for Reading Journal Articles
C. Your Own Sex History
D. Activities
    1. Developing a Survey Instrument
    2. Collecting Advice Columns
    3. Answering Advice Column Questions
    4. Comparing Journal and Popular Articles

Research Excerpt

Question: Has sexual behavior changed in the last 50 years? How do the Kinsey Reports (1948) differ from *Sex in America*, a 1994 study?

Sexual Behavior in the Human Male *
Alfred Kinsey, Wardell B. Pomeroy, and Clyde E. Martin

Total Sexual Outlet

A finer educational breakdown suggests that the sexually most active group is the one that goes into high school but not beyond tenth grade.

The single males who have the lowest frequencies of total sexual outlet are those who belong to the college level. The boys who never go beyond eighth grade in school stand intermediate between the high school and the college groups...

The social level picture for total outlet among married males is quite the same as for single males. The married males who have the highest total outlet are those who went to high school but not beyond. This is true for every age group between 16 and 40 years of age, and may be true at older ages...

(p. 337)

Masturbation

Ultimately, between 93 and 97 percent of all males have masturbatory experience...

Differences in incidence and frequencies of masturbation at different educational levels are even more striking among married males. At the grade school level, there are only 20 to 30 percent who masturbate in their early marital years, and the accumulative incidence figure climbs only a bit during the later years of marriage. The frequencies are very low. The high school group closely matches the grade school group in this regard. On the other hand, among the married males who have been to college, 60 to 70 percent masturbate in each of the age periods.

(p. 339)

Pre-marital Intercourse

Pre-marital intercourse, whatever its source, is more abundant in the grade school and high school levels, and less common at the college level. Even in the period between adolescence and 15 the active incidence includes nearly half (48% and 43%) of the lower educational groups, but only 10 percent of the boys who will ultimately go to college. In the later teens, 85 percent of the grade school group and 75 percent of the high school group is having pre-marital intercourse, while the figure for the college group is still only 42 percent. In later years the differentials are not so great, but compared with the grade school group, it is still only about two-thirds as many of the college males who have such intercourse.

The accumulative incidence figures for pre-marital intercourse show much the same differences. About 98 percent of the grade school level has experience before marriage, while only 84 percent of the high school level and 67 percent of the college level is involved.

(p. 347)

Nudity

Most amazing of all, customs in regard to nudity may vary between the social levels of a single community. In our American culture, there is a greater acceptance of nudity at upper social levels, and a great restraint at lower social levels. Compared with previous generations, there is a more general acceptance of nudity in the upper social level today. There is an increasing amount of nudity within the family circle in this upper level. There is rather free exposure in the home for both sexes, including the parents and the children of all ages, at times of dressing and at times of bathing. Still more significant, there is an increasing habit among upper level persons of sleeping in partial or complete nudity. This is probably more common among males, though there is a considerable number of upper level females who also sleep nude. Among the males of the college level, nearly half (41%) frequently sleep nude, about one-third (34%) of the high school males do so, but only one-sixth (16%) of the males of the grade school level sleep that way.

Finally, the upper level considers nudity almost an essential concomitant of intercourse. About 90 percent of the persons at this level regularly have coitus nude. The upper level finds it difficult to comprehend that anyone should regularly and as a matter of preference have intercourse while clothed. This group uses clothing only under unusual circumstances, or when variety and experimentation are the desired objectives in the intercourse. On the other hand, nude coitus is regularly had by only 66 percent of those who never go beyond high school, and by 43 percent of those who never go beyond grade school.

(p. 366)

*Reprinted by permission of The Kinsey Institute for Research in Sex, Gender, and Reproduction, Inc.

Sex in America

Michael, Gagnon, Laumann, and Kolata (1994) in *Sex in America* interviewed 3,432 subjects. They found that, among Americans from eighteen to fifty-nine, about 60% of the men and 40% of the women said they masturbated in the past year. This study also showed that since the average age of marriage is now in the mid-twenties, few Americans wait until they marry to have sex. Social class also plays a role, with less-educated people marrying earlier than better-educated people. However, the more educated people were, the more partners they had over their lifetime.

Reactions to nudity are also of interest. Some age differences exist, with 81% of 18-44-year-old women and 67% of 45-49-year-old women liking to watch their partners undress. Among men, 93% of the younger men (18-44) and 87% of older men enjoy the same activity.

Research Excerpt Reaction Questions

1. Kinsey found that college-educated males had a lower frequency for sex than did high school or grade school educated males. The 1994 study, however, seemed to show that more highly educated persons have more marriages or primary relationships over their lifetimes than do high school or grade school educated persons. Why do you believe these differences exist?

2. Masturbation rates have shifted from 1948 until 1994. Present male masturbation rates are more like the 1948 rates for college males. This would imply that grade school and high school educated male rates have increased. Why do you believe there has been a change?

3. Comfort with nudity among grade school and high school educated males also has increased from the time of the Kinsey study until the *Sex In America* study. How do you interpret these differences?

Tips for Reading Journal Articles

Academic journal articles are among the most reliable sources of information concerning sexuality. These articles are written by professionals in the field of human sexuality, and are reviewed prior to publishing by the author's academic peers to insure their accuracy.

The most important journals devoted to sex research are:

American Journal of Psychiatry
Archives of Sexual Behavior
Family Planning Perspectives
Journal of Homosexuality
Journal of Marriage and Family Counseling
Journal of Marital and Family Therapy
Journal of Marriage and the Family
Journal of Reproductive Medicine
Journal of Sex and Marital Therapy
Journal of Sex Education and Therapy (publication suspended 1995)
Journal of Sex Research
Sex Roles
Sexuality and Disability
Sexually Transmitted Diseases
SIECUS Report (Sex Information and Education Council of the United States)

Research articles usually have six sections: Abstract, Introduction or Review of the literature, Method, Results, Discussion and Summary, and References.

The <u>Abstract</u> section is a summary of the article, and is usually one to three paragraphs which are indented and placed at the beginning of the article. Read this portion first. Oftentimes, this will provide sufficient information for you to determine if you wish to read the remainder of the article.

The <u>Introduction</u> usually consists of the main questions (hypotheses) to be studied and a <u>literature review</u> of other studies which have preceded this particular study. It gives you an idea of the author's reasons for pursuing this particular topic.

The <u>Methods</u> section tells you how the study was undertaken. It describes the subjects of the study as well as the materials (tests, surveys, etc.) and procedures used to complete the study.

The <u>Results</u> section gives the outcome of the research. This is usually reported in numerical form, oftentimes using simple to complex statistical measures.

The <u>Discussion and Summary</u> portion pulls together the Introduction and Methods and Results Sections. It compares the results of this study with previously mentioned studies and attempts to explain any differences. Oftentimes this section concludes by suggesting areas of future research and study.

The <u>Reference</u> section is a bibliography of all the sources of information quoted in the research article.

As you read research studies, be a good consumer. Think critically! Even though these are scholarly articles that have been reviewed, there can be biases that can be challenged. A good research reader is one who may be a good future researcher--one who reads critically and asks questions which may be the source of future hypotheses and future studies.

Your Own Sex History

The Kinsey studies and the *Sex in America* study began with sex histories--approximately 18,000 for Kinsey, and 3,400 for *Sex in America*. Researchers and their colleagues in both studies sat with their subjects for many hours and collected information about their sexual beliefs, values, and behaviors. The following sex history format will allow you to do the same for yourself. Answer each of the questions as honestly as you can. If you wish to add more than space allows, just add your own paper and complete your answers. This is confidential and for your personal use only.

Background Information

1.   Gender: Male _____   Female   X

2.   Age: _20_

3.   Your birth order is _only_ (oldest, middle, youngest, only).

4.   The number of siblings in your family:
     Sisters _____   Half-brothers _____
     Brothers _____   Step-sisters _____
     Half-sisters _____   Step-brothers _____

5.   Your parents are:
     Married _____   Deceased _____
     Divorced __X____   Never married _____
     Separated __X____

6.   What are your thoughts about your parents' marital status?
     disappointed

7.   Your marital status is:
     Single __X___   Married _____
     Cohabiting _____   Divorced/Separated _____
     Engaged _____   Widowed _____

8.   What are your thoughts about your marital status?
     content but eager for more stability

9.   Are you sexually active?   YES X
                                  NO _____

10. What are your thoughts about your sexual activity level?
     reluctant of past but ambitious for future

11. What is your sexual orientation?
    Heterosexual _____X_____
    Homosexual _____
    Bisexual _____X_____

12. What are your thoughts about your orientation?
    content

13. With whom are you presently living?
    father

14. Which one relationship in your own life do you presently value most? Why?
    father — closest bond

15. Which one relationship in your own life do you presently value least? Why?
    past reoccuring friends —
    there were reasons why we grew
    for apart

Sex Education

1. Describe your formal sex education in school.
   thorough — all grades.

2. Describe your church, synagogue, or mosque sex education.
   none — catholic beef not consistant

3. Describe the sex education you received from your parents.
   good — always open & informative

4. What is your mother's ethnicity? white

   A. How has this affected you?
      hasn't

5. What is your father's ethnicity? white

   A. How has this affected you?
      hasn't

      it's simpley life

6. How would you describe your parents' relationship?

    neutral

7. How would you describe your parents' sexual relationship?

8. What impact has your parents' marital and sexual relationship had on you?

    I value honesty & affection more & more

9. What are the expectations that your parents have for your sexuality?

    cautious & smart — I deserve better than what I've chosen.

10. What do you feel about your parents' sexual values?

    Dignified.

11. How would you describe your relationship with your mother?

    Stronger now after traumatic events but has always been loving & strong.

12. How would you describe your relationship with your father?

    Strong as well. very important aspect of my life.

13. What was your informal sex education from your siblings and peers?

    usually "talked-up" & made

Social and Sexual Experiences as a Child

1. Describe any sex play that you engaged in as a child.

2. What did you think about your gender and your body as a child?

3.   What were your negative sexual experiences as a child?

4.   How have these negative experiences affected you as an adult?

5.   What were your positive sexual experiences as a child?

6.   How have these positive experiences affected you as an adult?

Puberty and Adolescence

1.   When did you first learn to masturbate?

2.   How did you learn to masturbate?

3.   Did you use fantasies or certain materials or objects to masturbate? Explain.

4.   What percentage of the time did you masturbate to orgasm?

5.   Has your masturbation pattern stayed the same or changed? Explain.

6.   (Females only) When did menstruation begin?

7.   How were you prepared for menstruation?

8.   What was your emotional response to menstruation?

9.   (Males only) When did you have your first nocturnal emission (wet dream)?

10.   How were you prepared for this experience?

11.   What was you emotional reaction to wet dreams?

12.   How was high school for you socially?

13.   How was high school for you sexually?

14.   In high school, what did you think about your body?

15.   When was your first intercourse with a partner?

16.   What was your reaction to your first intercourse experience?

17.   What sexual experience did you have in adolescence with same-sex peers?

18.   What were your thoughts about these same-sex sexual experiences?

19.   What were your experiences with pregnancy in adolescence?

20.   What were your experiences with sexually transmitted diseases as an adolescent?

21.   What was your most negative or confusing adolescent sexual experience?

22.   What was your most positive adolescent sexual experience?

Adult Sexuality

1.   What is adulthood like socially and sexually?

2.   What are your best sexual and relationship experiences in adulthood?

3.   What are your most difficult sexual and relationship experiences?

4.   As you review your total dating and sexual history, what were your most positive experiences?

5.   As you review your total dating and sexual history, what were your most negative experiences?

6.   What are the parts of your sexuality that you enjoy the most?

7.   What are the parts of your sexuality that you enjoy least?

Activities

1. **Developing a Survey Instrument**
   Write ten questions (True/False or Strongly Agree to S
   sex research topic such as attitudes toward masturbatio
   harassment. Give these questions to five to ten friends
   Compile the results. Think about your biases in choice
   choice of subjects interviewed.

2. **Collecting Advice Columns**
   Collect "Dear Abby," "Ann Landers," and other newspaper and magazine advice
   columnists for a set period of time (1 week, 2 weeks, etc.). What are the standards being
   reinforced by the columnist? How, if at all, do the columnists use any social science
   research?

3. **Answering Advice Column Questions**
   Collect "Dear Abby," "Ann Landers," and other newspaper and magazine advice
   columnists for one week. Write your own answers to ten of the questions. Are your
   answers similar to or different from the advice given by the "experts?" Why?

4. **Comparing Journal and Popular Articles**
   Choose any topic of interest in human sexuality. Find one popular article (newspaper or
   magazine) and one research journal article on the same topic. Compare the two articles
   in terms of goals, methods used, data collected, and references.

CHAPTER 3

YOUR BODY:
ITS PARTS AND WORKINGS

"In the first place, it's not so easy even to find your vagina. Women go weeks, months, sometimes years without looking at it. I interviewed a high-powered businesswoman who told me she was too busy; she didn't have the time. Looking at your vagina, she said, is a full day's work."

Eve Ensler, *Vagina Monologues*, 1998

You are housed in your own body. Do you know how it works? What are the beliefs that you carry with you about your own workings? Is it harder for you to learn about your sexual self than other parts of your body? This chapter helps you assess your own beliefs about your body and the impact of those beliefs on your behavior.

Chapter 3 Contents:

A.   Sex Talk and Reaction Questions
B.   Rating Your Parts
C.   Your Body: Reaction Questions
D.   Research Excerpt: " Knowledge of and Ability to Learn Genital Terminology" and Reaction Questions
E.   Activities
    1.   Sex Talk
    2.   Culture and Sex Talk
    3.   Erotic Art
    4.   Sex Reassignment
    5.   Self-Examination

Sex Talk

     As you grow up you hear many different names for your sexual parts. Many of these names are not the anatomically correct ones. This use of euphemisms (good words) or slang terms for the anatomical parts often gives you a sense of shame about your anatomy.

     Listed below are terms for various parts of the male and female anatomy, sexual behaviors, and other sex practices. In column A, write the word that you used as a substitute when you were growing up. In column B, write all the additional terms you have heard for that particular term.

	A	B
1. Genitals		
2. Vagina		
3. Clitoris		
4. Penis		
5. Scrotum		
6. Testicles		
7. Breasts		
8. Buttocks		
9. Nipples		
10. Orgasm		
11. Rectum/Anus		
12. Pubic Hair		
13. Masturbation		
14. Menstruation		
15. Urination		
16. Defecation		
17. Intercourse		
18. Gay Man		
19. Lesbian		

"Sex Talk" Reaction Questions

1.   Which of the "Sex Talk" terms did you use as a child? Which do you use as an adult?

2.   Are there any terms above that you, as an adult, do not like to hear? Which ones? Why?

3.   Describe your first experience in discussing sexual anatomy. Was it with a parent? With a peer?

4.   Was your initial information on sexual body parts accurate or inaccurate?

5.   At what age did you first become aware of the word "clitoris" and the sexual organ to which it refers? Why are girls and boys not taught this term as they are taught the term "penis?"

Rating Your Parts

In the blanks below, rate each of your parts according to the following scale:

1..............Very Satisfied
2..............Satisfied
3..............Dissatisfied
4..............Very Dissatisfied

1)_____ hair   14)_____ chest/breasts

2)_____ face   15)_____ arms

3)_____ mouth   16)_____ hands

4)_____ eyes   17)_____ hips

5)_____ nose   18)_____ knees

6)_____ teeth   19)_____ legs

7)_____ ears   20)_____ ankles

8)_____ smile   21)_____ feet

9)_____ chin   22)_____ abdomen

10)_____ facial hair   23)_____ back

11)_____ thighs   24)_____ buttocks

12)_____ neck   25)_____ genitals

13)_____ shoulders

Add your columns of ratings. The possible total score ranges from 25 to 100. The greater your score (60 or above), the more dissatisfied you are with your body. The lower your score (40 or lower), the more satisfied you are with you body.

Your Body: Reaction Questions

1.   What is your first memory about your body?

2.   When you were a child, what comments did others make about your body?

3.   When you were an adolescent, were you self-conscious about your body? In what ways?

4.   When did you first notice that male and female bodies were different?

5.   (Females only) When did you first begin to menstruate?

        A.   What did you think when you first began to menstruate?

        B.   With whom did you discuss your menstruation?

6.   (Males only) Have you had a nocturnal emission (wet dream)?

        A.   What did you think when this occurred?

        B.   With whom did you discuss your wet dreams?

7.   Have you experienced orgasm?

        A.   What did you think when this first occurred?

8.   What do you think when you look at yourself nude in a mirror?

9.   What do you think when your partner looks at you nude?

10.   What do you like most about your body?

11.   What do you like least about your body?

12.   What is your favorite part of a man's body?

13.   What is your favorite part of a woman's body?

14.   What is your least favorite part of a man's body?

15.   What is your least favorite part of a woman's body?

Research Excerpt

Question: Should we teach children correct names for sexual body parts?

Preschoolers' Knowledge of and Ability to Learn Genital Terminology*
Sandy K. Wurtele, Ph.D., Anastasia M. Melzer, B.A., and Laura C. Kast, M.S.

The implicit goal of child sexual abuse (CSA) prevention programs is to prevent sexual exploitation. However, to enhance community acceptance and avoid conflict with schools and parents, the explicit goal is usually to teach personal safety, not sexuality education. Ironically, most programs attempt to teach children about sexual abuse without discussing sexuality. As an example of this compromise, very few programs teach children anatomically correct terms for genitals (Tharinger, Krivacska, Laye-McDonough, Jamison, Vincent, & Hedlund, 1988). Instead, programs refer to sexual organs as "private parts" or "private zones" (Dayee, 1982). The use of these abstract terms is inconsistent with another goal of CSA prevention programs; to enhance children's disclosures of abuse. In order to successfully disclose to others about sexual abuse, children need correct terms for labeling their genitals. Without knowing the terms, it is difficult for children to tell a resource person about an abusive touch.

Few studies have investigated children's knowledge of genital terminology. Schor and Sivan (1989) asked 144 children (ages 3 through 8) for the terms they used for sexual body parts. Older children (5 through 8 years) generally knew more accurate terms than 3- and 4-year olds ($n = 48$), but even most older children were unable to correctly label these body parts. Knowledge levels also differed for different body parts, as 54% of the children gave a "correct" label for penis, 32% knew buttocks, 31% knew breast, but only 18% knew vagina. Gordon, Schroeder and Abrams (1990) likewise found children (between 2 and 7 years) to be more knowledgeable about male than female genitals. For example, 30% of the 4-year-olds ($n = 32$) knew penis, 27% knew breast, but only 10% knew vagina. Overall, 2- through 5-year-old children demonstrated knowledge of less than 50% in the area of sexual body parts. These results suggest that preschool-age children are largely unaware of the correct terminology for genitals (especially females'). As findings from both studies are based on small samples of children from primarily upper-class families, one purpose of the present study was to replicate these findings with a larger population of children from families of lower income and more ethnic diversity.

Although the exclusion of genital terminology from CSA prevention programs may have been necessary for parental acceptance of these programs in the past, not all parents have reservations about including this material, as was previously feared. Indeed, results from recent surveys (Conte & Fogarty, 1989; Wurtele, Kvaternick, & Franklin, in press) suggest that parents may be receptive to having this information included in CSA prevention programs. For example, 85% of parents of preschoolers in the Wurtele et al. study (in press) slightly or strongly agreed that CSA prevention programs need to teach children the correct names for their genitals, and another 10% were unsure. One area of childhood sexuality yet to be investigated involves young children's ability to learn the correct labels for sexual body parts. As previous research has shown that older children know more genital labels than younger children (Gordon et al., 1990; Schor & Sivan, 1989), another purpose of this study was to determine whether preschoolers could learn correct genital terminology when taught by either teachers or parents.

RESULTS
Table 1 summarizes the labels children used for their body parts. Although almost all children knew the correct labels for their nongenital body parts, few knew the correct terms for breasts, vagina or penis. Over one-half the children used slang labels for the breasts and one-third used slang labels for penis. Few children could produce labels for the vagina, whereas over one-half knew the correct term for buttocks. Table 2 contains a partial listing of the slang labels offered by the children.

Table 1. Percentages (and Number) of Children Who Used Various Labels for Body Parts

Body Part	Incorrect		Slang		Private Part		Correct	
	%	(n)	%	(n)	%	(n)	%	(n)
Genital								
Breasts	33.9	(92)	52.4	(142)	5.5	(15)	8.1	(22)
Vagina	51.7	(140)	27.7	(75)	17.7	(48)	3.0	(8)
Penis	41.3	(112)	34.7	(94)	17.7	(48)	6.3	(17)
Buttocks	20.7	(56)	10.0	(27)	10.7	(29)	58.7	(159)
Nongenital								
Eyes	2.2	(6)	—		—		97.8	(265)
Arms	1.1	(3)	—		—		98.9	(268)
Legs	1.5	(4)	—		—		98.5	(267)

Table 2. Slang Labels Offered for Genitalia

Breasts	Vagina	Penis	Buttocks
Bobbies	Cat	Boner	Ass
Boobies	Cookie	Dingaling	Bootie
Booboos	Coochie	Dick	Booboo
Bumps	Dingle	Dingdong	Buns
Chichis	Feefee	Dink	Shiney
Titties	Fluzzy	Dodo	
Tits	Heinie	Dollywacker	
	Lapoopoo	Hose	
	Muffin	Monkey	
	Peepee	Nuts	
	Pie	Pee-dee	
	Pooch	(-pee; -wee)	
	Pussy	Peter	
	Teetee	Petereater	
	Weewee	Piddlewiddle	
	Winkie	ShinyInie	
	Winnie	Teetee	
		Tinker	
		Tweeter	
		Weenie	
		Weewee	
		Wiener	

DISCUSSION

Preschool-age children in this study were largely unaware of the anatomically correct terminology for their genitals. Although over one-half the children knew the correct term for buttocks, less than 10% of the children knew the correct terms for breasts, vagina, or penis. They offered many (and creative!) slang terms for the genitals. In contrast, almost all children knew the correct terms for their nongenital body parts (i.e., eyes, arms and legs). This finding indicates that preschoolers were capable of following the experimenter's instructions and offering labels for (nongenital) body parts, but that they lacked knowledge about both female and male sexual body parts.

The percentages of children who gave correct terms for penis, vagina, and breasts were considerably lower than those reported in other studies, which may have been due to our stringent criteria for a "correct" answer and/or to our lower-class subject sample. Gordon et al. (1990) found that children from lower socioeconomic backgrounds demonstrated less knowledge of sexuality than children from middle and upper social classes. In addition, these findings were obtained from a large sample of ethnically diverse children, in contrast to previous studies using small samples that were limited in terms of ethnic and socioeconomic backgrounds.

We were also trying to determine whether children could learn anatomically correct terms for their genitals when taught a personal safety program by either their parents or teachers. When taught the terms by their parents, children were able to learn the labels for breasts, vagina, penis and buttocks. In contrast, children taught the terms by their teachers showed a significant increase in knowledge only for penis. One possible explanation for this finding is that at school, children may not have had as many opportunities to rehearse the terms for their genitals, as they were taught in small groups where they may have simply mimicked the responses of either the teacher or other program participants. At home, children were taught on a one-to-one basis and were expected to respond on their own initiative. In addition, parents may have taken advantage of the multiple opportunities to label their children's genitals (i.e., while dressing, bathing, discussing siblings), and/or they may have been more sensitive to their children's comprehension and rate of skill acquisition (as suggested by Miller-Perrin & Wurtele, 1988).

An important objective of CSA prevention programs is to encourage children to report sexual abuse. Without knowing the correct term for their genitals, children may have difficulty describing inappropriate sexual contacts. Our results suggest that children can learn anatomically correct labels, which should facilitate their reporting of an abusive situation. There may be other advantages of teaching children correct genital terminology. For example, teaching children the names of all their body parts might enhance body pride and provide a foundation for later sexuality education. Such terms also help children learn about human anatomy and give them a vocabulary with which to ask questions about sexuality (Koblinsky, Atkinson, & Davis, 1980).

Recent surveys indicate that many parents want to play an active role in educating their children about personal safety (e.g. Wurtele et al., in press). Furthermore, recent studies have shown that parents are effective trainers of personal safety skills (e.g., Wurtele, Currier, Gillispie, & Franklin, 1991; Wurtele, Gillispie, Currier, & Franklin, 1992; Wurtele, Kast, & Melzer, in press). Although based on a small sample, findings from the present study indicate that parents are also effective trainers of genital terminology. Parents play an important role in educating their children about personal safety, and programmers should continue to encourage parental involvement in prevention efforts.

*Reprinted by permission of the *Journal of Sex Education and Therapy* and *AASECT*.

Research Excerpt Reaction Questions

1. Preschoolers have generally been taught to use the terms "private parts" or "private zones" to describe their sexual anatomical parts. Do you agree or disagree with this practice? Why?

2. Which of the slang labels offered for genitalia (Table 2) are familiar to you? Which are unfamiliar?

3. Are young children capable of learning the correct names for sexual body parts? How do we know this?

4. Who should be responsible for teaching sexual language to children? Why?

Activities

1. **Sex Talk**
   Talk with four of your friends or acquaintances about language used in their homes for body parts as they were growing up. How do they think of this practice? Would they respond similarly or differently with their own children?

2. **Culture and Sex Talk**
   Talk with two persons from a cultural group different than your own. What were their experiences growing up with words concerning body parts?

3. **Erotic Art**
   Look in the library and photocopy five works of art that show interest in penis size. Good sources are ancient Roman, Japanese, and Greek, as well as contemporary art. What are some of the myths about penis size? How are these myths supported in this art?

4. **Sex Reassignment**
   How would you react if one of your classmates told you he or she had gender reassignment surgery? If a friend told you? If a date told you? If your sibling said he/she planned on having reassignment surgery?

5. **Self-Examination**
   Do a breast or testicular self-examination following the diagrams on the next page. What is your reaction to this activity? How would you increase the frequency of completing this self-exam?

Breast Self-Examination

Check your breasts about one week after your period.
Press firmly with the pads of your fingers.
Move your *left* hand over your *right* breast in a circle, as shown.
Now check your *left* breast with your *right* hand in the same way.
If you detect any lumps, knots, or changes, tell your doctor right away.
Breast cancer may be cured if you find it early.

Testicular Self-Examination

Check your testicles once a month.
Roll each testicle between your thumb and finger, as shown.
Feel for hard lumps or bumps.
If you notice a change or have aches or lumps, tell your doctor
right away. Testicular cancer can be cured if you find it early.

CHAPTER 4

REPRODUCTIVE DECISION-MAKING

"Four decades after the advent of the birth control pill, the rate of unintended pregnancy in the United States remains high. According to one study, 49% of pregnancies in 1994 were unintended."

Perlman et al., 1988

How do you picture yourself five, ten, fifteen years from now? Do you imagine yourself having a family? Do you picture your family as being similar or different from your family of origin? Are you living now as if you are building for the future you have planned?

Chapter 4 Contents:

Assessing Your Readiness to Become a Parent*
Bryan Strong

Many factors have to be taken into account when you are considering parenthood. The following are some questions you should ask yourself and some issues you should consider when making this decision. Some issues are relevant to both men and women; others apply only to women. There are no "right" answers--you must decide for yourself what your answers reveal about your aptitude for parenthood.

Physical Health

Yes   **No**   1.   Are you in reasonably good health?

Yes   **No**   2.   Do you have any behaviors or conditions that could be of special concern?

_____ Obesity	_____	Anemia
_____ Smoking	_____	Diabetes
_____ Drug use	_____	Sexually transmissible diseases
_____ Hypertension	_____	Epilepsy
_____ Previous problems with pregnancy or delivery	_____	Prenatal exposure to DES (diethylstilbestrol)

Yes   **No**   3.   Are you under 20 or over 35 years of age?

Yes   **No**   4.   Do you or your partner have a history of a genetic problem that a baby might inherit?

_____ Hemophilia	_____	Phenylketonuria (PKU)
_____ Sickle cell anemia	_____	Cystic fibrosis
_____ Down's syndrome	_____	Thalassemia
_____ Tay-Sach's disease	_____	Other

Financial Circumstances

Yes   **No**   1.   Will your health insurance cover the costs of pregnancy, prenatal tests, delivery, and medical attention for the mother and baby before and after the birth?

Yes   **No**   2.   Can you afford the supplies for the baby: diapers, bedding, crib, stroller, car seat, clothing, food, and medical supplies?

Yes   **No**   3.   Will one parent leave his or her job to care for the baby?

Yes   **No**   4.   If so, can the decrease in family income be worked into the family budget?

Yes   **No**   5.   If both parents will continue to work, has affordable child care been set up?

Yes   **No**   6.   The first few years of raising a baby can cost $10,000; can you save and/or provide the necessary money?

Education, Career, and Child Care Plans

Yes   **No**   1.   Have you completed as much of your education as you want?

Yes   **No**   2.   Have you sufficiently established yourself in a career, if that is important to you?

Yes No 3. Have you investigated parental leave and company-sponsored child care?

Yes No 4. Do both spouses agree on child care arrangements?

Lifestyle and Social Support

Yes No 1. Would you be willing to give up the freedom to do what you want to do when you want to do it?

Yes No 2. Would you be willing to restrict your social life, to miss lost leisure time and privacy?

Yes No 3. Would you and your partner be prepared to spend more time at home? Would you have enough time to spend with a child?

Yes No 4. Are you prepared to be a single parent if your partner leaves or dies?

Yes No 5. Do you have a network of family and friends who can help you with the baby? Are there community resources you can call on for additional assistance?

Readiness

Yes No 1. Are you prepared to have a helpless being completely dependent on you 24 hours a day?

Yes No 2. Do you like children? Have you had enough experiences with babies, toddlers, and teenagers?

Yes No 3. Do you think time spent with children is time well spent?

Yes No 4. Do you communicate easily with others?

Yes No 5. Do you have enough love to give a child? Can you express affection easily?

Yes No 6. Do you feel good enough about yourself to respect and nurture others?

Yes No 7. Do you have safe ways of handling anger, frustration, and impatience?

Yes No 8. Would you be willing to devote a great part of your life, at least 18 years, to being responsible for a child?

Relationship with Partner

Yes No 1. Does your partner want to have a child? Is he or she willing to ask these same questions of himself or herself?

Yes No 2. Have you adequately discussed your reasons for wanting a child?

Yes No 3. Do either of you have philosophical objections to adding to the world's population?

Yes No 4. Have you and your partner discussed each other's feelings about religion, work, family, and child raising? Are your feelings compatible and conducive to good parenting?

Yes   No   5. Would both you and your partner contribute in raising the child?

Yes   No   6. Is your relationship stable? Could you provide a child with a really good home environment?

Yes   No   7. After having a child, would your partner and you be able to separate if you should have unsolvable problems? Would you feel obligated to remain together for the sake of the child?

*Reprinted by permission of Mayfield Publishing Company.

Reproductive Decision-Making: Your Life Plan

Imagine yourself one year from now, five years from now, and ten years from now. What is your picture of your adult life? What sort of lifestyle would you choose for yourself? Answer the following questions to give a clearer picture of a direction for yourself.

1.   Would you like to have children some day? Should you? Reasons why? Reasons why not?

2.   How old would you like to be when you have your first child? Why?

3.   How many children would you like to have? Why? What spacing would you like for your children? Why?

4.   Would you like to be married or in a committed relationship some day? Which would you prefer? Why?

5.   When would you like to be married or in a committed relationship? Why?

6.   Do you wish to wait until marriage to have sexual intercourse? Why or why not?

7.   How concerned would you be if you were to become pregnant (or responsible for a pregnancy) and not be married?

8.   How sad would you be if you or your partner were not able to have any children? Why?

9.   What do you believe are some reasons for female infertility?

10.   What do you believe are some reasons for male infertility?

11.   What are some good rules to follow for good prenatal care?

12.   If a gender-selection method that was absolutely accurate were to be developed, would you use it? What considerations determine your answer?

13.   Would you work when your children were young? When your children were in school? When your children were no longer in the home?

14.   How would having children affect your overall life goals?

15.   How would you parent children if your marriage were to end in divorce?

Research Excerpt

Question: What is the best birth control method for you and your partner?

Choosing a Contraceptive *
Merle S. Goldberg

Choosing a method of birth control is a highly personal decision, based on individual preferences, medical history, lifestyle, and other factors. Each method carries with it a number of risks and benefits of which the user should be aware.

Each method of birth control has a failure rate--an inability to prevent pregnancy over a one-year period. Sometimes the failure rate is due to the method and sometimes it is due to human error, such as incorrect use or not using it at all. Each method has possible side effects, some minor and some serious. Some methods require lifestyle modifications, such as remembering to use the method with each and every sexual intercourse. Some cannot be used by individuals with certain medical problems.

Spermicides Used Alone

Spermicides, which come in many forms--foams, jellies, gels, and suppositories--work by forming a physical and chemical barrier to sperm. They should be inserted into the vagina within an hour before intercourse. If intercourse is repeated, more spermicide should be inserted. The active ingredient in most spermicides is the chemical nonoxynol-9. The failure rate for spermicides in preventing pregnancy when used alone is from 20 to 30 percent.

Spermicides are available without a prescription. People who experience burning or irritation with these products should not use them.

Barrier Methods

There are five barrier methods of contraception: male condoms, female condoms, diaphragm, sponge, and cervical cap. In each instance, the method works by keeping the sperm and egg apart. Usually, these methods have only minor side effects. The main possible side effect is an allergic reaction either to the material of the barrier or the spermicides that should be used with them. Using the methods correctly for each and every sexual intercourse gives the best protection.

Male Condom

A male condom is a sheath that covers the penis during sex. Condoms are made of either latex rubber or natural skin (also called "lambskin" but actually made from sheep intestines). Only latex condoms have been shown to be highly effective in helping to prevent STDs. Latex provides a good barrier to even small viruses such as human immunodeficiency virus and hepatitis B. Each condom can only be used once. Condoms have a birth control failure rate of about 15 percent. Most of the failures can be traced to improper use.

Some condoms have spermicide added. This may give some additional contraceptive protection. Vaginal spermicides may also be added before sexual intercourse.

Some condoms have lubricants added. These do not improve birth control or STD protection. Non-oil-based lubricants can also be used with condoms. However, oil-based lubricants such as petroleum jelly (Vaseline) should not be used because they weaken the latex. Condoms are available without a prescription.

Female Condom

The Reality Female Condom was approved by the FDA in April 1993. It consists of a lubricated polyurethane sheath with a flexible polyurethane ring on each end. One ring is inserted into the vagina much like a diaphragm, while the other remains outside, partially covering the labia. The female condom may offer some protection against STDs, but for highly effective protection, male latex condoms must be used.

FDA Commissioner David A. Kessler, M.D., in announcing the approval, said, "I have to stress that the male latex condom remains the best shield against AIDS and other sexually transmitted diseases. Couples should go on using the male latex condom."

DISEASE PREVENTION

For many people, the prevention of sexually transmitted diseases (STDs), including HIV (human immunodeficiency virus), which leads to AIDS, is a factor in choosing a contraceptive. Only one form of birth control--the latex condom, worn by the man--is considered highly effective in helping protect against HIV and other STDs. Reality Female Condom, made from polyurethane, may give limited protection against STDs but has not been proven as effective as male latex condoms. People who use another form of birth control but who also want a highly effective way to reduce their STD risks, should also use a latex condom for every sex act, from start to finish.

In April, 1993, the FDA announced that birth control pills, Norplant, Depo-Provera, IUDs, and natural membrane condoms must carry labeling stating that these products are intended to prevent pregnancy but do not protect against HIV infection and other sexually transmitted diseases. In addition, natural membrane condom labeling must state that consumers should use a latex condom to help reduce the transmission of STDs. The labeling of latex condoms states that, if used properly, they will help reduce transmission of HIV and other diseases.

Male Condom

Diaphragm

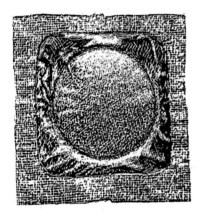

Female Condom

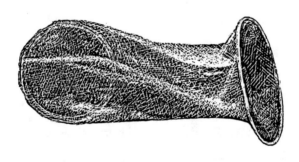

Norplant

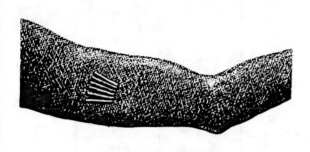

Intrauterine Device

Birth Control Pills

Depo-Provera

Type	Male Condom	Female Condom	Spermicides Used Alone	IUD	Diaphragm with Spermicide	Cervical Cap with Spermicide
Estimated Effectiveness	About 85%	An estimated 74-79%	70-80%	95-96%	82-94%	At least 82%
Risks	Rarely, irritation and allergic reactions	Rarely, irritation and allergic reactions	Rarely, irritation and allergic reactions	Cramps, bleeding; pelvic inflammat-ory disease; infertility; rarely, perforation of the uterus	Rarely, irritation and allergic reactions; bladder infection; very rarely, toxic shock syndrome	Abnormal Pap test; vaginal or cervical infections; very rarely, toxic shock syndrome
STD Protection	Latex condoms help protect against sexually transmitted diseases, including herpes and AIDS	May give some protection against sexually transmitted diseases, including herpes and AIDS; not as effective as male latex condom	Unknown	None	None	None
Convenience	Applied immediately before intercourse	Applied immediately before intercourse; used only once and discarded	Applied no more than one hour before intercourse	After insertion, stays in place until physician removes it	Inserted before intercourse; can be left in place 24 hours, but additional spermicide must be inserted if intercourse is repeated	Can remain in place for 48 hours, not necessary to reapply spermicide upon repeated intercourse; may be difficult to insert
Availability	Non prescription	Non prescription	Non prescription	Rx	Rx	Rx

Type	Pills	Implant (Norplant)	Injection (Depo-Provera)	Lunelle *	Periodic Abstinence (NFP)	Surgical Sterilization
Estimated Effectiveness	97-99%	99%	99%	Over 99%	Very variable, perhaps 53-86%	Over 99%
Risks	Blood clots, heart attacks and strokes, gallbladder disease, liver tumors, water retention, hypertension, mood changes, dizziness and nausea; not for smokers	Menstrual cycle irregularity; headaches, nervousness, depression, nausea, dizziness, change of appetite, breast tenderness, weight gain, enlargement of ovaries and/or fallopian tubes, excessive growth of body and facial hair; may subside after first year	Amenorrhea, weight gain, and other side effects similar to those with Norplant	Blood clots and blockage of blood vessels the most serious side effect; gall bladder disease; allergic reaction in some women	None	Pain, infection, and, for female tubal ligation, possible surgical complication.
STD Protection	None	None	None	None	None	None
Convenience	Pill must be taken on daily schedule, regardless of the frequency of intercourse	Effective 24 hours after implantation for approximately 5 years; can be removed by physician at any time	One injection every three months	One injection every month; quicker return of fertility than Depo-Provera	Requires frequent monitoring of body functions and periods of abstinence	Vasectomy is a one-time procedure usually performed in a doctor's office; tubal ligation is a one-time procedure performed in an operating room
Availability	Rx	Rx; minor outpatient surgical procedure	Rx	Rx	Instructions from physician or clinic	Surgery

* Hatcher et al., 2001, 2002; Perlman et al., 2001; Pharmacia & Upjohn, 2000

In a six-month trial, the pregnancy rate for the Reality Female Condom was about 13 percent. The estimated yearly failure rate ranges from 21 to 26 percent . This means that about 1 in 4 women who use Reality may become pregnant during a year.

Diaphragm

The diaphragm is a flexible rubber disk with a rigid rim. Diaphragms range in size from 2 to 4 inches in diameter and are designed to cover the cervix during and after intercourse so that sperm cannot reach the uterus. Spermicidal jelly or cream must be placed inside the diaphragm for it to be effective.

The diaphragm must be fitted by a health professional and the correct size prescribed to ensure a snug seal with the vaginal wall. If intercourse is repeated, additional spermicide should be added with the diaphragm still in place. The diaphragm should be left in place for at least six hours after intercourse. The diaphragm used with spermicide has a failure rate of from 6 to 18 percent.

In addition to the possible allergic reactions or irritation common to all barrier methods, there have been some reports of bladder infections with this method. As with the contraceptive sponge, TSS is an extremely rare side effect.

Cervical Cap

The cervical cap, approved for contraceptive use in the United States in 1988, is a dome-shaped rubber cap in various sizes that fits snugly over the cervix. Like the diaphragm, it is used with a spermicide and must be fitted by a health professional. It is more difficult to insert than the diaphragm, but may be left in place for up to 48 hours. In addition to the allergic reactions that can occur with any barrier method, 5.2 to 27 percent of users in various studies have reported an unpleasant odor and/or discharge. There also appears to be an increased incidence of irregular Pap tests in the first six months of using the cap, and TSS is an extremely rare side effect. The cap has a failure rate of about 18 percent.

Hormonal Contraception

Hormonal contraception involves ways of delivering forms of two female reproductive hormones--estrogen and progesterone--that help regulate ovulation (release of an egg), the condition of the uterine lining, and other parts of the menstrual cycle. Unlike barrier methods, hormones are not inert, do interact with the body, and have the potential for serious side effects, though this is rare. When properly used, hormonal methods are also extremely effective. Hormonal methods are available only by prescription.

Birth Control Pills

There are two types of birth control pills: combination pills, which contain both estrogen and a progestin (a natural or synthetic progesterone), and "mini-pills," which contain only progestin. The combination pill prevents ovulation, while the mini-pill reduces cervical mucus and causes it to thicken. This prevents the sperm from reaching the egg. Also, progestins keep the endometrium (uterine lining) from thickening. This prevents the fertilized egg from implanting in the uterus. The failure rate for the mini-pill is 1 to 3 percent; for the combination pill it is 1 to 2 percent.

Combination oral contraceptives offer significant protection against ovarian cancer, endometrial cancer, iron-deficiency anemia, pelvic inflammatory disease (PID), and fibrocystic breast disease. Women who take combination pills have a lower risk of functional ovarian cysts.

The decision about whether to take an oral contraceptive should be made only after consultation with a health professional. Smokers and women with certain medical conditions should not take the pill. These conditions include: a history of blood clots in the legs, eyes, or deep veins of the legs; heart attacks, strokes, or angina; cancer of the breast, vagina, cervix, or uterus; any undiagnosed, abnormal vaginal bleeding; liver tumor; or jaundice due to pregnancy or use of birth control pills.

Women with the following conditions should discuss with a health professional whether the benefits of the pill outweigh its risks for them:

- high blood pressure
- heart, kidney, or gallbladder disease
- a family history of heart attack or stroke
- severe headaches or depression
- elevated cholesterol or triglycerides; epilepsy or diabetes.

Serious side effects of the pill include blood clots that can lead to stroke, heart attack, pulmonary embolism, or death. A clot may, on rare occasions, occur in the blood vessel of the eye, causing impaired vision or even blindness. The pills may also cause high blood pressure that returns to normal after oral contraceptives are stopped. Minor side effects, which usually subside after a few months' use include: nausea, headaches, breast swelling, fluid retention, weight gain, irregular bleeding, and depression. Sometimes taking a pill with a lower dose of hormones can reduce these side effects.

The effectiveness of birth control pills may be reduced by a few other medications, including some antibiotics, barbiturates, and antifungal medications. On the other hand, birth control pills may prolong the effects of benzodiazepines such as Librium (chlordiazepoxide), Valium (diazepam), and Xanax (alprazolam). Because of the variety of these drug interactions, women should always tell their health professionals when they are taking birth control pills.

Norplant

Norplant--the first contraceptive implant--was approved by the FDA in 1990. In a minor surgical procedure, six matchstick-sized rubber capsules containing progestin are placed just underneath the skin of the upper arm. The implant is effective within 24 hours and provides progestin for up to five years or until it is removed. Both the insertion and the removal must be performed by a qualified professional.

Because contraception is automatic and does not depend on the user, the failure rate for Norplant is less than 1 percent for women who weigh less than 150 pounds. Women who weigh more have a higher pregnancy rate after the first two years.

Women who cannot take birth control pills for medical reasons should not consider Norplant a contraceptive option. The potential side effects of the implant include: irregular menstrual bleeding, headaches, nervousness, depression, nausea, dizziness, skin rash, acne, change of appetite, breast tenderness, weight gain, enlargement of the ovaries or fallopian tubes, and excessive growth of body and facial hair. These side effects may subside after the first year.

Depo-Provera

Depo-Provera is an injectable form of a progestin. It was approved by the FDA in 1992 for contraceptive use. Previously, it was approved for treating endometrial and renal cancers. Depo-Provera has a failure rate of only 1 percent. Each injection provides contraceptive protection for 14 weeks. It is injected every three months into a muscle in the buttocks or arm by a trained professional. The side effects are the same as those for Norplant and progestin-only pills. In addition, there may be irregular bleeding and spotting during the first months followed by periods of amenorrhea (no menstrual period). About 50 percent of the women who use Depo-Provera for one year or longer report amenorrhea. Other side effects, such as weight gain and others described for Norplant may occur.

Lunelle

Lunelle is a monthly hormonal contraception injection to prevent pregnancy. It contains hormones which have effects similar to the natural hormones, estrogen and progesterone, produced in your body. Lunelle is as effective as birth control pills and the failure rate is less than 1 percent per year. The side effects could be the formation of blood clots and blockage of blood vessels, some change in bone mineral density and, in some women, allergic reactions.

Intrauterine Devices

IUDs are small, plastic, flexible devices that are inserted into the uterus through the cervix by a trained clinician. Only two IUDs are presently marketed in the United States: ParaGard T380A, a T-shaped device partially covered by copper and effective for eight years; and Progestasert, which is also T-shaped but contains a progestin released over a one-year period. After that time, the IUD should be replaced. Both IUDs have a 4 to 5 percent failure rate.

It is not known exactly how IUDs work. At one time it was thought that the IUD affected the uterus so that it would be inhospitable to implantation. New evidence, however, suggests that uterine and tubal fluids are altered, particularly in the case of copper-bearing IUDs, inhibiting the transport of sperm through the cervical mucus and uterus.

The risk of PID with IUD use is highest in those with multiple sex partners or with a history of previous PID. Therefore, the IUD is recommended primarily for women in mutually monogamous relationships.

In addition to PID, other complications include perforation of the uterus (usually at the time of insertion), septic abortion, or ectopic (tubal) pregnancy. Women may also experience some short-term side effects-- cramping and dizziness at the time of insertion; bleeding, cramps and backache that may continue for a few days after the insertion; spotting between periods; and longer and heavier menstruation during the first few periods after insertion.

Periodic Abstinence

Periodic abstinence entails not having sexual intercourse during the woman's fertile period. Sometimes this method is called natural family planning (NFP) or "rhythm." Using periodic abstinence is dependent on the ability to identify the approximately 10 days in each menstrual cycle that a woman is fertile. Methods to help determine this include:

•   **The basal body temperature method** is based on the knowledge that just before ovulation a woman's basal body temperature drops several tenths of a degree and after ovulation it returns to normal. The method requires that the woman take her temperature each morning before she gets out of bed.

•   **The cervical mucus method**, also called the Billings method, depends on a woman recognizing the changes in cervical mucus that indicate ovulation is occurring or has occurred. There are now electronic thermometers with memories and electrical resistance meters that can more accurately pinpoint a woman's fertile period. The method has a failure rate of 14 to 47 percent.

Periodic abstinence has none of the side effects of artificial methods of contraception.

Surgical Sterilization

Surgical sterilization must be considered permanent. Tubal ligation seals a woman's fallopian tubes so that an egg cannot travel to the uterus. Vasectomy involves closing off a man's vas deferens so that sperm will not be carried to the penis.

Vasectomy is considered safer than female sterilization. It is a minor surgical procedure, most often performed in a doctor's office under local anesthesia. The procedure usually takes less than 30 minutes. Minor post-surgical complications may occur.

Tubal ligation is an operation-room procedure performed under general anesthesia. The fallopian tubes can be reached by a number of surgical techniques, and, depending on the technique, the operation is sometimes an outpatient procedure or requires only an overnight stay. In a minilaparotomy, a 2-inch incision is made in the abdomen. The surgeon, using special instruments, lifts the fallopian tubes and, using clips, a plastic ring, or an electric current, seals the tubes. Another method, laparoscopy, involves making a small incision above the navel, and distending the abdominal cavity so that the intestine separates from the uterus and fallopian tubes. Then a laparoscope--a miniaturized, flexible telescope--is used to visualize the fallopian tubes while closing them off.

Both of these methods are replacing the traditional laparotomy.

Major complications, which are rare in female sterilization, include: infection, hemorrhage, and problems associated with the use of general anesthesia. It is estimated that major complications occur in 1.7 percent of the cases, while the overall complication rate has been reported to be between 0.1 and 15.3 percent.

The failure rate of laparoscopy and minilaparotomy procedures, as well as vasectomy, is less than 1 percent. Although there has been some success in reopening the fallopian tubes or the vas deferens, the success rate is low, and sterilization should be considered irreversible.

* Reprinted by permission of *FDA Consumer*.

Research Excerpt Reaction Questions

1. Do you talk to your partner about birth control?

2. Have you ever had sexual intercourse and not used birth control? Why?

3. Do you talk to your partner about birth control before or after intercourse? Why?

4. What are your feelings about purchasing birth control devices?

5. There are three major categories of birth control methods: barrier methods, hormone methods, and natural family planning methods. Which category would be best for you? Why?

6. Which methods would be best for a person in a committed relationship? Which would be best for someone with multiple partners? Why?

Values Issues in Birth Control

What do you think about each of the birth control methods described in the previous article? Rank each of the methods listed by its number on each of the two continuum questions below.

1. Male Condom
2. Female Condom
3. Spermicides Used Alone
4. IUD (Intrauterine Device)
5. Diaphragm with Spermicide
6. Cervical Cap with Spermicide
7. Birth Control Pills
8. Norplant
9. Depo-Provera Injection
10. Lunelle
11. Natural Family Planning (NFP)
12. Surgical Sterilization

Q: What is your personal reaction to each of the contraceptive methods?

Very Unacceptable	Neutral	Very Acceptable

Q: What are your beliefs about other persons using these methods?

Very Unacceptable	Neutral	Very Acceptable

What factors affect your choice of birth control device? Answer the following questions with a **T** (true) or **F** (false). Tabulate your choices. Do your results match your choices above?

True / False

_____ 1. You like to be spontaneous about sex and not be bothered with thinking about contraception at the time of sex.

_____ 2. You want protection against sexually transmitted diseases.

_____ 3. You want a contraceptive that involves you and your partner.

_____ 4. You have sex frequently.

_____ 5. You have sex infrequently.

_____ 6. You are forgetful and have a variable routine.

_____ 7. You have one sexual partner.

_____ 8. You have more than one sexual partner.

_____ 9. You want the option of having a pregnancy immediately after discontinuing contraception.

_____ 10. You want no possible side effects from your contraceptive device.

_____ 11. You want a contraceptive that requires no advance planning or doctor visits.

_____ 12. You have completed your family.

_____ 13. You have beliefs that do not allow for any contraceptive method that interferes with fertilization.

If you answered **T (true)** to the statement numbers listed on the left, the method on the right might be a good choice for you. You may have several choices that could serve you and your partner well.

2, 3, 5, 6, 7, 8, 9, 10, 11 ....Male Condom

2, 3, 5, 6, 7, 8, 9, 10, 11 ....Female Condom

5, 6, 7, 9, 10, 11 ....Spermicide Used Alone

1, 4, 6, 7, 9, 12 ....IUD

2, 3, 5, 7, 8, 9, 10 ....Diaphragm with Spermicide

2, 5, 7, 8, 9, 10 ....Cervical Cap with Spermicide

1, 4, 7, 9 ....Birth Control Pills

1, 4, 6, 7 ....Norplant

1, 4, 6, 7 ....Depo-Provera

1, 4, 6, 7, 9 ....Lunelle

3, 5, 7, 9, 10, 13 ....Natural Family Planning

1, 4, 6, 7, 12 ....Surgical Sterilization

Exploring Your Thoughts Concerning Abortion

The debate over abortion has been an issue in this country since the US Supreme Court ruled in Roe vs. Wade in 1973. The decision of the Court was that the individual woman, not the government, should have the final say in the determination of whether or not to continue a pregnancy. Strong feelings, pro-choice and pro-life, exist among most persons, and are often based on family and religious values. Where do you stand on this issue? What is the source of your beliefs?

On the scale below, mark an X where you believe you stand on abortion.

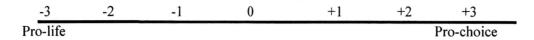

| -3 | -2 | -1 | 0 | +1 | +2 | +3 |

Pro-life   Pro-choice

1. Do you believe abortion should be legal in the United States? Why?

2. Do you believe abortion should be allowed if the woman is pregnant as a result of a rape? Why?

3. Do you believe abortion should be allowed if the life of the mother is endangered? Why?

4. Do you believe abortion should be allowed if having a baby is a financial burden on the family? Why?

5. Do you believe abortion should be allowed because the couple forgot to use birth control? Why?

6. Do you believe abortion should be allowed if it is known that the fetus is defective? Why?

7. Do you believe women should be able to have as many abortions as they wish? Why?

Exploring Your Thoughts Concerning Modern Reproductive Technologies
Nadja Tizer

"It goes without saying that human cloning does not involve, or need to involve, sexual intercourse. As one probes the seeming asexuality of cloning, one is initially drawn to the metaphors that feed and follow the asexual nature of technology" (McGee, 2000). McGee (2000) refers to cloning as "the reproductive technology least tied to human intimacy." This is probably a safe assertion but it should also be pointed out that human embryos are not currently being cloned, although it is possible the technology for this procedure may be available in the very near future. Cloning is not a possibility yet, but there are a variety of reproductive technologies already in existence for the general public. These technologies range from sperm donation and in vitro fertilization to surrogate motherhood. As more Assisted Reproductive Technologies (ART) become available there is increasing debate about the ethics surrounding the use of these technologies, particularly as they relate to assessing the health of the fetus and promoting fertility.

Most couples use some type of family planning. Many couples decide together what will be the best time to conceive a child. Most of the time this goes smoothly, but on some occasions couples have trouble conceiving. When a couple has tried to conceive for a year or more without success they are often told they have infertility problems and medical intervention is sometimes recommended. The couple must then choose to either terminate their pregnancy attempts, adopt, or employ the aid of ART, and potentially costly medical procedures.

What would you do if you and your partner had trouble conceiving? Would you adopt? Would you give ART a try? The following questionnaire is designed to help you evaluate your own attitudes about the reproductive technologies available today and some of the technologies that may be available in the future.

Using the scale below, mark an **X** where you believe you stand on ART (Assisted Reproductive Technology):

-3	-2	-1	0	+1	+2	+3
Anti-ART						**Pro-ART**

Your Attitudes About Modern Reproductive Technologies

Answer the following questions in the space provided:

1. If you learned that you and your partner could not conceive without the help of ART, would you give up trying? _____

2. If you and your partner could not conceive, would you consider adoption? _____
Why?_____
Why not?_____

_____

3. If you and your partner could not conceive would you consider ART? _____

4. ART procedures are generally costly. Would you and your partner be willing to spend up to $80,000 to conceive? _____

5. ART procedures are often invasive. Would you and your partner be willing to deal with invasive procedures that might not initially work and might need to be repeated several times? _____

6. Intrauterine Insemination or Artificial Insemination (AI) is a procedure that allows sperm to be deposited inside the woman in cases where the man's sperm count is low. It can also be used by women with no available partner or for lesbian couples who wish to conceive. Would you consider AI as a fertility option? _____

7. In vitro fertilization (IVF) is a procedure that begins in the laboratory when an oocyte is combined with sperm in a dish and is later implanted into the woman's uterus. Would you and your partner consider this procedure? _____
Would you still consider it knowing that each try costs about $8,000 and that this procedure must generally be repeated several times? _____

8. GIFT is a procedure where male sperm and female eggs are collected from both partners and deposited in the woman's fallopian tube. If the procedure is successful there are often several viable fetuses. This procedure is more invasive that IVF. Would you and your partner consider this procedure? _____
Would you abort any of the fetuses to help the others survive? _____
Why?_____
Why not?_____

9. ZIFT is a procedure similar to GIFT, only in this process the eggs and sperm are first combined in the laboratory and then implanted in the fallopian tube. Would you consider this procedure? _____

10. Intercytoplasmic sperm injection (ICSI) is a process where a single sperm is combined with an oocyte in the laboratory. Later it is implanted in the female. Would you and your partner consider this procedure? _____

11. Surrogate motherhood is when one woman bears a child for another who cannot bear children. A woman's egg is often combined with the male's sperm and then implanted in a surrogate who is often paid a large sum of money to carry the child to term. Would you and your partner consider using a surrogate to help you bear a child of your own? _____
Why?_____ Why not?_____
How much would you be willing to pay for this service? _____

12. If cloning were an option would you consider having yourself cloned? _____
Someone you know cloned? _____
Someone cloned who possesses the qualities you would like in your child? _____
What is your thinking pro and con concerning cloning?_____
_____

13. If a fetus could be tested and genetically altered would you consider having your child altered? _____
Under what circumstances? _____
If your child had a genetic disorder? _____
If your child were mentally deficient or handicapped? _____

14. If a gay gene were isolated and your child could be "fixed" in utero, would you consider having your child altered? _____
What is your thinking pro and con on this
issue?_____
_____

Activities

1. **Sex Education and Your Former High School**:
    Call your former high school guidance counselor or nurse. What sex education programs exist at the present time? Is the school nurse free to give contraceptive information to students? What are the restrictions for this information in this school? Is parent permission required to take advantage of services? Are any contraceptive devices available to the students? Is there any cost for these services? What are your views regarding the availability of these services in your school?

2. **Contraceptive Responsibility**
    Who do you believe is responsible for contraception in a single encounter? In an ongoing relationship? In a marriage? Interview 10 students, asking the above three questions. What is the consensus of these students?

3. **Two Interviews: Pro-life and Pro-choice**
    Interview someone who is pro-life and someone who is pro-choice. Make a list of questions you will ask each of them including why they hold these views, what they think about the different legal issues involved, and what they think about the use of an abortion pill.

4. **Community Resources for Abortion**

    Because of all the controversy concerning abortion and recent attacks on doctors and staff at places that perform abortions, there are many communities where it is difficult to find a place to have one done. Call family planning clinics in your area to see if there is access to abortion counseling and abortions. Are services available? Have these clinics had any community opposition?

5. **Abortion Law**

    If you had the power to write a new abortion law, how would you write it?

CHAPTER 5

SEXUALITY OVER THE LIFESPAN

"The attitude of the parents should be to socialize for privacy rather than to punish or forbid."

Dr. Mary Calderone, 1983

Your adult sexuality is often a reflection of your childhood experience. What sex-positive and sex-negative experiences did you have that affect your present actions? Can these adult behaviors be changed? What about your future? As you get older do you believe that your ideas about your sexuality will change? What sort of sexual 80-year-old do you wish to be?

Chapter 5 Contents:

A. **Childhood Sex Education**

B. **Questionnaire: "Retrospective Reports of Childhood Experiences With Nudity and Sleeping in the Parental Bed"**

C. **Research Excerpt: "The Relationship Between Adult Sexual Adjustment and Childhood Experiences Regarding Exposure to Nudity, Sleeping in the Parental Bed, and Parental Attitudes Toward Sexuality" and Reaction Questions**

D. **Adolescent Sex Education**

E. **Questionnaire: Sexuality and Aging**

F. **Activities**
   1. **Sex Learning in Childhood**
   2. **Adolescent Sexuality and Television Series**
   3. **Myths About Menopause**
   4. **Aging and Sexuality: Analyzing Birthday Cards**

Childhood Sex Education

How did you receive your sex education? Most sex education comes informally, as you grow up in your family and in your neighborhood. You observe those around you and the media messages in your home. You learn from your friends. From all of these sources you put together your picture of what is acceptable and what is not acceptable, what does or does not fit for you.

1. Who was your main sex educator?

2. What was the first thing you remember hearing about sex?

3. What did you think when you heard this?

4. What did you think sex was about when you were a child?

5. When did you first make a connection between male erections and sexual arousal? When did you first make a connection between female lubrication and sexual arousal? What were your thoughts about this?

6. Were you comfortable asking your parents about sex?

7. If your parents talked to you about sex, what do you remember they told you?

Retrospective Reports of Childhood Experiences With Nudity and Sleeping in the Parental Bed *
Robin J. Lewis and Louis H. Janda

Answer the following questions and then compare your results with the research excerpt in this chapter, "The Relationship Between Adult Sexual Adjustment and Childhood Experiences Regarding Exposure to Nudity, Sleeping in the Parental Bed, and Parental Attitudes Toward Sexuality."

Respond to items 1-10 using the following scale:

```
1----------------2----------------3----------------4----------------5
almost never     rarely          sometimes        often        very often
```

_____ 1. When you were between the ages of 0-5, how often do you remember seeing your mother naked?

_____ 2. When you were between the ages of 6-11, how often do you remember seeing your mother naked?

_____ 3. When you were between the ages of 0-5, how often do you remember seeing your father naked?

_____ 4. When you were between the ages of 6-11, how often do you remember seeing your father naked?

_____ 5. When you were between the ages of 0-5, how often do you remember seeing your same-sex siblings or friends naked?

_____ 6. When you were between the ages of 6-11, how often do you remember seeing your same-sex siblings or friends naked?

_____ 7. When you were between the ages of 0-5, how often do you remember seeing your opposite-sex siblings or friends naked?

_____ 8. When you were between the ages of 6-11, how often do you remember seeing your opposite-sex siblings or friends naked?

_____ 9. When you were between the ages of 0-5, how often do you remember sleeping in the same bed as your parents?

_____ 10. When you were between the ages of 6-11, how often do you remember sleeping in the same bed as your parents?

Parental Attitude Items
Respond to items 11-14 using the following scale:

```
1----------------2----------------3----------------4----------------5
extreme      moderate    neither comfort   moderate      extreme
discomfort   discomfort  nor discomfort    comfort       comfort
```

_____ 11. In general, over the course of your childhood, please rate the degree of comfort you felt in talking about sexual matters with your mother:

_____ 12. In general, over the course of your childhood, please rate the degree of comfort you felt in talking about sexual matters with your father:

_____ 13. While you were growing up, please rate the degree of comfort you think your mother felt when talking about sexuality:

_____ 14. While you were growing up, please rate the degree of comfort you think your father felt when talking about sexuality:

_____ 15. How would you characterize your mother's attitude toward sexuality when you were growing up?

```
1----------------2----------------3----------------4----------------5
extremely    moderately  neither positive  moderately    extremely
negative     negative    nor negative      positive      positive
```

_____ 16. How would you characterize your father's attitude toward sexuality when you were growing up?

```
1----------------2----------------3----------------4----------------5
extremely    moderately  neither positive  moderately    extremely
negative     negative    nor negative      positive      positive
```

_____ 17. Overall, how well do you feel that your upbringing prepared you to deal with issues of sexuality and sexual relationships?

```
1----------------2----------------3----------------4----------------5
not at all     poorly     adequately   pretty well    very well
```

_____ 18. How often do you remember issues of sexuality being discussed in your home when you were growing up?

```
1----------------2----------------3----------------4----------------5
almost never   rarely     sometimes      often       very often
```

_____ 19. In general, how often was there physical contact/affection displayed in your family?

```
1----------------2----------------3----------------4----------------5
almost never   rarely     sometimes      often       very often
```

Sexual Adjustment Items

Use the following scale for items 20-29:

1----------------2----------------3----------------4----------------5

| strongly | somewhat | neither agree | somewhat | strongly |
| disagree | disagree | nor disagree | agree | agree |

_____ 20. I feel good about myself.

_____ 21. I experience guilt or anxiety when it comes to my sex life.

_____ 22. I am happy with my sex life.

_____ 23. I am heterosexual.

_____ 24. I have sex more often than most people of my age and situation (e.g. married vs. single).

_____ 25. I tend to engage in casual sexual relationships.

_____ 26. I have experienced sexual problems.

_____ 27. I would like my sex life to be more active than it is.

_____ 28. I am very consistent in making certain that birth control is a part of my sexual encounters.

_____ 29. I am knowledgeable about sex.

_____ 30. Regarding physical contact and affection in your family how often do you remember having feelings of discomfort about this contact?

1----------------2----------------3----------------4----------------5

almost never   rarely   sometimes   often   very often

* Reprinted by permission of Plenum Publishing Company

Research Excerpt

Question: Is there a relationship between childhood exposure to nudity and adult sexual functioning?

The Relationship Between Adult Sexual Adjustment and Childhood Experiences Regarding Exposure to Nudity, Sleeping in the Parental Bed, and Parental Attitudes Toward Sexuality.*

Robin J. Lewis, Ph.D. and Louis H. Janda, Ph.D.

DISCUSSION

The results suggest that childhood exposure to nudity and sleeping in the parental bed are not related to poor sexual adjustment. In fact, for boys, exposure to nudity in early childhood appears to be modestly related to greater comfort levels with regard to physical contact/affection.

Exposure to nudity between ages 6 and 11 appears to be modestly related to increased sexual activity for both boys and girls. While some might interpret this as support for the harmful effects of nudity in the family, we suggest an alternative explanation. It is possible that the nudity experiences are related to increased comfort with sexuality and one's body, and this enables one to feel more comfortable pursuing sexual relationships. Although our question regarding casual sex has negative connotations, it is possible that respondents considered having sex outside of marriage or a love relationship to be "casual." Thus, a kind of sexual freedom/openness may be a more appropriate explanation of these findings. At any rate, the mean scores on this item suggest that while there was a difference in a tendency to engage in casual sex between respondents who reported differing childhood experiences, neither group saw themselves as having a strong tendency to engage in casual sex. It is noteworthy that late childhood (6-11) nudity exposure was modestly related to increased self-esteem and sexual knowledge for males, but not for females, suggesting that there may be a positive side effect of seeing others nude during childhood.

Examination of parental nudity in particular revealed a modest relationship with increased sexual activity. Again, some may interpret these data as supporting their position on the harmful effects of parental nudity, since increased sexual activity may be seen as problematic. However, increased sexual activity in the absence of guilt, anxiety, sexual dysfunction, and other adjustment problems also lends itself to the interpretation we favor, namely, that increased exposure to nudity in the family fosters an atmosphere of acceptance of sexuality, one's body, and increased comfort in this arena. Certainly additional investigation of this issue is warranted before either of these positions is completely accepted.

Although some experts have suggested that sleeping in the parental bed is stimulating and results in negative effects on later adjustment, our results do not support this position. Rather, for boys, sleeping in bed with the parents was related to increased self-esteem and less guilt and anxiety. Sleeping in bed with the parents also was modestly related to increased sexuality, again suggesting a possibility that these individuals are more comfortable with their bodies and their own sexuality permitting more freedom with regard to sexual encounters. For girls, sleeping in bed with parents was modestly related to increased comfort with physical contact and affection as well as increased sexuality.

The role of the parents in good sex education has been accurately emphasized in previous literature (Carrera, 1981; Chamberlin, 1974). In providing sex education for their children certainly *what* the parent says is important. Our data suggest that *how* the parents say it and their attitudes as perceived by their children are important as well. For males, a positive paternal attitude toward sex was modestly related to higher self-esteem, increased sexual activity, and more comfort about physical contact and affection. Sons who felt comfortable talking about sex with their fathers did report more sexual activity. Discussion of sexuality in the home was modestly related to less sexual dysfunction and more comfort about physical contact and affection. Males' comfort level about physical contact and affection was related to positive parental attitudes toward sex and perceived parental comfort dealing with sexuality issues.

Taken together these findings suggest a positive attitude toward sexuality expressed in the family can be beneficial for a child's comfort with his sexuality.

For females, daughters who felt comfortable talking about sex with their mothers and who perceived a positive maternal attitude toward sex tended to feel better about themselves. Paternal attitudes and comfort talking about sex with fathers were modestly related to a happier sex life. Discussion of sexuality in the home was also modestly related to increased sexual activity for girls. These findings also suggest that a positive attitude toward sexuality in the family is beneficial for a girl's comfort with her sexuality.

Regarding gender differences in perception of parental attitudes and comfort discussing sexual issues, it is interesting that men and women did not differ in their perceptions regarding maternal attitudes, mother's comfort level dealing with sexuality, or their own comfort discussing sex with mother. This may be interpreted as being consistent with the finding that mothers do most of the sexual education for children (Thornburg, 1981; Roberts et al., 1978) and implying that mothers deal with their sons and daughters similarly around issues of sexuality. Gender differences did emerge, however, when reports of paternal attitudes and comfort regarding sexuality were examined. Seventy-seven percent of females, compared to 52% of the males, were uncomfortable discussing sex with their father, whereas 21% of males and only 8% of the females were comfortable discussing sex with their fathers. More males tended to perceive their fathers as comfortable talking about sex compared to females (25 vs. 11%) and 69% of the females compared to 42% of the males indicated their fathers were extremely or moderately uncomfortable talking about sex with their fathers. Finally, males tended to perceive a more positive paternal attitude toward sex than did females (39 vs. 18%).

In addition to responding to specific questions, subjects were also invited to comment on their reactions to family practices regarding nudity and sleeping in the parental bed, and without exception such comments reflected a positive attitude toward such experiences. A representative comment for both men and women was "It always gave me a feeling of security to know that if I had a bad dream I could crawl into bed with my mom and dad." Although it might be argued from a psychoanalytic perspective that one would have repressed any memories of ill effects of such experiences, it does seem significant that not one man or woman reported any negative experiences from such family practices.

Although a number of significant relationships between recollected childhood experiences and adult sexual adjustment were found to exist, these relationships were quite modest. It was rare when as much as 10% of the variability of the sexual adjustment items was accounted for by the items pertaining to childhood experiences. Perhaps one of the most important findings of this research, however, is the *absence* of any relationships between retrospective reports of parental nudity, exposure to nudity in general, sleeping in the parental bed, and sexual adjustment problems. Further, the correlation between perceived parental attitudes toward sex and sexual adjustment were generally larger than those between specific family practices and sexual adjustment. It seems that the attitudes toward sex that the parents convey to their children may be more important to their subsequent sexual adjustment than any particular family practice.

This study represents a first attempt to provide some empirical basis for the advice any number of experts have provided to parents regarding the issues of childhood exposure to nudity and children sleeping in the parental bed. Certainly the limitations of this study due to its retrospective design and college student subject population need to be acknowledged. Data from retrospective reports present potential problems with its accuracy and ability to be verified. Further, results from college student samples are not necessarily generalizable to the population at large without additional empirical investigation. Thus, any conclusions drawn from this research must be tentative until the results are replicated with prospective studies and extended using other subject populations. It is clear, however, that there is no basis for the warning of the Cassandras of parental permissiveness regarding sexual issues. Indeed, it appears that parents who have a casual attitude toward family nudity and who permit their children to sleep in their bed may have children with better self-esteem and who feel more comfortable with their sexuality.

*Reprinted by permission of Plenum Publishing Company

Research Excerpt Reaction Questions

1. One result of the previous research article suggested that boys sleeping in bed with the parents was related to increased self-esteem and less guilt and anxiety. What is your explanation for this?

2. This research indicates that the manner and tone of a parent's sex education is as important as what the parent says. Give examples from your own life concerning this issue.

3. Why do you believe that so many girls and boys in this sample were more comfortable discussing sexuality with their mothers than with their fathers?

4. Are you surprised with the finding that exposure to parental nudity and sleeping occasionally in the parental bed did not lead to adulthood sexual adjustment problems? Explain.

Adolescent Sex Education

1. When were you first aware of your adolescent sexuality changes?

2. What did you first notice about your bodily changes?

3. How did you react to these changes?

4. Were you aware of changes among your peers? What did you notice?

5. What did your parents tell you about sexuality in adolescence?

6. When did you begin to notice a physical attraction to other persons? Describe.

7. What was your first adolescent experience that you would describe as sexual?

8. How did your sexual ideas in adolescence differ from your friends'? How were they alike?

Sexuality and Aging

Answer **T (true)** or **F (false)** to indicate your belief about the accuracy of the following statements.

     1. Couples who have sex after 50 are more likely to view their marriages as happy ones.

     2. Adultery is fairly common among sexually active couples over 50 years of age.

     3. Evidence shows that frequency of sex decreases throughout the life span.

     4. Age does not necessarily lead to a decrease in sex drive.

     5. Older women's continued sexuality is more dependent on their spouse's availability than is an older man's sexuality.

     6. There is less decline over age in masturbation for women than for men.

     7. The success rate of treating sexual dysfunction in older couples about equals the success rate of younger couples.

     8. Menopause has a generally negative effect on a woman's sexual desire.

     9. Abstinence from sex for long periods can lead to atrophy of genital tissue.

     10. The best predictors of continued sexual expression in older men are past sexual experience and health.

     11. The best predictors of continued sexual expression in older women are social class and age.

(Answers: 1 = T, 2 = F, 3 = T, 4 = T, 5 = T, 6 = T, 7 = T, 8 = F, 9 = T, 10 = T, 11=F.)

Activities

1. **Sex Learning in Childhood**
    List one or more "facts" that you learned in childhood (prior to 12) about sex from:

    a. your parents

    b. your siblings

    c. your friends

    d. your school

    e. your church

    f. the media (TV, magazines)

    Do you remember engaging in any sex play as a child? If so, how was your sex play treated by your family members?

2. **Adolescent Sexuality and Television Series**
    During one week watch five episodes on television that feature at least one adolescent. What are the sexual messages received by the adolescent? Who are the sources of the information? Is the information accurate or inaccurate? How does this compare to your adolescent experiences?

3. **Myths About Menopause**

   React to the following myths of menopause by writing a brief paragraph to counter the widely-held beliefs. (Internet sources or other research sources may be beneficial.)
   a. Menopause is abnormal.
   b. Menopause leads to a lowered sex drive.
   c. Menopause is accompanied by depression or anxiety.
   d. During menopause all women suffer from debilitating hot flashes.

4. **Aging and Sexuality: Analyzing Birthday Cards**

   Go to a card store and read through birthday cards for 20, 30, 40, 50, 60, and 70-year-olds. What are the messages about sensuality and sexuality as the person progresses through the successive decades? List the common phrases used in these cards to describe sexuality.

CHAPTER 6

MALE AND FEMALE, MASCULINE AND FEMININE

"What are little girls made of?
Sugar and spice and everything nice,
and that's what little girls are made of.
What are little boys made of?
Snips and snails and puppy dog tails,
and that's what little boys are made of."

Children's rhyme

"Is it a boy or a girl?" This was probably the first question uttered in your presence as you slipped out into the world. The answer to this question probably set in motion a multitude of thoughts and behaviors on the part of many of the people around you, and eventually to you. How did you think about your gender? Were you satisfied? Dissatisfied?

Chapter 6 Contents:

A. Gender and Sexual Identity Questions
B. Questionnaire: "How Androgynous Are You?" and Reaction Questions
C. Double Standard Scale
D. Research Excerpt: "Characteristics of the Ideal Sex Partner: Gender Differences and Perceptions of the Preferences of the Other Gender" and Reaction Questions
E. Activities
   1. Advantages and Disadvantages of Gender
   2. Toys as Gender Messages
   3. Sexist Remarks
   4. Androgyny

Gender and Sexual Identity Questions

When do you first remember being aware of being a boy or girl? What were the messages from others about your gender? Was your gender an acceptable one, or did the messages you received indicate otherwise?

1. How were you dressed as a child?

2. What sorts of toys do you remember from your childhood? What was your favorite toy?

3. When do you first remember being curious about the genitals of a same or opposite sex person?

4. How did you satisfy your curiosity about your own genitals? Alone? With same sex friends? With opposite sex friends?

5. How was nudity handled in your family? Was there a difference between same sex and opposite sex nudity in your home? Describe.

6. Do you remember anything about the label "sissy" or "tomboy?" How was this seen in your family or school?

7. Are males who act like females less valuable in our culture? What does this say about sexism in our culture?

8. What messages did you receive about being a boy or a girl?

9. Would you as a parent repeat the messages about masculinity and femininity that you received as a child? Which messages would you change and why? Which messages would you retain and why?

How Androgynous Are You?*

Robert F. Valois and Sandra Kammermann

DIRECTIONS: Use the scale below to indicate how well each of the following characteristics describes you. Write the number from the scale that is appropriate for each characteristic in the space provided.

1	2	3	4
Usually Not True	Occasionally True	Quite Often True	Almost Always True

_____	1. aggressive	_____	21. defends own beliefs
_____	2. affectionate	_____	22. yielding
_____	3. ambitious	_____	23. strong personality
_____	4. compassionate	_____	24. cheerful
_____	5. assertive	_____	25. analytical
_____	6. gentle	_____	26. shy
_____	7. athletic	_____	27. have leadership abilities
_____	8. loving toward children	_____	28. easily flattered
_____	9. competitive	_____	29. willing to take risks
_____	10. loyal	_____	30. feminine
_____	11. dominant	_____	31. make decisions easily
_____	12. sensitive to others	_____	32. eager to soothe hurt feelings
_____	13. forceful	_____	33. masculine
_____	14. sympathetic	_____	34. inefficient
_____	15. independent	_____	35. acts like a leader
_____	16. tender	_____	36. childlike
_____	17. self-reliant	_____	37. individualistic
_____	18. understanding	_____	38. doesn't use harsh language
_____	19. willing to take a stand	_____	39. self-sufficient
_____	20. warm	_____	40. gullible

SCORING: Add up your rating for all the odd-numbered items. This is your MASCULINITY SCORE.

Now add up your ratings for all the even-numbered items. This is your FEMININITY SCORE.

Subtract the lower score from the higher score. If the difference is less than ten (10), this is an indication that you have a well-rounded personality and to some degree you are an "androgynous" individual. If the difference is greater than ten, this is an indication that you tend to exhibit, more often, traditional gender role behavior. The higher of your two scores (masculinity and femininity) would indicate the traditional gender role behavior that you exhibit most often.

Androgyny Reaction Questions

In the questionnaire "How Androgynous Are You?" (previous page) the odd-numbered items are traditionally masculine items and the even-numbered items are traditionally feminine items. Answer the following questions noting your responses on the previous questionnaire.

1. Which characteristics did you choose to describe yourself (3's and 4's) which are gender-traditional items?

2. Which items did you choose to describe yourself (3's and 4's) which are gender non-traditional?

3. Are there gender non-traditional traits you would like to increase? Decrease?

4. Are there gender-traditional traits you would like to increase? Decrease?

5. Do you believe that society's definitions of gender roles are preventing you from behaving or developing in the ways you would most like? Explain.

Double Standard Scale

Circle the number that reflects the extent to which you agree or disagree with each of the following statements.

	Strongly Disagree		Neutral		Strongly Agree
1. It's better for a male to lose his virginity at an earlier age than a female.	1	2	3	4	5
2. It is more acceptable for a male than it is for a female to have sex on a first date.	1	2	3	4	5
3. Multiple partners are more acceptable for a male than for a female.	1	2	3	4	5
4. It's primarily the man's role to initiate sexual activity.	1	2	3	4	5
5. A man should be more sexually experienced than his female partner when he gets married.	1	2	3	4	5
6. A woman who initiates sex is too aggressive.	1	2	3	4	5
7. One questions the character of a woman who has many sex partners.	1	2	3	4	5
8. One admires a guy who has sex with many women.	1	2	3	4	5
9. It is more acceptable for women to fake orgasms than men.	1	2	3	4	5
10. Men should be the primary breadwinners in a relationship.	1	2	3	4	5
11. In most cases it is not appropriate for women to ask men for a date.	1	2	3	4	5
12. It is more appropriate for a woman to date someone older than it is for a man to date someone older.	1	2	3	4	5
13. It is more important for a man to have an orgasm during sex than it is for a woman.	1	2	3	4	5
14. If a woman accepts an expensive gift from a man, she's implying she will have sex with him.	1	2	3	4	5
15. It is more acceptable for a man than for a woman to have sex with someone with whom he's not in love.	1	2	3	4	5

Add together your circled numbers. Compare your score to the following:

15 – 30	Strongly against a double standard for men and women.
31 – 59	Mixed emotions about a double standard for men and women.
60 - 75	Strongly favor a double standard for men and women.

Reaction Questions

1. What are your reactions to your score on this "double standard" scale?

2. Would you like any of your responses to change? Which ones?

3. Which standards would you pass on to your children? Which would you change for your children?

Research Excerpt

Question: What makes for the ideal sex partner? Are there gender differences in these desired characteristics?

Characteristics of the Ideal Sex Partner: Gender Differences and Perceptions of the Preferences of the Other Gender*

Kerry E. McGuirl, Michael W. Wiederman

What makes for the ideal sex partner? Are there gender differences in these desired characteristics? How accurately do men and women perceive the preferences of the other gender? These are questions for which we have little empirical data. Much research has been conducted on men's and women's reported preferences regarding long-term mates (Allgeier & Wiederman, 1994; Buss, 1994; Wiederman & Allgeier, 1994). However, research on preferences in sexual partners has been relatively scarce.

Hatfield, Sprecher, Pillemer, Greenberger, and Wexler (1989) had undergraduates rate several characteristics and activities as to whether the respondent would prefer his or her partner to exhibit each of them more or less than the partner currently does during their sexual interaction. With only one exception (talk more lovingly), there were no gender differences with regard to the characteristics and activities related to love and intimacy (e.g., be more caring, considerate, complimentary, warm, involved, and seductive). However, there were gender differences on several of the items related to partner initiative and sexual variety. In each case, men indicated more than did women that they wished their partners would exhibit more frequently such characteristics or activities. These included being rough, dominant, experimental, variable, and impulsive during sex as well as taking the initiative more and providing more instructions.

Similar to Hatfield and colleagues, Purnine, Carey, and Jorgensen (1994) asked college students to respond to several items having to do with preferences for characteristics and activities related to one's sexual partner. There were many notable gender differences including men's greater preference for use of alcohol, drugs, and erotica with a partner as well as men's greater interest in oral sex. In contrast, women demonstrated greater preference than did men for emotionally intimate, romantic settings, as well as nongenital forms of sexual expression and stimulation. Danny, Field, and Quadagno (1984) also found that with regard to sexual interaction, male undergraduates placed the most emphasis on intercourse, whereas female undergraduates most valued foreplay.

These few studies that have compared men's and women's preferences for sexual partners have been fairly consistent in finding that men place relatively greater emphasis on genital stimulation and desire partners who exhibit greater initiative and erotophila. Compared to men, women may desire more nongenital expressions of affection as well as romantic settings for sexual activity. The extent to which men and women accurately perceive the preferences of the other gender is a question not explored in previous research.

The purpose of the current study was to further examine gender differences in a varied set of characteristics in a sexual partner (within the presumed context of an ongoing relationship) and to investigate the extent to which men and women accurately estimate the preferences of the other gender. This latter aspect of the current study may have important implications for sexual counseling and education; inaccuracy in assessing the other gender may lead to confusion, frustration, self-imposed pressure, and unsatisfying sexual interactions between men and women.

Table 1. Comparison of Men (n = 185) and Women (n = 244) with Regard to Rated Importance of Particular Characteristics in Long-Term Sex Partners

Partner Characteristic	Men Mean	(SD)	Women Mean	(SD)	F (1,427)	p<	d
1. Be open to discussing sex	5.19	(.86)	5.50	(.75)	15.82	.0001	.38
2. Be uninhibited	4.36	(1.19)	4.37	(1.12)	.02	.89	.02
3. Be physically attractive	5.21	(.82)	4.75	(.91)	29.88	.0001	.51
4. Be knowledgeable about sex	5.01	(.91)	5.21	(.85)	5.66	.02	.23
5. Pay me compliments during sex	4.41	(1.09)	4.72	(1.00)	9.59	.002	.29
6. Clearly communicate desires	5.10	(.91)	5.11	(.73)	.00	.98	.01
7. Be easily sexually aroused	4.59	(1.07)	4.57	(1.01)	.04	.85	.02
8. Experience orgasm easily	4.32	(1.01)	3.73	(1.19)	29.57	.0001	.51
9. Like erotic videos, books, magazines	3.48	(1.32)	3.08	(1.35)	9.36	.003	.30
10. Take the dominant role during sex	3.91	(.99)	4.19	(1.01)	8.24	.005	.28

Table 2. Comparison of Men's (n = 185) Self-Reported Preferences for Particular Characteristics in Long-Term Sex Partners and Women's (n = 244) Estimates of Male Preferences

Partner Characteristic	Men's Actual Mean	(SD)	Women's Estimates Mean	(SD)	F (1,427)	p<	d
1. Be open to discussing sex	5.19	(.86)	4.84	(1.05)	13.75	.001	.35
2. Be uninhibited	4.36	(1.19)	4.45	(1.21)	.70	.41	.08
3. Be physically attractive	5.21	(.82)	5.36	(.70)	4.38	.04	.20
4. Be knowledgeable about sex	5.01	(.91)	4.85	(.96)	2.78	.10	.16
5. Pay me compliments during sex	4.41	(1.09)	5.06	(.92)	45.33	.0001	.62
6. Clearly communicate desires	5.10	(.91)	4.86	(.89)	7.89	.005	.26
7. Be easily sexually aroused	4.59	(1.07)	4.98	(.95)	16.23	.0001	.39
8. Experience orgasm easily	4.32	(1.01)	4.60	(1.10)	7.01	.005	.26
9. Like erotic videos, books, magazines	3.48	(1.32)	4.22	(1.35)	31.96	.0001	.53
10. Take the dominant role during sex	3.91	(.99)	3.98	(1.16)	.45	.51	.06

Table 3. Comparison of Women's (n = 244) Self-Reported Preferences for Particular Characteristics in Long-Term Sex Partners and Men's (n = 184) Estimates of Female Preferences

Partner Characteristic	Men's Estimates		Women's Actual		F		
	Mean	(SD)	Mean	(SD)	(1,427)	p<	d
1. Be open to discussing sex	4.95	(.93)	5.50	(.75)	46.24	.0001	.63
2. Be uninhibited	4.11	(1.14)	4.37	(1.12)	5.51	.02	.23
3. Be physically attractive	4.96	(.93)	4.75	(.91)	5.81	.02	.23
4. Be knowledgeable about sex	5.05	(.85)	5.21	(.85)	3.71	.06	.19
5. Pay me compliments during sex	4.77	(.95)	4.72	(1.00)	.27	.61	.05
6. Clearly communicate desires	4.83	(.95)	5.11	(.73)	11.40	.001	.33
7. Be easily sexually aroused	4.32	(1.15)	4.57	(1.01)	5.63	.02	.23
8. Experience orgasm easily	3.33	(1.01)	3.73	(1.19)	9.97	.002	.30
9. Like erotic videos, books, magazines	3.06	(1.25)	3.08	(1.35)	.02	.90	.01
10. Take the dominant role during sex	4.24	(1.06)	4.19	(1.01)	.31	.58	.05

DISCUSSION

Considering the mean ratings in Table 1, both men and women rated eight of the ten characteristics as generally positive in a long-term sexual partner. The exceptions were that men slightly disagreed that an ideal partner would like erotic media and would take the dominant role during sex. Women slightly disagreed that an ideal sex partner would like erotic media and would attain orgasm easily. Despite a high degree of overall agreement as to the general positive nature of most of the partner characteristics, there were several gender differences with regard to how highly each was rated. Compared to the other gender, men placed relatively more value on a sexual partner who is physically attractive, experiences orgasm easily, and likes erotic media, whereas women placed relatively more value on a sexual partner who is open to discussing sex, provides compliments during sex, and takes the dominant role during sex.

The findings that perhaps have the greatest implications for intervention are those reported in Tables 2 and 3. In comparing the perceptions of the other gender with the actual ratings from each gender, several misperceptions were apparent. First, both men and women underestimated the value that the other gender places on a partner who is open to discussing sex and who clearly communicates desires. Yet for both men and women these characteristics were among the most highly rated. To the extent that members of each gender misperceive the high value members of the other gender place on communication by a sexual partner, individuals are liable to refrain from such communication. Acting on these misperceptions may result in an increased likelihood of unsatisfying sexual interactions as well as negative consequences that can result from sexual situations lacking in partner communication such as sexually transmitted diseases, sexual coercion, and hurt feelings.

The other apparent misperception may place both men and women at risk of self-imposed pressure to perform to a certain standard when involved in a sexual interaction. Specifically, women overestimated men's preference for a sexual partner who likes erotic media and easily becomes aroused and attains orgasm. Men overestimated women's dislike for a sexual partner who attains orgasm easily. This set of misperceptions may result in men and women being their own worst critics of sexual performance. Women may believe that they are not erotophilic enough and do not respond physically to sexual stimuli as their partner would like, whereas men may believe that they do not refrain long enough from ejaculating to meet their partners' expectations.

Research Excerpt Reaction Questions

1. What are the major gender differences in desired characteristics of long-term sex partners?

2. A previous study by Denny, Field, and Quadagno (1984) found what major difference between men and women in their sex preferences?

3. According to this study, how accurately do men and women estimate the preferences of their sexual partners?

4. What are the common misperceptions that men and women have about each other's sexual preferences?

Activities

1. **Advantages and Disadvantages of Gender**
   On a blank sheet of paper write "male" on the front, and "female" on the back. Divide each side into two columns, one labeled "Advantages," the other labeled "Disadvantages." List the advantages and disadvantages of being male and female in our culture. Ask five friends to add to your lists.

   After completing the lists, what do you notice?
   a. Which list is longer?
   b. What is the significance, if any, of the length of the list?
   c. Which qualities may have genetic components?
   d. Which qualities are primarily behavioral or societal?
   e. Would you like to change any aspects of your lists? Which ones?
   f. How could you change aspects of the list?

2. **Toys as Gender Messages**
   Visit the children's toy section of your favorite store. If you knew nothing about gender except that which you could gather from toys and the pictures on the box covers of toys, what generalizations could you make about boys and girls in our culture? Give examples.

3. **Sexist Remarks**
   Keep track and list all sex-biased remarks (both male and female) that you hear in a single day. Were there more female than male comments? Who gives the most comments, males or females? What are the settings for these remarks? Explain.

4. **Androgyny**
   Find two advertisements in print that portray androgyny. How does this differ from more traditional advertising?

CHAPTER 7

LIKING, LOVING, AND PHYSICAL ATTRACTION

"To be in love is merely to be in a state of perceptual anesthesia--to mistake an ordinary young man for a Greek god or an ordinary young woman for a goddess."

H.L. Mencken, 1919

Who might you like? Who might you love? Glance around a room full of persons who you do not know and attempt to answer the above questions. Do you have a template or pattern that you carry in your mind that helps you to determine who will be likeable and lovable? Who and what are the sources of your template? Do you tend to fall in love with the wrong persons? Does your template need to change?

Chapter 7 Contents:

A. Physical Attraction: What Counts?
B. Non-negotiables/Negotiables
C. Questionnaire: "Are You in Love? The Love Scale"
D. Research Excerpt: "Dating Preferences of University Women: An Analysis of the Nice Guy Stereotype" and Reaction Questions
E. Activities
    1. Loving versus "In Love"
    2. TV Relationships
    3. Love Songs
    4. Love versus Craziness
    5. Love Language
    6. Fairy Tales

Physical Attraction: What Counts?

As a heterosexual male or female, what physical qualities do you look for in the opposite sex? As a homosexual male or female, what physical qualities do you look for in the same sex? What do you assume others are looking for in you? Are your assumptions correct? Make a list of the three physical qualities you most admire in the same or opposite sex (depending on your sexual orientation).

1.

2.

3.

What three physical qualities do you assume others are looking for in you?

1.

2.

3.

Compare your answer with the results of the studies reported on the following page.

1. In what areas are you similar to the reported norms?

2. In what areas are you dissimilar from the reported norms?

What Men Find Erotic in Men
(Bell, 1974; Howard et al., 1987)

Pleasant face   Tallness

Youthfulness   Lack of baldness

Athletic build

Broad shoulders   Large penis
tapering to
the waist   Large
        scrotum

        Small buttocks

What Women Find Erotic in Women
(Bell et al., 1978; Kleinke et al., 1980; Howard et al., 1987)

Attractive face, hair and eyes Tall

Feminine body type
and frame   Absent body hair

       Medium-sized
       breasts

Athletic build   Small buttocks

       Small hips

What Men Find Erotic in Women
(Luria et al., 1979; Buss, 1994; Cunningham et al., 1995)

Shiny, full hair   Clear-skinned
       Expressive eyebrows
Physically attractive
Symmetrical face Large smile
Large eyes   Small nose and chin

Medium-sized
breasts   Thin body
       Small waist
Small hips,
buttocks,
thighs

Long legs

What Women Find Erotic in Men
(Gagnon, 1977; Cunningham et al., 1995)

  Adult jaw profile Tallness
  Large male chin   Slimness

  Facial hair   Muscular neck
        Muscular arms
V-shaped body,   and shoulders
tapering to
waist   Hairy, muscular
       chest
Flat stomach
       Small buttocks
Average penis   Long legs

Non-Negotiables/Negotiables

1. What are your non-negotiables? In other words, what are the qualities or traits (emotional and physical) that you <u>must</u> have in a partner to thrive in a relationship?

    1.   6.
    2.   7.
    3.   8.
    4.   9.
    5.   10.

2. What are your negotiables? In other words, what are the qualities or traits you would like in a partner but are not absolute necessities?

    1.   6.
    2.   7.
    3.   8.
    4.   9.
    5.   10.

Reaction Questions:

1. On what do you base your lists? Where do you believe your desire for these qualities originated?

2. Do you know anyone who possesses all of these traits?

3. What will occur if you cannot find someone who possesses all of these qualities?

4. How many of the qualities on your non-negotiable list do you feel you possess? Which are you missing?

5. Imagine your parents choosing your relationship partner. Which qualities would they select as most important? Least important?

6. How do your views about an ideal partner for yourself compare with your parents' ideas about an ideal partner for you?

7. Write one sentence about your requirements for your partner on each of the following criteria:

    a. Money:

    b. Religion:

    c. Ethnicity:

    d. Parenting interests:

    e. In-law interaction:

    f. Social interaction:

    g. Education level:

    h. Relative age of partner:

    i. Relationship history of partner:

    j. Sexual history of partner:

Are You in Love? The Love Scale *

S.A. Rathus and J.S. Nevid

The following measure of romantic love was developed at Northeastern University in Boston. To complete the scale, insert the name of your dating partner in the blank space for each item (or, if you've been busy, repeat the scale for other dating partners) and indicate the degree to which the item is true or false for you by circling the appropriate number. Then add the circled numbers together to arrive at your total love score and compare your score with those from a sample of 220 undergraduates at Northeastern University (age range 19-24, mean age = 21).

Directions: Circle the number that best shows how true or false the items are for you according to this code:

7 = definitely true	**3 = somewhat false**
6 = rather true	**2 = rather false**
5 = somewhat true	**1 = definitely false**
4 = not sure, or equally true and false	

1. I look forward to being with _____ a great deal.	1	2	3	4	5	6	7
2. I find _____ to be sexually exciting.	1	2	3	4	5	6	7
3. _____ has fewer faults than most people.	1	2	3	4	5	6	7
4. I would do anything I could for _____.	1	2	3	4	5	6	7
5. _____ is very attractive to me.	1	2	3	4	5	6	7
6. I like to share my feelings with _____.	1	2	3	4	5	6	7
7. Doing things is more fun when _____ and I do them together.	1	2	3	4	5	6	7
8. I like to have _____ all to myself.	1	2	3	4	5	6	7
9. I would feel horrible if anything bad happened to _____.	1	2	3	4	5	6	7
10. I think about _____ very often.	1	2	3	4	5	6	7
11. It is very important that _____ cares for me.	1	2	3	4	5	6	7
12. I am most content when I am with _____.	1	2	3	4	5	6	7
13. It is difficult for me to stay away from _____ for very long.	1	2	3	4	5	6	7
14. I care about _____ a great deal.	1	2	3	4	5	6	7

Total Score for Love Scale: _____

The table below shows the mean (average) scores for 220 Northeastern University undergraduate students. Students were asked to indicate whether they were "absolutely in love," "probably in love," "not sure," "probably not in love," or "definitely not in love" with a person they were dating. Mean scores for men and women were not significantly different, so they were combined to form the means. If your own score is 85, your feelings of love toward your partner would fall between those of the Northeastern students who said that they were "probably in love" and those who reported being "absolutely in love" with their partners.

Let us caution, however, that arguments have erupted between dating partners whose love scores for one another differed by a few points! The Love Scale is meant to be a crude index of the intensity of love, not a scientifically precise measurement. Don't take your score so seriously. The scale is meant to be fun, so rely on your feelings toward one another, not on your score *per se*.

Love Scale Scores of Northeastern University Students

Condition	N*	Mean Score
Absolutely in love	56	89
Probably in love	45	80
Not sure	36	77
Probably not in love	40	68
Definitely not in love	43	59

*Number of students

* From *Adjustment & Growth, 5th Edition* by Spencer Rathus. Copyright © 1992 by Spencer Rathus. This material is used by permission of John Wiley & Sons, Inc.

Research Excerpt

Question: What types of men do women consider most desirable?

> **Dating Preferences of University Women: An Analysis of the Nice Guy Stereotype***
> Edward S. Herold and Robin R. Milhausen
>
> Many researchers have attempted to discover what types of men women consider most desirable for relationship partners. This study investigated university women's (N = 165) perceptions of "nice guys," specifically whether women perceived nice guys to be more or less sexually successful than guys who are considered not nice. Both quantitative and qualitative analyses were used. The qualitative analysis was useful in understanding women's different interpretations of the nice guy label. More than one half of the women agreed that nice guys have fewer sexual partners. However, more than one half also reported a preference for a nice guy over a bad boy as a date. As hypothesized, women who placed a lesser emphasis on the importance of sex, who had fewer sexual partners, and who were less accepting of men who had many sexual partners were more likely to choose the nice guy as a dating partner. The findings indicate that nice guys are likely to have fewer sexual partners but are more desired for committed relationships.
>
> ## DISCUSSION
>
> The objective of this research was to explore women's perceptions and preferences regarding men considered to be nice guys. Consistent with past research, the majority of the women reported a preference for a nice guy (Buss & Barnes, 1986; Regan, 1998) who had limited sexual experience (O'Sullivan, 1995). However, when asked about behaviors rather than their preferences, more than one half of the women (56%) agreed that nice guys do tend to have less sexual success with women. Also, more than one half of the women (56%) reported that they knew of women who had selected an experienced, not-so-nice guy over a nice, less experienced male. However, unlike Sprecher et al. (1997), who reported that almost all women prefer a "chaste partner" over those with moderate or extensive sexual experience, almost all of the women (95%) in our study were willing to date a male who had had at least one other previous partner.
>
> What, then, is the answer to the question "Do nice guys finish last?" It appears that the measurement instruments used strongly influence the answer to this question. First, research findings to date proclaiming the popularity of kind, sensitive men have overemphasized women's partner preferences obtained through checklists while neglecting to study their actual relationship choices. Although many women report that nice guy characteristics are the most desired in a partner, women's actual choices do not always coincide with what they report they want in checklist studies of mate preferences. For example, although the women in our study reported preferring dating partners with limited sexual experience, more than one third reported having dated someone who had had more sexual partners than they would have liked. These findings show the value of analyzing both preferences and behaviors.
>
> Second, determining success also depends on whether the criteria for success are focused on sexual or relationship factors. More than one half of the women agreed nice guys were likely to have fewer sexual partners. However, when relationship criteria were used, as when the women were asked about dating preferences, nice guys were favored by the majority. Most researchers have measured women's preferences for dating or marriage partners. However, only a few studies asked what traits or characteristics women might seek in sexual partners. Women emphasize different characteristics as important when choosing sexual rather than relationship partners. For example, although Sadalla et al. (1987) found male dominance to increase women's ratings of sexual attractiveness, dominant men were considered less likeable and not desirable as spouses. As well, Regan and Berscheid (1997) found that

although sensitivity, honesty and kindness were women's most preferred characteristics in a marriage partner, physical attractiveness was most desired in a sexual partner, with women considering nice guy characteristics to be of only moderate importance. The assumption in the literature has been that all women are more interested in relationships than sex. Yet for some women, the sexual aspect of a relationship is primary (Kalof, 1995). In particular, women who are more permissive and who are willing to engage in sex are more attracted to bad boys. Thus, bad boys tend to be more sexually successful with these women. Our study supports previous research which found that women who have had many partners prefer men who also have had many partners (Istvan & Griffit, 1980). However, nice guys are popular among women who are not so sexually active. Thus, while nice guys may not be competitive in terms of numbers of sexual partners, they tend to be more successful with respect to longer-term, committed relationships.

An important contribution of this study is the qualitative analysis of women's responses to the open-ended question "Do nice guys finish last?" Although the expression, "Nice guys finish last," is widely used, research has not addressed what the nice guy construct encompasses. Specifically, researchers have made assumptions about what characteristics are associated with being a nice guy and what these characteristics might mean to women (Jensen-Campbell et al., 1995; Trapnell & Meston, 1996). Our results revealed that different meanings are associated with the nice guy label. Some women offered flattering interpretations of the nice guy, characterizing him as committed, caring, and respectful of women. Others, however, emphasized more negative aspects, considering the nice guy to be boring, lacking confidence, and unattractive. The bad boys were also perceived dichotomously, as either confident, attractive, sexy, and exciting or as manipulative, unfaithful, disrespectful of women, and interested only in sex. As these profiles came directly form the women's open-ended responses, they provided insight into the women's motivations for preferring nice or not-nice guys.

Simpson and Gangestad's (1992; Gangestad & Simpson, 1990) approach to sexual strategies can be used to explain differences in the women's perceptions of nice guys and bad boys and their preferences for date selection. Women who endorse a restricted sociosexual orientation would be more likely to select nice guys as partners and would be more likely to fear or dislike bad boys. On the other hand, women who adopt an unrestricted sociosexual orientation would choose partners who are more dominant, assertive, and physically attractive, while considering the nice guys to be uninteresting and unexciting. Our results support these categorizations. Women who had had fewer sexual partners (an indicator of restricted sociosexual orientation) were more likely to select the inexperienced, nice guy over the experienced, fun, attractive man as a dating partner. As well, women who considered sex to be less important to them and women who were less accepting of a partner with high levels of sexual experience were more likely to select the nice guy.

Our study provided two major contributions to the literature on nice guys and women's preferences for dating partners. First, it analyzed both women's preferences and their actual behaviors in terms of selecting nice or not-nice guys. As well, the open-ended format allowed the women to describe their motivations for preferring a nice guy or a bad boy, whereas other research has ignored this component of partner selection.

This study was limited by its reliance on single item measures rather than scales. Further, social desirability may have influenced some of the women's responses.

To conclude, the answer to the question "Do nice guys finish last?" is complicated in that it is influenced both by the measurement instruments used and by subject characteristics. Although the majority of women report a preference for nice guys, these men tend to have fewer sexual partners. On the other hand, bad boys tend to be more sexually successful, perhaps because of their confident, assertive style of propositioning women as well as their popularity and attractiveness. Bad boys fare especially well with highly sexually experienced women who are looking for casual, short-term relationships. Although nice guys may be less successful in terms of number of sexual partners, they continue to be preferred for friendships and committed, intimate relationships. In this context, nice guys do not always finish last.

Research Excerpt Reaction Questions

1. According to this research excerpt, do nice guys finish last? Explain.

2. Are women's verbal preferences for partners consistent with their behavioral preferences? Explain.

3. Do you agree that nice guys have fewer sexual partners? What has your experience been on this topic?

4. Regan and Berscheid (1997) found that women desire different characteristics for a marriage partner than a sexual partner. What are these differences?

5. What are the differences in mate choices for sexually experienced or inexperienced women?

Activities

1. **Loving versus "In Love"**

   Interview two persons who have been in committed relationships for two or more years. Has their "love" changed over time? How do they describe these "love" changes? Do they see a difference between "infatuation" and "love?" Explain.

2. **TV Relationships**

   What is your favorite TV relationship? Watch two segments of this series and describe the qualities that you would wish to model in your relationship. Are there aspects that you do not admire?

3. **Love Songs**

   Write out the lyrics to two of your favorite love songs. What are the messages of importance to you in these lyrics? Have you had relationships that mirror these images? Describe.

4. **Love versus Craziness**

   How do you know when you are in love? What are the signs? What are the signs of emotional disturbance? Are there similarities between the two? How might this be explained psychologically and/or physiologically?

5. **Love Language**

   Generate a list of words or phrases that you have heard related to love, i.e., falling in love, being smitten, etc. What are the underlying assumptions regarding this language?

6. **Fairy Tales**

   Read a few fairy tales, i.e., *Cinderella, Sleeping Beauty*, etc. What are the love messages in these tales?

CHAPTER 8

COMMUNICATION AND SEXUALITY

In a Woody Allen movie, Woody's date says, "I believe in having sex as often, as freely, and as intensely as possible." Allen responds by embracing her and trying to kiss her.

"What do you take me for?" she replies angrily.

Allen asks himself, "How did I misread those signs?"

Play It Again Sam, Woody Allen

A definition of good communication is INTENT = IMPACT. In other words, does your language have the impact that you have intended? If you intend to get close to someone and, instead, they become angry and leave you, what has happened to your communication? Obviously, something has gone awry. Good communication takes not just practice, but correct practice to increase the probability that your words and actions are accurately perceived.

Chapter 8 Contents:

A. Problem Solving Rating Sheet and Reaction Questions
B. Questionnaire: "What's Your Gender Communication Quotient?" and Reaction Questions
C. Good Communication: The Root of Intimacy
D. Research Excerpt: "By the Semi-Mystical Appearance of a Condom: How Young Women and Men Communicate Sexual Consent in Heterosexual Situations" and Reaction Questions
E. Sexual Communication: Good and Bad Sex
F. Activities
   1. How Do People Meet Each Other?
   2. Dating Services
   3. Personal Ads
   4. Internet Dating Services
   5. Mutual Consent Policy

Problem Solving Rating Sheet

Does your <u>intent</u> equal your <u>impact</u>? In other words, do your words do what you want them to do? Are you communicating effectively?

The following rating sheet will allow you to evaluate your own style of communication and that of your partner. You might find it helpful to copy this sheet and have your partner complete one as well. To understand the "Guidelines" use the following definitions.

1. **Start with positives** - when asking for a change in behavior, start your request with a related behavior that your partner is already doing well (e.g. "I really like it when you hug me at home. Could you do it when we are out?")

2. **No Zapping** - Avoid any sarcastic comment, name-calling, or non-verbal messages such as eye-rolling, frowning.

3. **No Generalizations** - Avoid use of the words "always" or "never" or use of general traits, e.g. "irresponsible," "lazy," rather than a specific request.

4. **Use Feeling Language** - Use of "I" and feeling words rather than blaming with "you" words and sentences.

5. **Admit Your Role** - Take some responsibility for a problem situation before casting all blame on your partner.

6. **Don't Bring Up the Past** - Concentrate on the present problem with future plans for change, not elaborating on past issues.

7. **One Problem at a Time** - Do not go off on tangents. Stick with first problem until it is resolved.

8. **Don't Infer Motives** - Avoid mind-reading. Ask a person what they are feeling rather than assigning them a feeling or belief.

9. **No Interrupting** - Let your partner complete an idea before you share your idea. By not interrupting, you increase the chance that you are listening effectively.

After completing your ratings on the next page answer the following questions:

Rating Sheet Reaction Questions

1. What are your strengths?

2. What are your weaknesses?

3. How might you improve your weaker areas?

Rate your behavior and that of your partner by circling the number below that represents how well you think you and your partner do on these measures. Use the directions and definitions on the previous page.

GUIDELINES		Inadequate								Adequate
1. Start with positives	Self	1	2	3	4	5	6	7	8	9
	Partner	1	2	3	4	5	6	7	8	9
2. No zapping	Self	1	2	3	4	5	6	7	8	9
	Partner	1	2	3	4	5	6	7	8	9
3. No generalizations	Self	1	2	3	4	5	6	7	8	9
	Partner	1	2	3	4	5	6	7	8	9
4. Use feeling language	Self	1	2	3	4	5	6	7	8	9
	Partner	1	2	3	4	5	6	7	8	9
5. Admit your role	Self	1	2	3	4	5	6	7	8	9
	Partner	1	2	3	4	5	6	7	8	9
6. Don't bring up the past	Self	1	2	3	4	5	6	7	8	9
	Partner	1	2	3	4	5	6	7	8	9
7. One problem at a time	Self	1	2	3	4	5	6	7	8	9
	Partner	1	2	3	4	5	6	7	8	9
8. Don't infer motives	Self	1	2	3	4	5	6	7	8	9
	Partner	1	2	3	4	5	6	7	8	9
9. No interrupting	Self	1	2	3	4	5	6	7	8	9
	Partner	1	2	3	4	5	6	7	8	9

What's Your Gender Communications Quotient? *

Hazel R. Rozema and John Gray

How much do you know about how men and women communicate with one another? The 20 items in this questionnaire are based on research conducted in classrooms, private homes, businesses, offices, hospitals--the places where people commonly work and socialize. The answers are at the end of this quiz.

True False

_____ _____ 1. Men talk more than women.

_____ _____ 2. Men are more likely to interrupt women than they are to interrupt other men.

_____ _____ 3. There are approximately ten times as many sexual terms for males as females in the English language.

_____ _____ 4. During conversations, women spend more time gazing at their partner than men do.

_____ _____ 5. Nonverbal messages carry more weight than verbal messages.

_____ _____ 6. Female managers communicate with more emotional openness and drama than male managers.

_____ _____ 7. Men not only control the content of conversation, but they also work harder in keeping conversations going.

_____ _____ 8. When people hear generic words such as "mankind" and "he," they respond inclusively, indicating that the terms apply to both sexes.

_____ _____ 9. Women are more likely to touch others than men are.

_____ _____ 10. In classroom communications, male students receive more reprimands and criticism than female students

_____ _____ 11. Women are more likely than men to disclose information on intimate personal concerns.

_____ _____ 12. Female speakers are more animated in their conversational style than are male speakers.

_____ _____ 13. Women use less personal space than men.

_____ _____ 14. When a male speaks, he is listened to more carefully than a female speaker, even when she makes the identical presentation.

_____ _____ 15. In general, women speak in a more tentative style than do men.

_____ _____ 16. Women are more likely to answer questions that are not addressed to them.

_____ _____ 17. There is widespread sex segregation in schools, and it hinders effective classroom communication.

_____ _____ 18. Female managers are seen by both male and female subordinates as better communicators than male managers.

_____ _____ 19. In classroom communications, teachers are more likely to give verbal praise to females than to male students.

_____ _____ 20. In general, men smile more often than women.

(1 = T, 2 = T, 3 = F, 4 = T, 5 = T, 6-9 = F, 10-15 = T, 16 = F, 17 = T, 18 = T, 19-20 = F)

*Reprinted by permission of Hazel R. Rozema and John Gray, Department of Communication, University of Arkansas, Little Rock.

"Communications Quotient" Reaction Questions

1. Which of the answers to the above questions are most surprising?

2. Which of the above have you noticed most in your communication with the opposite sex?

3. Which of the above concerns have the most impact in your day-to-day interactions with others? Describe.

4. How might you use two of the above facts to strengthen your communication concerns?

Good Communication: The Root of Intimacy

"We want more intimacy," is a common complaint of many couples entering therapy. As the problems are discussed, "intimacy" is often the code word for talking. Women claim to want more talking. Men also ask for intimacy, but often operationalize it by asking for more sexual activity. What are ways to improve intimacy and communication?

Ask yourself the following questions. Each of these questions describe an area that relates to good communication and, therefore, increased intimacy.

True False

1. It is easy for you to express thanks for a gift or favor without feeling uncomfortable.
2. It is easy for you to compliment others.
3. It is easy for you to take responsibility for an error you might have made.
4. It is easy for you to express warmth or affection for someone you care for.
5. It is easy for you to talk over a problem rather than to worry about it silently.
6. It is easy for you to meet new people and make new acquaintances.
7. It is easy for you to express your innermost feelings with close friends.
8. It is easy for you to see another person's point of view in an argument.
9. It is easy to believe that someone who loves you could also be angry with you.
10. It is easy for you to express emotion in a physical way by touching, holding.

Reaction Questions:

1. Which of the above would you like to improve?

2. What would be some steps to improve yourself in one or more of these areas?

Research Excerpt

Question: How do men and women communicate sexual consent to one another?

**By the Semi-Mystical Appearance of a Condom: How Young Women and Men
Communicate Sexual Consent in Heterosexual Situations***
Susan E. Hickman and Charlene L. Muehlenhard

In the fall of 1990, students and administrators at Antioch College in Yellow Springs, Ohio, joined forces to develop a mutual sexual consent policy. It required, among other things, that all Antioch students obtain consent from their partners prior to engaging in any sexual contact and before proceeding to the next level of sexual intimacy, unless the sexual activity was mutually initiated. Consent was defined as "the act of willingly and verbally agreeing to engage in specific sexual contact or conduct" (Antioch College, 1990, p.1).

When the national press brought this policy to the attention of the general public in the fall of 1993, it created an international controversy. The policy was discussed and critiqued on the front pages of newspapers ranging from the *New York Times* to the *Bangkok Post*, on every major U.S. television network, and even on the comedy show *Saturday Night Live* (Guskin, 1994). In a response to the public's reaction, Alan Guskin (1994), President of Antioch College, discussed the reasoning behind the mutual consent policy. The goal of the policy was to enable women and men to communicate freely about their sexual wishes in an open and honest manner. Ideally, this would reduce the incidence of sexual assault on campus. Reflecting on the international press coverage this policy received, Guskin (1994) stated,

> I believe it's not just sex that has created the reaction, but the Antioch requirement that students
> talk about sex! Talking about it with someone whom you desire; getting consent before having sex;
> having to think about sexual acts that you are about to do; communicating with your partner about
> your interests. (p. 2)

Sexual consent is an important issue. Consent is a central issue in defining rape both in research and in legal cases (rape is often defined as sex without consent; see Burt & Albin, 1981; Estrich, 1987; Muehlenhard, Powch, Phelps, & Giusti, 1992; Sanday, 1996). It has even been suggested that gender-based misunderstandings regarding consent can lead to rape (Abbey, 1991; see also Crawford, 1995). Unfortunately, there has been little research to help clarify how people perceive and communicate sexual consent.

DISCUSSION

Sexual Consent Signals

Communicating sexual consent is far more complex than simply saying yes to a sexual initiation. The young women and men in this study reported that they use a variety of signals to indicate their consent, and that they view a variety of signals as indicative of sexual consent in heterosexual situations. These signals ranged from behaviors as vague as smiling to statements as straightforward as "I want to have sex with you." Most of the sexual consent signals in this study fell into indefinable categories of direct and indirect verbal and nonverbal consent signals.

Reported use of consent signals. Participants who had previously engaged in sexual intercourse reported that they used a wide repertoire of signals to indicate their sexual consent in actual situations: direct verbal signals, direct nonverbal signals, indirect verbal signals, and indirect nonverbal signals. They reported almost never using statements about their level of intoxication or direct refusals to signal their sexual consent; they did, however, frequently convey consent by not resisting. Self-reported use of consent signals was, at most, moderately related to ratings of how indicative the signals were of sexual consent in the scenarios. The use and interpretation of consent signals depended on other factors such as gender and the way in which sex was initiated.

Gender and Sexual Consent

Gender and the self-reported actual use of consent signals. Closer examination of the self-reported use of consent signals revealed that there were small differences between women and men in the kinds of consent signals they reported using. Women were more likely than men to use indirect verbal signals (e.g., asking if the other person has a condom), whereas men were more likely than women to use indirect nonverbal signals (e.g., touching, kissing, or caressing the other person), no response (e.g., not saying no), or statements about their level of intoxication (though the use of intoxication statements was relatively rare) to indicate their consent. These differences suggest the possibility of gender-based misunderstandings. Women and men may expect that their date would consent in the same way they would consent; if their date does or says something that they themselves would use to signal consent, they may mistakenly assume the date is signaling consent. However, the effect sizes of the differences between women's and men's self-reported use of these consent signals were small, suggesting that the actual differences are small. Additionally, both women and men reported using no response (e.g., not resisting) more frequently than other signals. They were equally likely to use direct verbal and direct nonverbal signals, and equally unlikely to use direct refusals to signal consent. There were far more similarities than differences in women's and men's self-reported use of consent signals.

Gender and perceptions of sexual consent. There were also gender differences in ratings of how indicative signals would be of one's own sexual consent in response to a date's sexual initiation in hypothetical scenarios. Men rated direct verbal signals, direct nonverbal signals, indirect verbal signals, indirect nonverbal signals, statements about intoxication, and no response as more indicative of their own sexual consent than did women. This is not surprising given that numerous studies have found that men rate women, other men, and even themselves more sexually than women do (e.g., Abbey, 1982; Johnson et al., 1991). It seems this tendency also affects perceptions of hypothetical self-consent ratings. The one exception was saying no to signal consent: Women and men rated a direct refusal—a no—as being equally unindicative of their sexual consent.

Women and men were in agreement about the meaning of their dates' sexual consent signals in hypothetical scenarios. Interestingly, although women and men have similar ideas about whether their dates' signals indicate consent, they mean different things when they themselves use these signals. That is, women interpret their male dates' signals the same way that men interpret their female dates' signals, but paradoxically, as discussed in the previous paragraph, men's signals indicate a greater level of sexual consent than do the same signals given by women. This difference sets up the potential for sexual miscommunication.

Further exploration revealed that men rated their female dates' direct verbal signals, direct nonverbal signals, indirect verbal signals, indirect nonverbal signals, and intoxication statements as more indicative of their female dates' sexual consent than women rated their own sexual consent signals. Likewise, men rated their own indirect verbal signals, indirect nonverbal signals, statements about intoxication, and no response as more indicative of their own sexual consent than women rated their male dates' signals. These findings, taken in combination with the differences between women and men in what they mean by different consent signals, suggest the potential for gender-based sexual miscommunication.

However, it is important not to exaggerate these gender differences. Although there were significant gender differences in the expected direction, effect sizes were small, and the actual ratings of signals were quite similar. Differences between women's and men's ratings of how they interpreted these signals were always *less than 1 point* on a 7-point scale, just as they were for ratings of how often they used these signals. Additionally, there was agreement on an important issue: Both men and women rated direct refusals as equally unindicative of sexual consent, suggesting that direct refusal is an unambiguous signal.

Gender and sexual initiations. There were also significant gender differences in ability to imagine oneself initiating sexual intercourse in the scenarios. More men than women were able to imagine themselves initiating sexual intercourse both verbally and nonverbally. This pattern fits with the traditional sexual script, in which men initiate sexual intercourse and women are the recipients of these initiations. It also has implications for sexual consent. It men typically initiate sexual intercourse, men will be interpreting women's consent signals more often than women will be interpreting men's consent signals. Thus, women's misinterpretations of men's consent signals are less relevant to most sexual situations than men's misinterpretations of women's sexual signals.

Verbal and Nonverbal Initiations

The way in which sexual intercourse was initiated influenced what behaviors were seen as indicative of consent. Women and men rated indirect verbal signals as more indicative of their and their dates' sexual consent in response to nonverbal initiations than in response to verbal initiations. Conversely, they rated indirect nonverbal signals as more indicative of their and their dates' sexual consent in response to verbal initiations than in response to nonverbal initiations. It seems that the meanings of indirect verbal and nonverbal signals are more situationally specific than are direct verbal and nonverbal signals. The unclear nature of indirect signals may force the initiator to look to the situation for cues as to whether the respondent has actually consented. The type of initiation did not affect how participants rated direct verbal signals or direct nonverbal signals. Further research is needed to clarify the role of the type of initiation on perceptions of sexual consent and to explore the situational specificity of consent signals.

Implications

Miscommunication and acquaintance rape. Many researchers have discussed the possibility that sexual miscommunication between women and men contributes to acquaintance rape (Abbey, 1982, 1987; Bart & O'Brien, 1985; Warshaw, 1994). Indeed, anecdotal evidence suggests that gender-based misunderstandings do sometimes lead to rape (Bart & O'Brien, 1985; Warshaw, 1994). Empirical research has also found support for this hypothesis. One study found that male and female participants had different understandings of resistance messages, particularly when the messages were indirect, suggesting that miscommunication about refusals could contribute to sexual assault (Motley & Reeder, 1995). Abbey (1987), examining naturally occurring misperceptions of sexual intent, found that such misperceptions are common between women and men. Significantly more women (72%) than men (60%) reported that they had had at least one experience in which a member of the "opposite sex" misperceived their friendly behavior as sexually-interested behavior. Although most misperceptions were minor in nature and were resolved quickly, some led to forced sexual activity, ranging from kissing to sexual intercourse. However, it is unclear from these data whether the respondents' signals were misunderstood or deliberately ignored.

As a result of the miscommunication hypothesis, women have been advised to clearly communicate their sexual intentions to prevent being raped. This "prevention strategy" is problematic, for it suggests that it is women's responsibility to ensure that men understand their sexual intentions, not men's responsibility to listen to their partner or date or to get clear consent before proceeding (Crawford, 1995). It encourages victim blaming, for women are held responsible when their communication efforts "fail" and they are raped (Crawford, 1995; Warshaw 1994). Also, this approach does not take into account women's concerns about the effect of direct messages, particularly direct refusals, on their relationship with the man involved (Motley & Reeder, 1995). Cupach and Metts (1991) suggested that both men and women prefer indirect communication because it enables them to gain sexual access and avoid explicit rejection. If the indirect communication is not responded to in a positive way, it can go unacknowledged. If it is accepted, then sexual activity can begin or continue.

Although this study found evidence that women and men do have different ideas about how indicative of sexual consent many signals are, the differences between women and men were generally quite small. Thus, it is unlikely that miscommunication about consent is a major contributing factor to acquaintance rape. It is more likely that sexually aggressive men selectively ignore or reinterpret what women say to fit what they want to hear, using miscommunication as an excuse for raping (Christopher & Frandsen, 1990; Warxhaw, 1994).

One finding in the present study did signal a cause for concern, however. Both women and men reported that they most frequently signaled sexual consent by not resisting: letting their partner undress them, not stopping their partner from kissing or touching them, not saying no. Unfortunately in some cases of rape, the aggressor proceeds without resistance from the victim, perhaps because the victim is frightened, confused, or embarrassed (Estrich, 1987; Meyer, 1984; Warshaw, 1994). Thus, it could be dangerous to use not resisting as a signal of consent.

Directions for Future Research

Numerous participants wrote comments indicating that being in a relationship affected how they signaled consent. One women wrote that "a smile does not mean consent in a bar to a guy I hardly know, but it does with my boyfriend." It may be that couples develop more idiosyncratic rules for interpreting each other's behavior and sexual signals as the relationship develops (Peplau et al., 1977). There may also be a sense of entitlement that encourages people to presume sexual consent in relationships (Shotland & Goodstein, 1992). Further research is needed in this area. Additionally, the current study was designed to assess how young women and men perceive and communicate consent in heterosexual situations. Further research is needed to examine how people of different ages, socioeconomic groups, ethnic groups, and sexual orientations infer and convey consent.

*Reprinted by permission of *The Journal of Sex Research*.

Research Excerpt Reaction Questions

1. How are consent and rape related? Give examples with which you are familiar.

2. What are the ranges of behaviors that might signal sexual consent?

3. How do consent signals differ between men and women?

4. Give examples of verbal and non-verbal sexual consent. How might these be misread by a partner?

5. How do you believe that miscommunication could lead to acquaintance rape? Give any examples with which you are familiar.

Sexual Communication: Good and Bad Sex

Think of four or five of the best sensual or sexual experiences that you have had. Think of four or five of the worst sensual or sexual experiences you have had. List as many details of these experiences (without naming names) as you can recall. Be specific. What made these good and bad experiences particularly memorable?

Good Sex	Bad Sex

Reaction Questions

1. Review your good and bad sex lists. Which is the longer list? Why?

2. What would you like to do to improve upon your good sex list?

3. Do you assume that female and male lists would be similar or different?

4. How might you communicate more effectively what specific sexual or sensual requests you desire in a relationship?

Activities

1. **How Do People Meet Each Other?**
    Briefly interview five persons who you know are in a relationship. How did they meet their partners? What seems to be the best sources for you to meet persons to date? What is your opinion of the pros and cons of the following sources:

    a. friends:

    b. school:

    c. work:

    d. leisure activities:

    e. dating services:

2. **Dating Services**
    Look in *The Yellow Pages* of the phone book for "dating services." Call two of the listings that look of interest and describe what they offer. Were there any surprises? Would you ever consider using one of these services? Under what conditions would you use these services?

3. **Personal Ads**
    Review the "Personals" of a local newspaper. Write out several of the ads that seem of interest to you. What caught your eye? Under what conditions would you pursue these ads? Write an example of an ad you would write for yourself for this particular newspaper following their requested format.

4. **Internet Dating Services**

Check out an internet dating service such as love.com, match.com, or oneandonly.com. Would you recommend any of these as a method of meeting partners? What do you like about these services? What don't you like about them?

5. **Mutual Consent Policy**

Based on the Antioch College Sexual Consent Policy described in the research excerpt in this chapter, write your own brief mutual consent policy. How is it similar to the Antioch policy? How is it different from the Antioch policy?

CHAPTER 9

SOLITARY SEX: MASTURBATION AND FANTASY

"Masturbation is the primary sexual activity of mankind. In the nineteenth century it was a disease; in the twentieth, it's a cure."

Thomas Szasz

Is sex only to be shared? Or is solitary sex an alternative? Kinsey found in his sample of case histories in the 1930s and 1940s that those persons who had reached orgasm via self-touch (or any other method) prior to marriage had a more satisfying sex life in marriage. One's private sex life is just that: it is private. Sexual fantasies and behaviors can be shared with another or they can be enjoyed in and of themselves in a way that enhances one's private sexuality.

Chapter 9 Contents:

A. **Solitary Sexual Activity: Does the Language Matter?**
B. **Research Excerpt: "Masturbatory Guilt and Sexual Responsiveness Among Post-College-Age Women: Sexual Satisfaction Revisited" and Reaction Questions**
C. **"Solitary Sex: Behavior and Fantasy Questionnaire"**
D. **Research Excerpt: "Gender Differences in Sexual Fantasy and Behavior in a College Population: A Ten-Year Replication" and Reaction Questions**
E. **Activities**
  1. **Sexual Fantasy**
  2. **Written Erotic Material**
  3. **Visual Erotic Material**
  4. **Masturbation**

Solitary Sexual Activity: Does the Language Matter?

Think of the following words and phrases: "solitary sex," "self-pleasuring," "autoerotic behavior," "self-touch," "masturbation." What do these words connote? Do you have separate feelings for each of these? Now say the same words out loud. What reactions do you notice? If you felt comfortable with the first three but not the fourth, "masturbation," you are not alone. Most persons are still uncomfortable talking about masturbation. Since research shows that most individuals masturbate, it would seem reasonable to explore the discrepancy between your behavior and your reactions to that behavior.

Respond to the following questions and then share your answers with a trusted friend or partner.

1. How would you define masturbation?

2. How do you believe that males masturbate? Do you believe that all males masturbate in a similar fashion or are there differences?

3. How do you believe females masturbate? Do you believe that all females masturbate in a similar fashion or are there differences?

4. Why are college students and adults reluctant to talk about masturbation?

5. What are the positive aspects of masturbation?

6. Could masturbation ever be problematic? Explain.

7. Do you assume that couples in stable relationships also masturbate? Together? Alone?

8. What are your beliefs about the normalcy of masturbation? Circle a number representing your beliefs.

Abnormal			Neutral			Normal
-3	-2	-1	0	+1	+2	+3

Research Excerpt

Question: The ex-Surgeon General of the United States, Dr. Joycelyn Elders, created a controversy when she suggested in a speech that teaching masturbation to teens as an alternative to intercourse might be commendable. Why was this so controversial?

Masturbatory Guilt and Sexual Responsiveness Among Post-College-Age Women: Sexual Satisfaction Revisited.*
J. Kenneth Davidson, Sr. and Carol Anderson Darling

During the nineteenth century, and especially during the Victorian era, women were viewed as being essentially devoid of sexual feelings. This legacy from the Victorian era has so dominated their sexual attitudes and behaviors that until the 1960s most women tried to hide their sexual interests and desires for fear of being considered social deviants (Allgeier et al., 1991). The feminist movement that began during the 1960s supported and promoted the claim of women that they were sexual beings in their own right rather than having to subordinate their sexual desires to those of men. The sexual autonomy model that emerged in the 1970s depicted women as independent sexual agents, self-sufficient, and in control of their own sexuality (Weinberg et al., 1983). As a consequence, the experience of orgasm came to be perceived as a woman's right. By focusing on empowering women to insist upon that right, women's sexuality has now been elevated to the same status as men's sexuality (Williams, 1987). Further, many women today argue that greater knowledge of their own sexuality places them in control of their sexual needs and, consequently, frees them from dependence on men for receiving sexual gratification (Stockard et al., 1992).

REVIEW OF THE LITERATURE

Women are seemingly becoming more accepting of masturbation as they are receiving psychological permission, instruction, and support in learning about their own bodies (Laws et al., 1977). Consequently, the beneficial aspects of masturbation have taken on special meaning for women. It is now often used not only as a means of sexual self-expression, but as a form of sex therapy for those who are unable to experience an orgasm through sexual intercourse. Through masturbation, women can become aware of the kind of stimulation that gives them the most pleasure as well as learn to be comfortable with their own bodies and sexual responses (Lips, 1993). Masturbation also can be used to experience orgasm during menstruation, which may help to alleviate menstrual cramps if aesthetics, circumstances, physical discomforts, or personal values do not permit access to sexual intercourse (Stewart et al., 1979).

Among college women, the incidence of masturbation has continued to increase. During the 1980s, the reported percentages for college women ranged from 46% (Davidson, 1984) to 85% (Person, 1989). As the 1990s begin, masturbation as a sexual outlet among college women remains evident as others have found a similar range: 53% to 84%. Thus, most college-educated women today appear to have utilized this sexual outlet by their mid-30s (Davidson, 1989).

However, not all women feel comfortable with masturbation. In a study of college women, 30% reported "shame" as the major reason for not engaging in masturbation (Atwood et al., 1987). More recently, others have found that only 50% of college women believe that masturbation is a "healthy practice" (Weiss et al., 1992). So, even with the apparent increasing incidence of masturbation, considerable data suggest negative feelings toward self-stimulation still deter many women from choosing this source of sexual fulfillment. And, of those who do engage in masturbation, they do so much less frequently than men (Jones et al., 1990). The reported mean frequency for college women was 3.3 times per month in comparison to 4.8 times per month for men (Weiss et al., 1992). In a large-scale

---

sample of college-educated women, without regard to marital status, the reported frequency of masturbation was 7.1 times per month (Davidson et al., 1989). By contrast, high-school educated, married women engaged in masturbation only 3.7 times per month (Hulbert et al., 1991). In general, women are more likely to report guilt feelings about their masturbatory activity than men (Davidson et al., 1986). Further, substantial evidence suggests guilt feelings may interfere with the physiological and/or psychological sexual satisfaction derived from masturbation (Mosher, 1985; Davidson et al., 1989). The presence of guilt also has other implications for female sexuality. Guilt feelings associated with masturbation have been found to inhibit the insertion of the diaphragm as a contraceptive technique, since its utilization requires the handling of the genitals (Gerrard, 1987). Women with high levels of masturbatory guilt also experience more emotional trauma if they contract a sexually transmitted disease and have greater fear about telling their sex partner than women with low masturbatory guilt (Houck et al., 1986). Masturbatory guilt, likewise, may inhibit women from responding to foreplay as a prelude to sexual intercourse (Gunderson et al., 1979). Finally, since masturbation is the most efficient way to produce intense orgasms, masturbatory guilt also may play an important role in the lack of adequate sexual responsiveness and sexual satisfaction. Given these circumstances, the purposes of this investigation were to determine the degree of masturbatory guilt, if any, and its effects on the sexual responsiveness and sexual satisfaction of adult women.

SUMMARY AND CONCLUSIONS

Based on findings on 671 female respondents, it is readily apparent that most adult women (88.5%) engage in masturbation. And, marital status does not appear to affect the likelihood of the presence or absence of masturbatory guilt. Further, as might be anticipated, the annual rate of masturbatory frequency was found to be greatest among those women never experiencing masturbatory guilt. With regard to attitudes toward masturbation, those women never feeling guilty about masturbation were less likely to feel ashamed about admitting to masturbation and less likely to believe masturbation to be a sin, an unhealthy practice, or a sign of poor marital adjustment and to approve of their female acquaintances engaging in masturbation. These findings suggest that the origins of masturbatory guilt can be traced to early socialization experiences. Since the women who felt guilty more often expressed guilt about not experiencing an orgasm during sexual intercourse than the not guilty women, they apparently were less likely to have psychological permission to use self-stimulation to experience orgasm than not guilty women. Finally, in terms of sexual satisfaction, the not guilty women were more likely to receive more intense physiological and psychological reactions from masturbating than the guilty women. In addition, they reported higher levels of overall sexual adjustment as well as greater physiological and psychological sexual satisfaction than the guilty women.

What are the meanings and implications for these findings about masturbatory guilt? It would appear that the guilty women are more dependent upon men for their orgasmic release. This argument is supported by the fact that these women more often feel guilty if they do not experience an orgasm associated with sexual intercourse.

Since masturbation has emerged as a potential sexual outlet as well as a means to engage in personal body exploration for women, these findings have substantial implications. Some college women, for example, report having never engaged in masturbation because the practice is contrary to their personal and/or religious values, yet they report having unprotected sexual intercourse with a number of different sex partners. Women should be encouraged to continue to explore their own sexuality within the context of the many physiological and psychological factors that may produce greater degrees of sexual satisfaction. Yet, masturbation still remains, for many women, a source of considerable psychological discomfort and concern. Therefore, what is the impact of masturbatory guilt on the interpersonal dynamics of a sexual relationship? And what of those women who must deal with the presence of masturbatory guilt in their sexual lives along with its influence on the quality of their overall sexual satisfaction?

It is of crucial importance that therapists, counselors, theologians, sexuality educators, and physicians begin to address the negative connotation of masturbation in our society and its attendant impact on sexual satisfaction.

Research Excerpt Reaction Questions

1. What were your early learnings about masturbation? Did these learnings lead to comfor shame about self-stimulation activities?

2. Why is it that females oftentimes do not use masturbation for a sexual outlet until they reach their 30s?

3. Why do 30% of women still feel sexual shame about masturbation?

4. Does the lower frequency of female than male masturbation mean that females have a lower sex drive then men? Why or why not?

5. How could sex educators and other community leaders be involved in lessening the shame that seems to pervade our society's beliefs concerning masturbation?

Solitary Sex: Behavior and Fantasy

Until recently, fantasy has not been discussed openly as a sexual topic. Some religious writings concerning sexual thoughts are interpreted to mean that fantasy or thought equals behavior and is therefore wrong. As a result, many persons have felt shame at having sexual thoughts. Sex therapists know, however, that sensual and sexual thoughts can be healthy additions to your sexual repertoire. Persons allowing themselves to think in sensual and sexual ways are those who have fewer sexual dysfunctions and often have a richer, more rewarding, sex life.

The following research excerpt, "Gender Differences in Sexual Fantasy and Behavior in a College Population: A Ten-Year Replication," is based on a study of behaviors and fantasies of graduate and undergraduate students. You can compare your experiences and fantasies with those of the students in the study. There were 67 reported sexual experiences and 55 reported fantasies. Simply check YES or NO depending on whether you have had these experiences and these fantasies. After completing your checklists, compare your answers with those of the men and women in the study (Table 1--Behaviors and Table 2--Fantasies).

Sexual Experiences*

Have you ever had this experience?	YES	NO
1. Kissing of sensitive areas (nongenital)		
2. Stroking/petting partner's genitals		
3. Naked caressing and embracing		
4. Breast petting (nude)		
5. Kissing nude breasts		
6. Genitals caressed by partner		
7. Having your genitals orally stimulated		
8. Erotic embrace (clothed)		
9. Kissing on the lips		
10. Deep kissing		
11. Watching partner undress		
12. Mutual undressing		
13. Sexual intercourse		
14. Male petting female breasts (clothed)		
15. Mutual petting of genitals to orgasm		
16. Oral stimulation of partner's genitals		
17. Walking hand in hand		
18. Intercourse/male superior		
19. Male lying prone on female (clothed)		
20. Intercourse/female superior		
21. Having partner masturbate you		
22. Intercourse side by side		
23. Masturbating sexual partner		
24. Intercourse sitting position		
25. Reading/watching pornography		
26. Masturbating alone		
27. Mutual oral stimulation of genitals		
28. Intercourse/unusual positions		

29. Intercourse/vaginal entry from rear		
30. Being seduced		
31. Seducing a sexual partner		
32. Having sex that lasts for hours		
33. Using dirty language		
34. Intercourse/unusual locations		
35. Caressing partner's anal area		
36. Having anal area caressed		
37. Watching a sexual partner masturbate		
38. Performing sex acts before a mirror		
39. Sex with a virgin		
40. Having partner watch you masturbate		
41. Dressing with erotic garments		
42. Being discovered making love		
43. Sex with a stranger		
44. Using artificial devices		
45. Anal intercourse		
46. Watching others make love		
47. Being forced to submit to sexual acts		
48. Seeing pictures/film of self making love		
49. Forcing partner to submit		
50. Being tied/bound during sex activities		
51. Sex with two or more people		
52. Exhibiting body in public		
53. Being tortured by a sexual partner		
54. Being whipped or beaten by a partner		
55. Whipping/beating partner		
56. Torturing sexual partner		
57. Degrading sexual partner		
58. Sex with a close relative		
59. Watching someone make love to partner		
60. Being sexually degraded		
61. Dressing in clothes of opposite sex		
62. Being involved in a sexual orgy		
63. Mate swapping		
64. Performing sexual acts for an audience		
65. Homosexual experience if heterosexual, heterosexual experience if homosexual		
66. Being a prostitute		
67. Sexual relations with animals		

* Reprinted by permission from Bing Hsu, M.D.

Sexual Fantasy*

Have you ever had this fantasy?	YES	NO
1. Touching/kissing sensuously		
2. Watching partner undress		
3. Being sensuously touched		
4. Oral-genital sex		
5. Naked caressing		
6. Walking hand in hand		
7. Seducing partner		
8. Sex in unusual locations		
9. Being seduced		
10. Sex that lasts for hours		
11. Intercourse in unusual positions		
12. Having partner masturbate you		
13. Sex with a virgin		
14. Masturbating your partner		
15. Making love with the possibility of being discovered		
16. Two or more lovers		
17. Sex with a mysterious stranger		
18. Watching partner masturbate		
19. Using dirty language		
20. Sex with a famous person		
21. Gaining love of a rejecting lover		
22. Melting the heart of a cold partner		
23. Performing sex acts before a mirror		
24. Forbidden lover in sex adventures		
25. Sex with a much older person		
26. Watching others make love		
27. Anal intercourse		
28. Being involved in an orgy		
29. Sex with a much younger person		
30. Having your partner watch you masturbate		
31. Getting married		
32. Being forced to submit		
33. Forcing partner to submit		
34. Seeing pictures/videos of yourself having sex		
35. Being tied up or bound during sex		
36. Dressing in special costumes		
37. Being brought into a room against your will		
38. Mate swapping		
39. Being rescued from danger by one who will become my lover		
40. Whipping/beating partner		
41. Homosexual fantasies if heterosexual, heterosexual fantasies if homosexual		
42. Fantasizing that you are the opposite sex		
43. Exhibiting body in public		

44. Being whipped/beaten by a partner		
45. Being attracted to someone with a physical abnormality		
46. Being sexually degraded		
47. Sex with a close relative		
48. Performing sex before an audience		
49. Being a prostitute		
50. Being tortured by a sex partner		
51. Dressing in clothes of the opposite sex		
52. Watching someone else make love to your partner		
53. Degrading sex partner		
54. Torturing sex partner		
55. Sexual relations with animals		

* Reprinted by permission from Bing Hsu, M.D.

Research Excerpt

Question: Are your fantasies and behaviors identical? Are there male and female differences?

Gender Differences in Sexual Fantasy and Behavior in a College Population: A Ten-Year Replication*

Bing Hsu, Arthur Kling, Christopher Kessler, Kory Knapke, Pamela Diefenback, and James E. Elias

The purpose of this study was to examine the temporal stability (or lack thereof) in sexual fantasy and sexual behavior in a population of university students. Of particular interest is the issue of whether gender differences in sexual fantasy and behavior have altered over the past decade.

To accomplish this, we attempted to replicate a study conducted approximately 10 years ago by Person et al., (1989). In that study, Person and her colleagues found that even though men fantasized more than women, they did not have more sexual experiences.

Since the Person et al. study, there has been widespread attention to the AIDS epidemic and a continuing evolution in the role of women in our society. We would expect these factors to impact on contemporary sexual behavior.

DISCUSSION

Male subjects consistently endorsed slightly more items than female subjects for both fantasy and experience. This is quite different from the results reported by Person et al., (1989). In their study, for the fantasy samples, the males endorsed almost twice as many items as the females. But for the experience samples, the two sexes endorsed a similar number of items. Thus, there was a narrowing of the gender difference, with respect to the variety of fantasy in which individuals engaged, in the intervening ten years. In contrast, there is a gender difference for the experience items which was not present in the Person et al. study.

Similarly, in comparing the relative degree of gender influence between sexual behavior and sexual fantasy, Person et al.'s study demonstrated a dramatic gender difference in sexual fantasy, but little gender difference in sexual behavior. Our data suggest that a similar trend still exists, though the differences are less dramatic.

Even though females continue to use sexual fantasy less than males, this difference has decreased in the past 10 years.

Previous studies have demonstrated that there is a tendency for a lessening of gender differences over time, especially with respect to certain sexual experiences.

The growing awareness and acceptability of variety in sexual activity may provide our subjects the opportunity to practice the behaviors about which they fantasize. Yet, females consistently showed a higher degree of correlation than males. An explanation may be that males entertain certain fantasies which *do not* correlate with engaging in the matched experience, while the same is *not* true for females. Men do fantasize about sexual activities that are out of the range of their individual experiences. Women do not. This difference in the manner in which each gender utilizes fantasy may help explain the gender differences noted earlier. Since men are more likely to have fantasies about sexual acts outside of their experience, it follows that we would find a gender difference in amount and type of sexual fantasies, and not in experience.

Further study in this area would be useful to clarify some of the trends noted. For example, does the trend we observed toward an increase in gender difference in sexual experience signify a reversal of the generally accepted trend that the two sexes are "converging?" It would also be of interest to control for ethnic and cultural differences.

Table 1
Sexual Experiences - College Population

Experience	Males %	Females %
1. Kissing of sensitive areas (nongenital)	98.1	92.5
2. Stroking/petting partner's genitals	96.3	92.5
3. Naked caressing and embracing	96.3	91.5
4. Breast petting (nude)	96.2	90.6
5. Kissing nude breasts	96.2	79.0
6. Genitals caressed by partner	94.4	91.5
7. Having your genitals orally stimulated	94.4	88.6
8. Erotic embrace (clothed)	94.4	93.4
9. Kissing on the lips	94.4	96.2
10. Deep kissing	94.4	96.2
11. Watching partner undress	94.4	92.4
12. Mutual undressing	92.6	89.5
13. Sexual intercourse	90.7	90.5
14. Male petting female breasts (clothed)	90.7	88.6
15. Mutual petting of genitals to orgasm	88.9	81.9
16. Oral stimulation of partner's genitals	88.9	88.6
17. Walking hand in hand	88.9	96.2
18. Intercourse/male superior	88.7	85.4
19. Male lying prone on female (clothed)	87.0	88.6
20. Intercourse/female superior	86.8	83.5
21. Having partner masturbate you	85.2	80.0
22. Intercourse side by side	85.2	79.0
23. Masturbating sexual partner	83.3	77.1
24. Intercourse sitting position	83.3	81.9
25. Reading/watching pornography	83.3	64.8
26. Masturbating alone	83.3	70.5
27. Mutual oral stimulation of genitals	77.8	82.9
28. Intercourse/unusual positions	77.8	80.0
29. Intercourse/vaginal entry from rear	76.9	79.0
30. Being seduced	75.9	75.0
31. Seducing a sexual partner	75.9	70.5
32. Having sex that lasts for hours	75.9	62.9
33. Using dirty language	70.4	51.4
34. Intercourse/unusual locations	66.7	65.7
35. Caressing partner's anal area	61.1	37.1
36. Having anal area caressed	61.1	49.5
37. Watching a sexual partner masturbate	55.6	51.4
38. Performing sex acts before a mirror	53.7	53.3
39. Sex with a virgin	47.2	24.0
40. Having partner watch you masturbate	44.4	43.8
41. Dressing with erotic garments	37.0	56.2
42. Being discovered making love	35.2	28.6
43. Sex with a stranger	32.1	18.1
44. Using artificial devices	25.9	31.4
45. Anal intercourse	22.2	26.7
46. Watching others make love	20.4	20.0

	Males %	Females %
47. Being forced to submit to sexual acts	18.5	24.8
48. Seeing pictures/film of self making love	17.0	8.6
49. Forcing partner to submit	15.4	9.5
50. Being tied/bound during sex activities	15.1	16.2
51. Sex with two or more people	13.2	8.6
52. Exhibiting body in public	11.3	9.5
53. Being tortured by a sexual partner	11.3	2.9
54. Being whipped or beaten by a partner	11.3	1.9
55. Whipping/beating partner	9.4	1.9
56. Torturing sexual partner	9.4	1.9
57. Degrading sexual partner	9.4	1.9
58. Sex with a close relative	5.7	2.9
59. Watching someone make love to partner	5.7	1.9
60. Being sexually degraded	5.7	7.6
61. Dressing in clothes of opposite sex	5.7	12.4
62. Being involved in a sexual orgy	5.7	2.9
63. Mate swapping	3.8	2.9
64. Performing sexual acts for an audience	3.8	0.0
65. Homosexual experience if heterosexual, heterosexual experience if homosexual	3.8	6.7
66. Being a prostitute	1.9	1.9
67. Sexual relations with animals	1.9	0.0

Table 2
Sexual Fantasies - College Population

Fantasy	Males %	Females %
1. Touching/kissing sensuously	98.1	97.2
2. Watching partner undress	98.1	84.0
3. Being sensuously touched	96.3	96.2
4. Oral-genital sex	96.3	83.8
5. Naked caressing	92.6	91.5
6. Walking hand in hand	92.5	91.4
7. Seducing partner	90.7	80.2
8. Sex in unusual locations	88.9	82.1
9. Being seduced	87.0	80.2
10. Sex that lasts for hours	87.0	74.5
11. Intercourse in unusual positions	87.0	81.9
12. Having partner masturbate you	85.2	67.9
13. Sex with a virgin	85.2	32.1
14. Masturbating your partner	83.3	74.5
15. Making love with the possibility of being discovered	77.8	49.1
16. Two or more lovers	75.9	45.3
17. Sex with a mysterious stranger	70.4	47.2
18. Watching partner masturbate	70.4	57.5
19. Using dirty language	68.5	53.8

20. Sex with a famous person	64.8	50.0
21. Gaining love of a rejecting lover	61.5	45.2
22. Melting the heart of a cold partner	61.1	48.1
23. Performing sex acts before a mirror	61.1	62.3
24. Forbidden lover in sex adventures	59.3	49.1
25. Sex with a much older person	57.4	36.8
26. Watching others make love	57.4	46.2
27. Anal intercourse	55.6	25.5
28. Being involved in an orgy	55.6	29.3
29. Sex with a much younger person	55.6	30.2
30. Having your partner watch you masturbate	55.6	53.3
31. Getting married	51.9	70.6
32. Being forced to submit	44.4	36.2
33. Forcing partner to submit	42.6	22.6
34. Seeing pictures/videos of yourself having sex	42.6	32.1
35. Being tied up or bound during sex	40.7	42.9
36. Dressing in special costumes	38.9	44.3
37. Being brought into a room against your will	33.3	27.4
38. Mate swapping	25.9	11.3
39. Being rescued from danger by one who will become my lover	25.9	46.2
40. Whipping/beating partner	22.2	3.8
41. Homosexual fantasies if heterosexual, heterosexual fantasies if homosexual	18.9	33.0
42. Fantasizing that you are the opposite sex	18.5	24.5
43. Exhibiting body in public	18.5	23.6
44. Being whipped/beaten by a partner	18.5	4.7
45. Being attracted to someone with a physical abnormality	18.5	10.4
46. Being sexually degraded	18.5	7.5
47. Sex with a close relative	16.7	8.5
48. Performing sex before an audience	16.7	18.9
49. Being a prostitute	14.8	18.9
50. Being tortured by a sex partner	13.0	4.7
51. Dressing in clothes of the opposite sex	13.0	13.2
52. Watching someone else make love to your partner	13.0	11.3
53. Degrading sex partner	9.3	3.0
54. Torturing sex partner	9.3	1.9
55. Sexual relations with animals	0.0	2.8

Research Excerpt Reaction Questions

1. How did your answers to the experience and fantasy questions compare to those in the previous tables? What surprises you?

2. Why might you expect that males consistently have more items than females in both the areas of experience and fantasy?

3. Why do you believe that a female's fantasy and experience are more similar to each other than a male's fantasy and experience?

4. Do you perceive that the fantasies and experiences on the two lists have a male or female bias? Explain.

5. Do you believe that fantasy is helpful to a relationship?

6. Do you believe that fantasy could be detrimental to a relationship? Explain.

7. Does fantasy mean that a person is dissatisfied in a present relationship? Explain.

8. What are your beliefs about the normalcy of fantasy? Circle the number representing your beliefs.

Abnormal			Neutral			Normal
-3	-2	-1	0	+1	+2	+3

9. Does the power of the fantasy change when fantasy becomes reality?

Activities

1. **Sexual Fantasy**
   As you are driving to and from work, create six or more sensual or sexual fantasies. Record your fantasies. What are your triggers for sexual fantasy in your surroundings, (i.e., billboards, people in cars, on the street, in parks, music in your car)?

2. **Written Erotic Material**
   Find a portion of a novel that for you is highly erotic. Why do you find this section particularly erotic? What are the components that make this scene erotic? Explain.

3. **Visual Erotic Material**
   Describe a scene in a movie that for you is highly erotic. Why do you find this scene particularly erotic? What are the components that make this scene erotic? Explain.

4. **Masturbation**
   Ask three men and three women for their views on masturbation. Growing up, how did they learn about masturbation? Have their views changed since childhood?

CHAPTER 10

SAME-SEX LOVING

"They gave me a medal for killing two men and a discharge for loving one."

Gay Vietnam Veteran,
Leonard Matlovich

When was your first crush? Kindergarten? First or second grade? Adolescence? What do you remember about your first love relationship? Was your first crush on someone older? Younger? Your age? Your gender? The other gender? Why do you believe that some persons are attracted more to their own gender than the other? When does that attraction begin? Understanding sexual orientation is difficult for many persons for it is hard to comprehend anything other than one's own experience. This chapter will aid in your understanding of differences and how these differences may develop.

Chapter 10 Contents:

A. Personal Assessment: Homosexuality Questionnaire
B. Myths vs. Facts: Your Basic Knowledge
C. Research Excerpt: "Assessing Latino(a) and non-Hispanic White College Students' Homophobia" and Reaction Questions
D. Did You Know? The Right to Privacy in the U.S.
E. Case Study and Reaction Questions
F. The Fluidity of Sexual Orientation
G. Activities
    1. Religion and Homosexuality
    2. Gay/Lesbian Support Groups
    3. Interview of a LGBT Person
    4. Fluidity of Sexual Orientation

Personal Assessment: Homosexuality Questionnaire

How do you feel about men and women who are homosexual? Answer the following questions as honestly as you can, using the 3-point scale below.

	Very Comfortable (2)	Neutral (1)	Very Uncomfortable (0)
Social Arena:			
1. You see two men holding hands in public. You feel:			
2. You are asked to participate in a gay rights march. You feel:			
3. You are asked to sign a petition against gay bashing or gay harassment. You feel:			
4. You are asked to support legislation for gays to be adoptive parents. You feel:			
Community Arena:			
5. You discover you have a gay religious leader (i.e., rabbi, priest, minister). You feel:			
6. You discover your psychologist (counselor or social worker) is gay. You feel:			
7. You discover that your physician is gay. You feel:			
8. You discover that your neighborhood is home to many gay persons. You feel:			
Workplace:			
9. You are assigned a work project with a gay person. You feel:			
10. You discover that your office-mate is gay. You feel:			
11. You are approached for a date by a same-sex work-mate who is gay. You feel:			
12. You find that you are attracted to someone at your office who is gay. You feel:			
Family:			
13. You are watching a film with your family that includes same-sex affection. You feel:			
14. Your brother or sister comes out to your family as gay. You feel:			
15. Your child's teacher or coach is gay. You feel:			
16. Your young adult child indicates that he/she is gay. You feel:			

This scale measures your comfort or lack of comfort with homosexuality. Add your total score. The possible range of scores is 0-32. A score from 17-32 implies that you are overall accepting of persons who are homosexual in orientation. A score of 9-16 indicates a mild discomfort with homosexuality. A score of 0-8 indicates a very negative attitude toward homosexuality.

Myths versus Facts: Your Basic Knowledge

Mark the following statements true or false.

	TRUE	FALSE

1. Homosexual behavior is very rare (less than 1 in 100 of the population).

2. Psychologists and psychiatrists consider people who are homosexual mentally ill.

3. Homosexuality is caused by a weak father and a dominant mother.

4. Homosexuality is the result of children being seduced or recruited by adult gays and lesbians.

5. Some homosexual people marry and have children.

6. Most women and men who are gay and lesbian are unhappy with their orientation.

7. AIDS is more common among homosexual men than homosexual women.

8. Bisexuality is always a cover for homosexuality.

9. Gay males are more likely than heterosexual males to be pedophiles.

10. Gays all fit the stereotype of a certain appearance.

11. In a long-term gay male couple relationship, one man assumes the role of the "wife" and one the role of the "husband."

(Answers: 1-F, 2-F, 3-F, 4-F, 5-T, 6-F, 7-T, 8-F, 9-F, 10-F, 11-F.)

Research Excerpt

Question: Do attitudes toward homosexuals vary from one ethnic group to another?

Assessing Latino(a) and non-Hispanic White College Students' Homophobia*
Suki S. Montgomery, Ph.D.

Homophobia, the negative attitudes one holds toward people who identify as lesbian or gay, is a serious problem on college campuses in the United states for all students (Berrill, 1992; Herek, 1993b; D'Augelli, 1990). In order to begin to make college campuses and their communities safe for gay and lesbian students, homophobia and its impact must be understood.

Background of the Problem

The Stonewall Riots in New York City in 1969, a rebellion of gay, lesbian, bisexual, and transgendered people against police brutality, are generally thought of as the beginning of the Gay Movement. The 1973 decision by the American Psychiatric Association to eliminate homosexuality from the *Diagnostic and Statistical Manual (DSM)* was another landmark event that opened the gay and lesbian community to be more visible and celebrated. In Colorado alone, there are more than 300 organizations specifically aimed at providing community services and support for gay, lesbian, bisexual, and transgendered persons (Pink Pages, 1999). However, despite the increasing awareness and acceptance in the heterosexual mainstream community regarding gay, lesbian, bisexual, and transgendered persons, many incidents of violence and hatred as well as negative attitudes toward people who identify as lesbian, gay, or bisexual have been documented (Elia, 1993; Garnets, Herek, and Levy, 1993; Herek, 1993a; Reiter, 1991). In addition, states across the country are passing laws to ban gay marriages, often considered an institutional type of homophobia. Therefore, it is clear that attitudes toward homosexuality impact not only those people who identify as lesbian or gay, but also have far-reaching influence in our relationships and in our communities (Herek, 1984a).

Justification for the Study

Gregory Herek's "Attitudes Towards Lesbians and Gay Men Scale" (ATLG) has been shown to measure the construct of homophobia with White (Herek, 1984b, 1987, 1988) and African American samples (Herek and Capitanio, 1995). Homophobia has been studied mainly in non-Hispanic White, college-educated populations. As stated, very few studies have used Latino(a) samples and even fewer have used Mexican American samples. Studies done with non-Hispanic White samples have shown that negative attitudes toward lesbians and gay men are related to traditional beliefs about women and gender roles, negative or no previous personal contact with lesbians or gay men, belief that one's friends hold similar negative attitudes, adherence to a conservative religious ideology, and gender (usually male) (Aguero, Bloch, and Byrne, 1984; Cotton-Huston and Waite, 2000; D'Augelli and Rose, 1990; Herek, 1994, 1988; Marsiglio, 1993).

Statement of the Problem

Researchers have found that there is a link in Latino(a) populations between one's attitudes toward lesbians and gay men and attitudes toward people with AIDS (Alcalay, Sniderman, Mitchell, and Griffin, 1990). Accurate information about AIDS is lacking in Latino(a) communities (DiClemente, Boyer, and Morales, 1988). Further, according to adult and adolescent Latino(a) samples studied, it is assumed that if a man is gay, he must have AIDS (DiClemente, et al., 1988). One direct consequence of this lack of information is the increase in HIV/AIDS in the Hispanic community, according to the Centers for Disease Control and Prevention. Describing HIV/AIDS prevention programs that need to happen in Hispanic communities, they write, "Messages targeted to these populations must be based on an understanding of their cultural attitudes toward homosexuality and bisexuality, which may be different from those of other populations at high risk for infection" (HIV/AIDS among Hispanics in the United States, 2001).

Homophobia and Related Variables: Studies with non-Hispanic White and African American Samples

In the classic study of public attitudes toward homosexuality in American adults done as part of the 1970 National Survey by the Institute for Sex Research, Levitt and Klassen (1974) found that those respondents who were more homophobic were likely to have specific characteristics (they used the term "homosexphobia" that is considered similar to what is currently called "homophobia"). They found that those respondents who scored higher on homophobia measures tended to be rural, White, raised in the

Midwest or South, and more conservative and less lenient about accepting sex and sexual behavior in general. Further, they were more likely to claim a strong belief in a religion, with a tendency toward a more fundamentalist one. On the other hand, they found that variables such as age, sex, education level, marital status, and occupation were unrelated to homophobia scores.

Review of Research

An investigation of the subgroups of the Latino(a) sample found that there were no differences between the Mexican American sample and other groups in their attitude toward homosexuality. The difference that was found, however, was that the males across the Latino(a) subgroups with lower levels of education and more conservative scores on scales measuring beliefs about sexuality were less tolerant concerning attitudes toward homosexuality. These results are consistent with those found in studies with both Black and non-Hispanic White samples (Baker and Fishbein, 1998; Coltton-Huston and Waite, 2000; D'Augelli and Rose, 1990; Herek and Capitanio, 1995; Herek and Glunt, 1991, 1993; Irwin and Thompson, 1978; Kurdek, 1988).

Education level (which Bonilla and Porter point out is closely related to level of acculturation) was found to be a good predictor of attitudes toward the civil liberties of GLBT persons in the Latino(a) sample. That is, those who were more educated were more likely to express more open attitudes toward the civil liberties of gay men and lesbians. Bonilla and Porter's investigation of attitudes toward homosexuality in Latino(a), Black, and non-Hispanic White samples is the only specific information about homophobia in a Mexican American sample currently available.

*Reprinted by permission of Suki S. Montgomery, Ph.D.

Research Excerpt Reaction Questions

1. What are some of the events initiating the gay movement in the United States?

2. Do you agree that the banning of gay marriages is a form of institutional homophobia? Explain briefly.

3. Negative attitudes toward lesbians and gay men are related to what beliefs?

4. Why might Latino populations often link homophobia and AIDS? Explain briefly.

5. Why do you assume that education level and homophobia are related? Explain briefly.

The Right to Privacy in the U.S.*

 States with laws regulating oral and/or anal sex between consenting partners

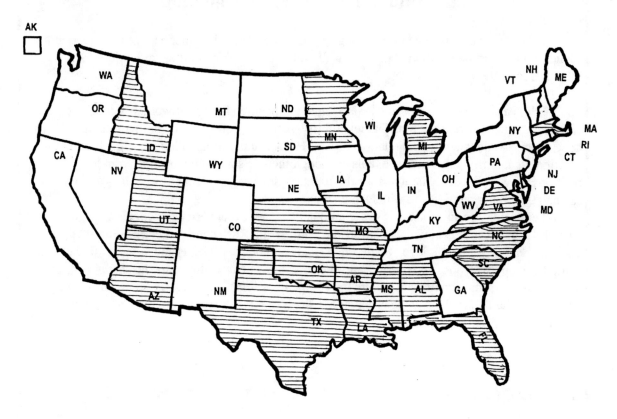

Alabama	Oral or anal sex with someone other than your spouse receives a maximum penalty of one year in prison.
Florida	Anal sex is considered an "unnatural and lascivious act," leading to a sentence of 60 days in prison and/or a $500 fine.
Georgia	In 1998, the Georgia Supreme Court overturned the state's sodomy law after reviewing a case in which a man was serving a five-year term for having consensual oral sex with a woman.
Idaho	Anal sex is considered an "infamous crime against nature," receiving a life (five years minimum) sentence.
Kentucky	In 1992, Kentucky's Supreme Court struck down that state's sodomy law, aimed specifically at homosexuals, stating, "We need not sympathize, agree with, or even understand the sexual preference of homosexuals in order to recognize their right to equal treatment before the bar of criminal justice."
Tennessee, Montana, and Maryland	Courts in Tennessee and Montana struck down those states' same-sex sodomy laws in 1996, and Maryland followed in 1998.
Virginia	A Virginia law that forbids oral and anal sex between either hetero- or homosexual individuals was upheld by both a state and federal court in 1975. The ruling indicates that "individual states have the right to regulate sexual behavior for your own good."

* National Gay and Lesbian Task Force (2000)

Case Study: Heidi, 23, College Student

"What I am--and have been for as long as I can remember--is someone whose gender and sexuality have just never seemed to mesh well with the available cultural categories" (Sandra Lipsitz Bem, 1993).

Heidi is a twenty-three-year-old Asian female. She attends a small women's college on the east coast. She is currently dating Daniel, a thirty-year-old professional who lives nearby. They have a very passionate physical relationship but Heidi usually turns to her close girlfriends for emotional support. Sometimes she feels as though there is something missing from her relationship with Daniel. She longs for the intimacy she shares with her girlfriends and wishes she had this in her relationship with Daniel.

When Heidi was an adolescent she shared her first sexual experience with another girl named Kasha. Kasha is now in a relationship with April. Kasha and April are committed, devoted, and very much in love. Sometimes Heidi watches her friends and wonders if she too could be happy with another woman. She enjoys the physical relationship she shares with Daniel but socially and emotionally she prefers the company of females. She wonders if she should tell Daniel that she thinks she may be bisexual but she is not even certain about her own sexual feelings

Reaction Questions

1. What are your beliefs about Heidi's sexual orientation?

2. How might Heidi resolve her mixed feelings about her attractions to men and women?

The Fluidity of Sexual Orientation

Nadja Tizer

Cases like Heidi's are not all that uncommon. Within the present day social construct there is a prevalent desire to see things from a dualist perspective. It is easiest to categorize both people and their behaviors into distinct boxes. This is common in the case of both gender norms and sexual orientation. There are only two genders recognized in the current social construct, masculine and feminine. Anything outside these prescribed genders and their stereotypical behavior norms is considered deviant. The same is applicable in the case of sexual orientation. One is either "gay" or "straight." This framework provides little or no room for fluidity and is of concern considering that the spectrum of gender attributes and sexual orientation in reality may be as varied as snowflakes.

One of the chief components that create stereotypes about orientation is society's formula for gender norms. Men are supposed to engage in typical "male" pastimes. They must behave in a manner that is masculine, meaning they must avoid all behavior termed female or feminine. They must be dominant and sexually aggressive. A man who does not follow these prescribed norms is a "sissy," "faggot," or "queer." Women also are expected to conform to a feminine norm. They must keep up an appearance of sexual purity and submissiveness. A woman who does not follow these norms may be called a "tramp," a "slut," or a "dyke." It is by creating prescribed gender categories that society sets up a model of what specific sexual orientation should look like.

Through categorization and assumptions our world only prescribes to one lens. The far side of that lens boxes everything, including gender and orientation, into strict little compartments. Arguably, this makes a more convenient social structure. At the same time, it is incredibly limiting. In a world where nothing fits a compartment in reality, it is not fair to see orientation categorically. Some theorists suggest there are several components that make up orientation. These include such standards as sexual behavior, attractions, and fantasies, as well as emotional, social, and community preferences, not to mention the question of self-identity. When one looks at all these components it shows just how difficult it can be to label one's own, let alone anyone else's, identity or orientation.

What are your beliefs about the fluidity of sexual orientation? Do you believe that sexual orientation is fluid or fixed at birth?

Fluid   **Neutral**   **Fixed at Birth**

+3   +2   +1   0   -1   -2   -3

Activities

1. **Religion and Homosexuality**

   What do your religious teachings say about homosexuality? Is your denomination having any debates over the role of homosexuals within your church? What are the differences of opinion on this matter? Do your churches, synagogues, or mosques permit gay/lesbian leaders? Ask your religious leader about these issues.

2. **Gay/Lesbian Support Groups**

   Check at your college or university and in *The Yellow Pages* for support groups for gays and lesbians. What do these services do? What are the needs met by these school and community organizations?

3. **Interview of a Lesbian, Gay, Bisexual, or Transgendered (LGBT) Person**

   Request from your college or university LGBT organization the name(s) of someone who would be willing to talk briefly with you about their orientation. When were they clear about their orientation? What, if any, negative experiences have they had on campus with their orientation? What positive experiences have they had? What is your reaction to meeting and talking with this person?

4. **Fluidity of Sexual Orientation**

   Interview someone who has presented themselves as having a fluid sexual orientation. How is this fluidity demonstrated? Is this fluidity confusing or calming for this person? Explain.

CHAPTER 11

ATYPICAL AND PARAPHILIC SEXUAL BEHAVIOR

"People are like snowflakes. Each person is unique in their particular arousal triggers."

Sharon, phone sex operator in *Videocases in Human Sexuality*

What images trigger your sexual thoughts? Do you remember your first kiss? Is that sensation still special to you as an adult? Do your arousal images match those in *Playboy* or *Playgirl* magazines or are your images more those in *Better Homes and Gardens* or *Popular Mechanics*? The first connections you make as a child to sensuality and sexuality often set the stage for your later arousal triggers. Some triggers are healthier than others. Some may get you in trouble with the law; some are merely annoying while others are harmless. Think of your early childhood triggers. How have they served you in adulthood?

Chapter 11 Contents:

A. Questionnaire: Typical to Variant; Normal to Paraphilia and Reaction Questions
B. Research Excerpt: "Are Transvestites Necessarily Heterosexual?" and Reaction Questions
C. Questionnaire: Sexual Attitudes and Legal Sanctions and Reaction Questions
D. Research Excerpt: "Sexuality in the Internet: From Sexual Exploration to Pathological Expression" and Reaction Questions
E. Activities
   1. Continuum: Normal to Paraphilia
   2. Media Paraphilia
   3. Sensory Arousal

Questionnaire: Typical to Variant; Normal to Paraphilia

What does it mean to be defined by others as "normal" in our society? For many of you, a behavior is normal only if it fits into certain categories of right or wrong; for others, there is more flexibility.

Using the continuum below, circle the number that best represents your <u>attitudes</u> toward this behavior. In general, your number does <u>not</u> indicate your own personal behavior, it simply means that you judge the behavior to be normal or abnormal for people in general.

Behavior	Abnormal			Neutral			Normal
1. Nude sleeping	-3	-2	-1	0	+1	+2	+3
2. Nudity around the home	-3	-2	-1	0	+1	+2	+3
3. Masturbation when alone	-3	-2	-1	0	+1	+2	+3
4. Masturbation with a partner	-3	-2	-1	0	+1	+2	+3
5. Oral sex	-3	-2	-1	0	+1	+2	+3
6. Group sex	-3	-2	-1	0	+1	+2	+3
7. Frottage (rubbing against a stranger in a public place for arousal)	-3	-2	-1	0	+1	+2	+3
8. Female prostitution	-3	-2	-1	0	+1	+2	+3
9. Anal sex	-3	-2	-1	0	+1	+2	+3
10. Phone sex	-3	-2	-1	0	+1	+2	+3
11. Extramarital sex	-3	-2	-1	0	+1	+2	+3
12. X-rated films	-3	-2	-1	0	+1	+2	+3
13. Reading sexually explicit material	-3	-2	-1	0	+1	+2	+3
14. Male prostitution	-3	-2	-1	0	+1	+2	+3
15. Male homosexuality	-3	-2	-1	0	+1	+2	+3
16. Female homosexuality	-3	-2	-1	0	+1	+2	+3
17. Bestiality/sex with animals	-3	-2	-1	0	+1	+2	+3
18. Having an abortion	-3	-2	-1	0	+1	+2	+3
19. Sex play among children	-3	-2	-1	0	+1	+2	+3
20. Interracial marriage	-3	-2	-1	0	+1	+2	+3
21. Cohabitation	-3	-2	-1	0	+1	+2	+3
22. Sex without love	-3	-2	-1	0	+1	+2	+3

Reaction Questions

1. List the items from the questionnaire on the previous page that you rated most abnormal. Trace any religious and/or family beliefs on these topics that may have impacted your beliefs.

2. What were your criteria for judging a behavior as abnormal or normal? Would your answers have been different if the scale had used the terms "natural" or "unnatural?" Explain. Would your answers have been different if the scale had used the terms "moral" or "immoral?" Explain.

3. Do you believe that community standards on any of the above have changed in the past twenty years? Which ones? Explain.

4. Do you believe community standards on any of the above will change in the next twenty years? Which ones? Explain.

Research Excerpt

Question: What assumptions do you make about men who cross-dress?

Are Transvestites Necessarily Heterosexual?*
Bonnie Bullough, R.N., Ph.D. and Vern Bullough, R.N., Ph.D.

A survey of 372 male cross-dressers gathered data about present and childhood experiences and attitudes in light of the growing knowledge about transvestism. This article focuses on data related to sexual orientation, particularly in relationship to the definition of transvestism in the *Diagnostic and Statistical Manual of Mental Disorders* of the American Psychiatric Association. It is argued that transvestism is not necessarily a heterosexual phenomenon.

Childhood Experiences
The median age at which this group started to cross-dress was 8.5 and 32% of the sample cross-dressed before they were 6. This is slightly younger (about 1 year) than the median age reported in other studies. Most of the subjects in this research were clandestine cross-dressers as children, and 56% (by their accounts) were never caught; although 93% of the sample indicated that they were afraid of being caught. An open-ended question solicited the reasons they feared being caught. Their answers could be coded into four groups shown (Table III).

Table III. What Did You Fear Would Happen
if You Were Caught Cross-Dressing? (N=312)

Fears	N	%
Rejection	148	47.4
Sissy Label	78	25.0
Crazy, mentally ill label	71	22.8
Sinful label	15	4.8

The most common fear was a fear of rejection which was emphasized by 47% of respondents: 25% feared a "sissy" label; 23% were afraid of a "crazy" label; and 5% figured cross-dressing was a sin. The sissy category also included those who feared being called a "faggot" or a "queer" as well as those that used the term "sissy." From the context of the answers it seemed that *sissy* sometimes meant girlish and weak and sometimes it meant a homosexual orientation. This confusion is a part of the childhood culture because labels are often applied before the participants know what the words mean. Even *queer* can mean "strange," "girlish," or "silly" rather than denoting a sexual orientation. In addition some of the answers which were primarily focused on parental or peer rejection included a secondary fear that they would be rejected because they were sissies or crazy. Nevertheless, the fact that these labels were used in variable ways did not lessen their stigma. Fear of a label was a powerful deterrent to open expression of feminine traits including an interest in women's clothing. It may have influenced the child to stick with a clandestine activity to express his gender feelings rather than seeking out a same-sex partner which would have been less secret.

Childhood and adolescent sexual experiences may also touch on the variable of sexual orientation. Ninety-seven persons or 26% of the group reported some homosexual experiences as a child or adolescent and 135 persons or 41% indicated they had some heterosexual experiences as children or adolescents. For most of the respondents this was a positive experience, but a small number reported negative feelings. Table IV shows these data.

Ten percent of the sample reported that they were raped or sexually assaulted as children and although there is some overlap between this group and the people who reported that they had a negative sexual experience, there were also those who reported both a rape and pleasant sexual experiences.

Table IV. Sexual Experiences as a Child or Adolescent

Experience	N	%
Homosexual		
Yes, a positive experience	42	12.5
Yes, ambivalent about it	31	8.4
Yes, negative	20	5.4
No homosexual experience	271	73.6
Heterosexual		
Yes, a positive experience	104	28.4
Yes, ambivalent about it	31	8.4
Yes, negative	20	5.4
No heterosexual experience	217	59.3

Discussion

These data clearly indicate that while a majority of transvestites are heterosexual, a significant portion are bisexual, homosexual, or not sexually active with another person. Although the DSM-IV (APA, 1994) definition of transvestism is better than the older definition, it seems to be in error on this issue.

There is support for this broader definition in the cross-cultural literature. Whitman studied cross-dressing communities in Java, Thailand, Guatemala, Peru, Brazil, and the Philippines and has found that the men who cross-dress are often homosexual. Some of them consider themselves preoperative transsexuals but few actually have sexual reassignment surgery. They have a distinctive name in each of the cultures. In Java for example, they are known as *waria*, and in Brazil they are known as *travesties* (Whitam and Mathy, 1986: Whitam, in press). Favorite occupations are hairdressing, prostitution, and entertainment including dancing, theater and other art forms. Whatever the local culture, Whitam (in press) reports that cross-dressing men outside of United States, Canada, and Western Europe have close ties to the gay community and in many countries are primarily homosexual.

The transvestite prostitutes of Costa Rica serve a clientele of heterosexual men who do not consider themselves homosexual because the client is the high-status person and the prostitute is a subordinate. This Latin American definition of the situation has more to do with power in the encounter than with sexuality (Schifter and Madrigal, in press).

The transgenderists who live in the opposite sex, both men and women, are a growing phenomenon (Devor, 1989; Boswell, 1991; Bornstein, 1994; Bolin, 1994). In this sample, the transgenderists were quite variable in their sexual orientation, with orientations towards the same sex, the opposite sex, or no sex at all.

The DSM model of obligatory heterosexual orientation for transvestites needs reconsideration since there is significant variation in sexual orientation among people who cross-dress.

Research Excerpt Reaction Questions

1. When do most transvestites initially begin to cross-dress?

2. What are the common fears of boys who cross-dress?

3. Are transvestites necessarily heterosexual? What is the percentage of transvestites who are heterosexual, homosexual, or bisexual?

4. What information do we have concerning other cultures and male practices in cross-dressing?

Questionnaire: Sexual Attitudes and Legal Sanctions

The following questionnaire asks you to rate the listed paraphilias (an unusual arousal pattern) and to determine what level of legal sanction, if any, you would recommend for this behavior. See the **Glossary** at the end of the workbook for definition of terms.

Your Attitude
  A. Normal
  B. Questionable
  C. Abnormal

Legal Sanction
  A. Make this a legal activity
  B. Mandatory counseling
  C. Misdemeanor, short-term
     sentence
  D. Felony, long-term sentence

Paraphilia	Attitude (A, B, or C)	Legal Sanction (A, B, C, or D)
1. Sadism and Masochism		
2. Bondage and Discipline		
3. Fetishism		
4. Transvestism		
5. Zoophilia		
6. Voyeurism		
7. Exhibitionism		
8. Telephone Scatalogia		
9. Frotteurism		
10. Necrophilia		
11. Pedophilia		
12. Sexual Addiction		
13. Coprophilia		
14. Urophilia		
15. Klismaphilia		
16. Infantilism		
17. Internet Sex Addictions		

Reaction Questions

1. What are the criteria on which you base your answers? Are the criteria different for your attitudes than for your recommendations for legal sanctions? Which are more liberal? Which are more conservative? Why?

2. Have you had any personal experiences with any of the above behaviors that influenced your beliefs? Explain.

Research Excerpt

Question: Is viewing of sex sites on the internet always pathological?

Sexuality on the Internet: From Sexual Exploration to Pathological Expression*
Alvin Cooper and Coralie R. Scherer, Sylvain C. Boies, Barry L. Gordon

A growing number of clients are presenting in therapy with problems related to their on-line sexual habits. Adults who had used the Internet for sexual pursuits at least once (*N=9,177*) completed a 59-item on-line survey. Men and women generally behaved differently, and most (92%) indicated their on-line sexual behaviors were not problematic. Heavy users (8%) reported significant problems typically associated with compulsive disorders. Problems were highly correlated with time spent on-line for sex. Results are discussed in terms of their research and practice implications, including diagnosis and treatment. Recommendations are made for outreach prevention programs and future policies.

Implications
Internet communication might be reflective of the demands of an increased pace and intensity that individuals in our society experience. Computers, the Internet, and E-mail allow for easy access to vast stores of information as well as the ability to have rapid and brief contacts with interested others. For most individuals, the availability of this type of communication and means of accessing information may increase their productivity and enhance their lives; however, the nature of this type of communication might also create problems for those individuals who are more susceptible to intense sexualized interactions.

Persons who spend large amounts of time on-line report more perceived problems. A significant correlation was found between time spent on-line for sexual pursuits and negative effects on one's life. The HU (Heavy Users) group preferred chat rooms to Web sites and reported higher frequencies on items that "most interfered" with and "most jeopardized" important aspects of their lives. This finding has also been reported in recent studies, suggesting that for both men and women the most powerful and potentially problematic types of interactions take place in chat rooms with other Internet users.

The finding that heavy users from both genders use chat rooms more than average users suggests that high use is associated with greater interaction with other Internet users. The relationship between these two variables seems to corroborate an association of sexually compulsive or addictive behavior with social isolation (Leiblum, 1997). It presupposes that individuals are motivated by a need for greater social contact which is consistent with Young's (1997) position that social support and sexual fulfillment serve as psychological reinforcements underlying computer-mediated communication.

The association between high use and interaction appears to be less strong for women, however. HU women were found to use Web sites twice as much as MU (Moderate Users) women. Thus, it seems that other variables mitigate this relationship in women. One possibility is that women who visit Web sites are more responsive to visual cues, a quality often attributed to men's sexuality. This is of particular interest when one considers that younger women represented a significant proportion of our sample. It suggests that younger women may feel freer to explore that aspect of their sexuality.

These findings lead to a number of important conclusions. The vast majority of on-line users generally seem to use Internet sexual venues in casual ways that may not be problematic. However, the strong correlation between time spent on-line for sexual pursuits and measures of distress, of sexual compulsivity, and of sensation seeking (sexual and nonsexual) suggest that these variables can serve as indicators in identifying individuals at risk for developing psychological difficulties. The finding that a significant minority of people who spend more than 11 hours a week on-line for sex had higher scores on these four measures than the rest of the sample reinforces the association between TOS (Time Spent On-line for Sexual Pursuits) and the manifestation of problematic behaviors.

The number of individuals for whom Internet sex can be problematic appears consistent with estimates made of this problem in the population at large. E. Coleman (personal communication, May 1998) estimated that 5% of the general population deals with issues of sexual compulsivity. The slightly higher percentage (8.5%) found in our study can be explained by the sample being entirely made up of individuals who go on-line for sexual pursuits.

The results of this study support previous findings (Young 1997) and the view of many clinicians that, for a vulnerable but significant minority of heavy Internet users, on-line sexual behavior can be detrimental. Although on-line sexuality appears to be a form of sexual exploration or recreation without negative consequences for most people, those who spend 11 hours or more time on-line in sexual pursuits show signs of psychological distress and admit that their behavior interferes with some area(s) of their lives. Consistent with Leiblum's (1997) position, it is likely that sexual problems can be best understood and treated when considered within a global understanding of a person's psychological functioning. These data are to be interpreted with caution, however. They are correlations and do not ascribe directionality or causality. At present these findings suggest only an association and do not explain whether these problems were caused by the availability of sexual outlets on-line or whether already existing issues were just being played out in a new form. The good and bad news is that only about an 8% minority could be characterized as compulsive users. This makes on-line sexual compulsivity a relatively rare condition among the on-line community. Hearing clients talk about sexual "surfing" on the Internet should raise our interest but not necessarily our alarm. We have much to learn about the wide variety of sexual offerings available on the Internet, both positive and negative, and may have to hold our assumptions in check until we understand what meaning it has in our clients' lives. This research might point to certain criteria that help provide concrete markers, such as a minimum amount of time on-line. However, clinicians need to be cautious about jumping to a diagnosis of an on-line sexual compulsion or addiction.

On the other hand, if the 8% of respondents in the study that were found to have sexually compulsive features were to generalize to the 57 million people who log on daily, a whopping 4,560,000 persons could be at risk. Thus, we should neither minimize not ignore the signs if we suspect our clients have problems where sex and the Internet intersect. We need to explore with clients whether their on-line usage is excessive and whether it is creating or resulting from problems that already exist in their lives.

The identification of four factors related to the on-line experience of users (Reflection, Action, Arousal, and Excitement) suggests that people can have different experiences or be involved in various psychic operations while pursuing sex on the Internet. This finding is particularly useful for one to consider when trying to determine where a problem lies for someone who experiences distress from their on-line behavior. It could provide a way to understand the needs and motivations underlying on-line experience. This model remains to be tested by gathering additional information about respondents' experiences and their psychological functioning. Therapeutic interventions that focus on the identified specific psychological processes could help foster awareness and change in clients.

Research Excerpt Reaction Questions

1. What amount of time spent viewing Internet sexual sites is likely to cause relationship problems?

2. Why might this form of sexual expression be prevalent in the future?

3. What are the gender similarities and differences in the use of sex sites on the Internet?

4. What are the indicators that identify persons at risk for developing psychological difficulties?

5. What percent of the population would be considered compulsive users? How might these persons be treated?

Activities

1. **Continuum: Normal to Paraphilia**
   Using the following behavioral series as an example, choose three other paraphilias and develop a continuum from normal to paraphilia. Where do you draw the line between normal and abnormal? When does normal behavior become a paraphilia?

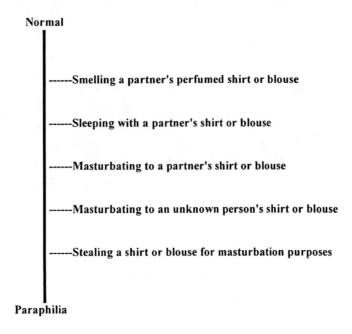

Normal

------Smelling a partner's perfumed shirt or blouse

------Sleeping with a partner's shirt or blouse

------Masturbating to a partner's shirt or blouse

------Masturbating to an unknown person's shirt or blouse

------Stealing a shirt or blouse for masturbation purposes

Paraphilia

2. **Media Paraphilia**
   Think about persons in the media who have used various sexual behaviors as part of their performances that have generated publicity, e.g. Madonna, Britney Spears. Name three to five of these persons. What is your view of them? What is the public's view of them?

3. **Sensory Arousal**
   Give specific examples in each of the following sensory categories of images that are arousing to you. What do you believe are the sources of your arousal to these stimuli?
   1. Hearing

   2. Taste

   3. Touch

   4. Vision

   5. Smell

CHAPTER 12

COERCIVE SEX:
RAPE, HARASSMENT, AND
ABUSE

"Being forced is poison for the soul."

Ludwig Borne, 1786-1837

What behavior is wanted? What is unwanted? Many persons are confused about desired and non-desired behavior. Hopefully from the confusion will come clarity. In the meantime it is important to attend to your communication style. Do your messages have the impact you have intended? Do you say no and behave in accordance with your words? Are your advances welcome or unwelcome? Have you gone too far?

Chapter 12 Contents:

A. Research Excerpt: "Feigning Sexual Desire: Consenting to Unwanted Sexual Activity in Heterosexual Relationships" and Reaction Questions
B. Myths About Rape: What Do You Believe?
C. What is Sexual Exploitation? and Reaction Questions
D. Case Study: Date Rape
E. Activities
   1. Sexual Harassment
   2. Therapist-Patient Sex
   3. Faculty-Student Sex

Research Excerpt

Question: Do college students consent to unwanted sex? Why do they do so?

Feigning Sexual Desire: Consenting to Unwanted Sexual Activity in Heterosexual Relationships*
Lucia F. O'Sullivan, Elizabeth Rice Allgeier

The prevalence rates of unwanted sexual activity indicate that a substantial portion of both men and women are at risk for experiencing unwanted (nonconsensual) sexual activity. However, little is known about the extent to which men and women consent to unwanted sexual activity, such as when a person indicates willingness to engage in a sexual activity at a time when he or she experiences no sexual desire. In the current study, 80 male and 80 female U.S. college students involved in committed dating relationships kept diaries of their sexual interactions for two weeks. More than one third (38%) of the participants reported consenting to unwanted sexual activity during this period. The most common motives for engaging in this behavior were to satisfy a partner's needs, to promote intimacy, and to avoid relationship tension. Most participants reported positive outcomes associated with these motives. The results indicate that previous estimates of the prevalence of unwanted (nonconsensual) sexual experiences may actually represent a confound of nonconsensual and consensual forms.

Discussion
We explored college students' reports of consenting to unwanted sexual activity in their committed heterosexual dating relationships. This study was based on the assumption that not all unwanted interactions are nonconsensual in nature. Approximately one quarter of the men and one half of the women who participated in this study reported consenting to unwanted sexual activity during a two-week period. This finding indicates that these experiences were not uncommon for our sample.

Consenting to Unwanted Sexual Activity
Sprecher et al. (1994) found that 55% of their participants reported having consented to unwanted sexual activity on more than one occasion, consistent with our finding that these experiences are apparently not isolated events. Also consistent with our findings, Sprecher et al. found that women were more likely than men to report consenting to unwanted sex. However, they obtained somewhat lower prevalence rates than those reported here. This discrepancy may reflect differences in survey methods: We used a self-monitoring procedure, whereas Sprecher et al. used retrospective reports. Moreover, Sprecher et al. surveyed only nonvirgin students and incidents related to participation in sexual intercourse--all of which may account for the lower rates. On the other hand, most of the experiences described by our sample involved participation in sexual intercourse. Thus, the rates obtained by Sprecher et al. from their larger, more diverse sample may more accurately reflect how common these experiences are, at least in college dating samples.

Although apparently a relatively common experience, consenting to unwanted consensual activity does not characterize most sexual interactions in committed dating relationships for our sample. Participation in sexual interactions during the two-week period of data collection was typically desired by both partners, a finding noted by other researchers assessing levels of desire (e.g., Byers & Lewis, 1988). We were surprised, however, that in only 13% of the cases did the participant refuse to participate in the unwanted sexual activity. In all other cases, participants reported that they had consented willingly.

One question that arises is whether the partner was truly unaware that the participant did not want or desire the sexual activity. Although participants typically rated their partner's level of desire as higher than their own, many reported some occasions in which they believed their partner felt less than desirous during a sexual encounter, and almost two thirds reported that they believed that their partner had consented to unwanted consensual activity in the past. These findings indicate that couples may have an implicit understanding with regard to consenting to unwanted sexual activity, similar to Shotland and

Goodstein's (1992) notion of a "sexual contract." As discrepancies in desire levels between committed sexual dating partners are relatively common (as indicated by participants' reports and what is known from past research; e.g., O'Sullivan & Byers, 1996), there may be a reciprocal agreement that the less ardent partner will accept unwanted advances on occasion, even feign desire in the sexual activity, unless he or she experiences strong inhibitions at a given time about doing so.

The reasons provided by participants for consenting to unwanted sexual activity support the hypothesis of this understanding between couples. Participants typically reported consenting to unwanted sexual activity to satisfy a partner's needs, to promote relationship intimacy, and to avoid relationship tension. Diminished intimacy and/or relationship discord may be a consequence of violating such an implicit contract. Shotland and Hunter (1995) also found that participants typically reported benefits associated with establishing or maintaining interest in the relationship and intimacy. The reasons for consenting to unwanted sexual activity may be quite different in sexual encounters between uncommitted couples--an area for future research.

It may also be important to consider the meaning given to sexual activity by men and women in heterosexual dating relationships. Sex may constitute an important symbolic means of establishing couplehood in a way that distinguishes the relationship from one of "mere" friendship. If so, refusing a partner's sexual advances may be construed as an attempt to dissolve or to diminish the relationship or, more symbolically, as refusing to recognize the intimate status of their partnership.

Characterizing Participants of Unwanted Consensual Sexual Interactions
Our prediction that endorsement of traditional masculine roles for men and feminine roles for women would be associated with reports of consenting to unwanted sexual activity was not supported. Employing a measure that assessed a less extreme stance toward gender roles may have differentiated the two groups successfully. On the other hand, perhaps sex and gender socialization are not useful factors for understanding this type of interaction. Women were more likely than men to report having consented to unwanted sexual activity during the two-week period. However, there were no differences in men's and women's lifetime and one-year incidence estimates for those participants who reported at least one incident. Moreover, we found few differences in men's and women's reports of their experiences, including their reasons for engaging in unwanted consensual sexual activity, contextual features, and outcomes.

Also contrary to our predictions, endorsement of normative beliefs about consenting to unwanted sexual activity was not predictive of reporting this behavior. Yet endorsement of norms seems to play a role in this decision: Almost one third of the participants who reported consenting to unwanted sexual activity reported that they had done so because they had engaged in the initiated sexual activity on a previous occasion or because they endorsed a norm to engage in sexual activity regularly. A more discriminating measure may have been one that assessed norms about participating in a particular type of unwanted consensual sexual activity or sexual activity generally, regardless of whether the sexual activity was desired.

Partial support was found for our prediction that men and women who reported more active dating and sexual histories would be more likely to consent to unwanted sexual activity. Participants who reported consenting to unwanted sexual activity reported a younger age of first intercourse. However, the differences in age between the two groups is small (approximately 8.5 months) and may have little practical significance. As none of the other sexual and dating history variables supported this hypothesis, it may be best to consider this a spurious finding.

Perceived Consequences
Researchers have frequently discussed their findings regarding experiences of unwanted sexual activity (broadly defined) in terms of therapeutic implications for those involved (e.g., Muehlenhard & Cook, 1988; Poppen & Segal, 1988; Zimmerman et al., 1995). However, we found that most respondents

characterized their experiences of unwanted sexual activity and their interactions with their partner as pleasant and identified a number of positive outcomes associated with the encounter, including the promotion of intimacy in the relationship. In addition, the quality of the dating relationship did not appear to suffer as a result of one partner engaging in unwanted sexual activity.

Despite reports of positive outcomes, negative outcomes were associated with more than one half of the interactions. The most frequently reported negative outcome was emotional discomfort, such as feeling uncomfortable about engaging in "meaningless sex" or feeling disappointed in oneself. The greater number of reported positive outcomes in relation to negative outcomes might reflect a certain degree of dissonance regarding one's participation in unwanted sexual activity. That is, respondents may have compensated for negative feelings associated with engaging in this discrepant behavior by overreporting positive outcomes and/or underreporting negative outcomes.

*Reprinted by permission of *The Journal of Sex Research.*

Research Excerpt Reaction Questions

1. What percentage of men and women in this study had consented to unwanted sexual activity?

2. Are men or women more likely to submit to unwanted sex? Why do you believe that this discrepancy exists?

3. Do partners know when sexual activity is not desired by their partner? Explain briefly.

4. What could be the positive and negative relationship outcomes of regularly consenting to unwanted sexual behavior?

Myths About Rape: What Do You Believe?

In some situations there is a very fine line between giving in to sex on a date and acquaintance rape. Where do you draw the line? How would you communicate to a partner your comfort area for sexuality? When should you share your beliefs with a partner? This questionnaire on myths explores many controversial facets of this question of drawing the line. Respond to the exercise, read the article, and think about your own experiences. Are these confusing to you or are you clear as to your beliefs?

Determine whether you agree or disagree with the following statements.

Statement	Agree	Disagree
1. Women "ask for it" by the way they act and dress.		
2. If a woman really did not want to get raped, she could prevent a man from having intercourse with her.		
3. Women accuse men of rape to get even with them.		
4. Women give sex to get love; men give love to get sex.		
5. Men have much stronger sexual drives than women and need to be controlled.		
6. Rape is a natural male reaction to wanting sex.		
7. Rapists are oversexed and need more outlets.		
8. Most women are teases.		
9. If a man spends money on a date for dinner or an outing, his partner owes him sex.		
10. Many women want sex; they have just been socialized to say "no."		
11. If a man gets his date drunk and then convinces her to have sex with him, he has raped her.		
12. Many men still hope the woman they marry will be a virgin or only have had a very few sexual experiences.		

Reaction Questions

1. Choose a few questions that generate your strongest responses. Which are your choices? What are your experiences that impact this response?

2. Share your responses with one person of the opposite sex. Do you agree on all of your responses? Describe any disagreements you have on your answers.

What is Sexual Exploitation?

The word exploitation used in the context of sexuality means the use of another person for your own advantage or profit. Evaluate each of the following behaviors and determine whether or not you believe they are exploitative.

Behavior	Normal			Neutral			Exploitative
1. A woman marries a wealthy man whose financial future is secure even though she can't stand to have him touch her.	-3	-2	-1	0	+1	+2	+3
2. A woman flirts with a guy at a bar, allows him to buy her drinks, lets him take her home and to bed and, after foreplay, says she doesn't want sex.	-3	-2	-1	0	+1	+2	+3
3. An investment broker greets all of his female clients with a hug and kiss on the mouth.	-3	-2	-1	0	+1	+2	+3
4. A 25-year-old man picks up a woman at a bar, invites her home, and seduces her.	-3	-2	-1	0	+1	+2	+3
5. An attendant at a nursing home fondles a female patient because the patient felt neglected.	-3	-2	-1	0	+1	+2	+3
6. A teacher takes nude pictures of a female student for a sociology project.	-3	-2	-1	0	+1	+2	+3
7. An art teacher uses student male and female nudes for class modeling.	-3	-2	-1	0	+1	+2	+3
8. A woman has sex with a male friend only because she wants a pregnancy	-3	-2	-1	0	+1	+2	+3
9. A father "wet kisses" his daughter.	-3	-2	-1	0	+1	+2	+3
10. A 16-year-old brother plays strip poker with his 10-year-old sister.	-3	-2	-1	0	+1	+2	+3
11. A college male spends his weekends trying to pick up women and "score."	-3	-2	-1	0	+1	+2	+3
12. A college fraternity pays a woman to strip for the freshman pledge class.	-3	-2	-1	0	+1	+2	+3
13. A coed sleeps with her physics professor to get a better grade.	-3	-2	-1	0	+1	+2	+3
14. A 17-year-old girl cuddles with her father on the sofa and then asks for a new car.	-3	-2	-1	0	+1	+2	+3

Reaction Questions

1. Which questions generate your strongest reactions? Explain briefly.

2. What criteria are you using to determine if exploitative behavior is in existence?

3. Discuss your answers with someone of the opposite sex. On which items is there strong agreement? Strong disagreement?

Case Study: Susan, 17, High School Student

Susan was getting ready to graduate from high school. She was really excited to take her spring break trip to Mexico. She knew this would be a great opportunity to meet people and get away from home for the first time. Susan was still a virgin, and she really believed that she would wait for the right person. She had some sexual experience, but nothing had ever gone too far. Mexico was like paradise for Susan and her friends. She had only been there for two days, but already had met so many friendly people.

On the third night there was a big party at a club for all the spring break guests. Susan was starting to let her guard down and decided to have a couple of beers. She was not very experienced at drinking, but everybody seemed to be enjoying themselves. Susan had met a boy the day before and thought he was very nice. The night of the party they ended up dancing together and kissing. He asked her to take a walk on the beach. She felt kind of dizzy from the alcohol and thought the fresh air would be helpful. She didn't tell any of her friends that she was leaving, because she thought she would be right back. Susan and her new friend started to walk on the beach. She started feeling kind of sick and decided to sit down. As soon as they sat down Susan's friend started kissing and touching her. At first she thought it was okay, but soon he started touching her beneath her clothing. She knew it was time to stop and she asked him many times. Before she knew it he was becoming forceful and she felt that the situation was out of control. Susan lost her virginity that night by force. Her friends took her to the hospital the next day. Susan went through a series of tests and interviews. Susan started counseling as soon as she got back to the U.S. She and her parents decided not to press charges. Susan relives that experience every day and wonders about how things could have been different.

Reaction Questions

1. How do you think Susan's decisions that night, i.e., drinking, not telling her friends where she was going, leaving with someone by herself, may have put her at risk for rape?

2. What emotions do you think Susan experienced during and after the assault?

3. What actions might Susan take to help her move forward?

Activities

1. **Sexual Harassment**

   Visualize a situation in which you might experience sexual harassment. Be specific in your depiction. How might this situation be avoided? How would you handle the situation if harassment were to occur?

2. **Therapist-Patient Sex**

   Many states in the United States have made it a felony for a therapist to have sex with a client, even if the client appears to consent. What is your opinion about this issue? Should adults be able to do whatever they wish? Is a therapist-patient relationship different from a physician-patient or an attorney-client or a minister-parishioner relationship? Explain.

3. **Faculty-Student Sex**

   Many college and graduate students are of adult age. Interview three college students about their thoughts on adult student and faculty sexual interactions. What are the ethical problems inherent in such relationships? Explain briefly.

CHAPTER 13

SEX PROBLEMS AND THEIR TREATMENT

"We are told that sex is dirty-- yet we are instructed to save it for someone we love!"

Lonnie Barbach, *For Each Other*

According to the research excerpt in this chapter many of you will likely experience one or more sexual problems in your adult life. The good news is that most are treatable and often can be positively resolved. What will your experience be? Will you try to correct the problem or will you resign yourself to living with the issue? Shame plays a major role in the acknowledgment of sexual concerns. How will you react?

Chapter 13 Contents:

What is Sex Therapy?
Mary Ann Watson, Ph.D.

Many of us worry about our sexual performance. We worry about our level of sexual desire. Is our desire for sex too high or too low? We are concerned about our arousal. Do we get erections quickly enough or lubricate adequately? We are concerned about our orgasms. Do we have orgasms, or are they seemingly too slow or too fast? Is intercourse painful?

These questions are the subjects for sex therapy as it is currently practiced in the United States. The practice of sex therapy grew out of the extensive research of Dr. William Masters and Dr. Virginia Johnson in their St. Louis clinic, and the additional work of Dr. Helen Singer Kaplan who added the desire component in her conceptualization of the sexual response cycle.

Sex therapy as presently practiced is a time-limited, goal-oriented form of cognitive and behavioral therapy. Individuals or couples who have the above concerns will typically contact a psychologist, social worker, psychiatrist, or psychiatric nurse who specializes in sex therapy. The goal of the therapy process is to educate the individual or couple as to their own sex education history and practice and to resolve the issues that bring them to therapy. Therapy is generally structured for the couple to practice various sexual techniques in order to resolve their presenting sexual concerns. The therapist gives "homework" assignments for the couple to practice in the privacy of their homes. A typical sex therapy process lasts approximately 12-20 weeks with hour-long sessions on a weekly basis. The success rate for the resolution of these concerns using the Masters and Johnson and Kaplan methods has been high, with success rates in the 80-90% range.

If you and your partner were to have any of these sexual concerns, how likely are you to consult a sex therapist?

1	2	3	4	5	6	7
Very Unlikely						Very Likely

Why? _____

Why not? _____

Sex Therapy Survey
Mary Ann Watson, Ph.D. *

Respond to the following survey as directed. When you have finished the questionnaire you may compare your responses to the results of the following research excerpt--"Silence About Sexual Problems Can Hurt Relationships."

	YES	NO	N/A
1. Do you have sex about as often as you or your partner would like?		X	
2. Is sex as pleasurable as you would like?	X		
3. Do you have difficulty attaining or maintaining lubrication until the end of sex? (women only)	X		
4. Are you orgasmic as much as you would like? (women only)		X	
5. Is intercourse ever physically painful for you? (women only)			
6. Do you ever have pain or spasms at the vaginal opening that don't allow for penetration? (women only)			
7. Do you notice urine loss during intercourse, orgasm, or other physical activity, e.g., sneezing, running? (women only)			
8. Do you avoid sex with a partner?			
9. Have you or your partner had any chronic disability or illness which has precipitated any sexual concerns, e.g., diabetes, heart disease, cancer, terminal illness?			
10. If yes to 9, what is the disability?			
11. Is it ever difficult for you to attain or maintain an erection of sufficient strength for intercourse? (men only)			
12. Is your ejaculation response slower than you would like? (men only)			
13. Is your ejaculation response absent at times when you would like it? (men only)			
14. Is your ejaculation response faster than you would like it? (men only)			
15. Is intercourse ever physically painful for you? (men only)			
16. If treatment were available for any of your above stated concerns, would you likely seek help?			

17. If treatment were available for any of these problems, would you prefer:
        a hospital/clinic setting_____
        private office_____
        no preference_____

18. Circle the number on the scale below which best describes the degree of happiness, everything considered, of your relationship:

1	2	3	4	5	6	7
Very Unhappy					Perfectly Happy	

MARITAL STATUS: Married _____ Single _____ Divorced_____ Widowed_____ Separated_____

* Reprinted by permission of Mary Ann Watson, Ph.D.

Research Excerpt

Question: How common are sexual dysfunctions?

Silence About Sexual Problems Can Hurt Relationships*

It's the kind of problem most people hope is a one-time occurrence. But when a man or a woman has difficulty becoming aroused or can't perform during sex with his or her partner, it's a real problem that has to be addressed.

Results from a national survey of people aged 18 to 59 years reported in the February 10, 1999, issue of *JAMA* indicate that sexual dysfunction was common among women (43%) and men (31%).

Most cases of sexual dysfunction are treatable. The first step is to realize that a problem exists and seek help from a professional.

TYPES OF DYSFUNCION
- **Inhibited sexual desire**—Lack of sexual desire or inability to become physically aroused during sexual activity. Caused by a variety of physical or psychological problems.
- **Painful intercourse**—Pain during intercourse can be caused by a number of physical or psychological problems, including hormonal changes, poor vaginal lubrication, **vaginitis** (inflammation of the vagina), sexually transmitted diseases, and the use of spermicides. The condition is known as **dyspareunia**.

FOR WOMEN
- **Lack of orgasm**—Inability to achieve orgasm. Caused by sexual inhibition, inexperience, lack of knowledge, or psychological factors such as anxiety or early sexual trauma.
- **Vaginismus**—A painful, involuntary spasm of the muscles that surround the vaginal entrance, which interferes with sexual intercourse. Usually occurs in women who fear that penetration will be painful and may stem from a previous traumatic or painful experience.

FOR MEN
- **Erectile dysfunction**—Inability to achieve or maintain an erection for satisfactory sexual intercourse. Also known as **impotence**. An estimated 20 million U.S. men, mostly older than 65 years, are affected but less than 10% of affected men actually receive treatment.
- **Ejaculatory disorders**—When ejaculation occurs before or soon after penetration (**premature**), ejaculation does not occur (**inhibited**), or the ejaculate is forced back into the bladder (**retrograde**).

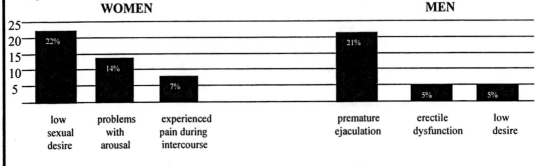

More women reported sexual dysfunction than men.

CAUSES OF DYSFUNCTION
- Physical causes-- Underlying physical conditions that can cause sexual problems include diabetes, heart disease, neurological disorders, pelvic surgery or trauma, side effects of medications, chronic disease like kidney or liver failure, hormonal imbalances, alcoholism and drug abuse, or heavy smoking.
- Psychological causes-- Stress or anxiety from work, concern about poor sexual performance, marital discord, unresolved sexual orientation, depression, previous traumatic sexual experience.

TREATMENT
Most types of sexual dysfunction can be corrected by treating the underlying physical or psychological problems. Discuss specific treatment options with your doctor.

* Reprinted by permission of the *Journal of the American Medical Association.*

Research Excerpt Reaction Questions

1. This study finds that sexual dysfunction is more common among women than men. Why do you believe this is so?

2. The most common disorders reported for women were low sexual desire and problems with arousal or lack of orgasm. Why do you believe this is so? Do you believe there are age differences in these two dysfunctions? Describe briefly.

3. The most common disorders reported for men are premature ejaculation, erectile dysfunction, and low sexual desire. Why do you believe that premature ejaculation is so frequently experienced?

4. Do you believe that most adults seek treatment for the above listed dysfunctions? Why or why not?

Why Have Sex?

A commonly stated rationale for low sexual desire is that the two persons in a relationship may have very different reasons for desiring sex. The answer to the question "Why have sex?" seems obvious enough to the average college student, yet this is one of the most common disagreements among couples who are experiencing low sex drive. One of the more telling activities is to ask each partner to list the reasons they wish to have sex with their partners. The partners then share their lists and negotiate the "good" reasons for sex in their relationship.

Read through the following reasons some persons choose to have sex. Evaluate your response to each on the following scale. After you have scored each response on the scale to the right, rank order from highest to lowest (1 is highest) your positive reasons for sex in the line before the statements. Rate your positives only.

Ranking	Reasons for Sex	Strongly Disgree		Neutral				Strongly Agree
_____	1. To express love to your partner	-3	-2	-1	0	+1	+2	+3
_____	2. To have a pregnancy	-3	-2	-1	0	+1	+2	+3
_____	3. To be playful, have fun	-3	-2	-1	0	+1	+2	+3
_____	4. For lust or horniness	-3	-2	-1	0	+1	+2	+3
_____	5. For lessening insecurity	-3	-2	-1	0	+1	+2	+3
_____	6. For money or gifts	-3	-2	-1	0	+1	+2	+3
_____	7. To fall asleep	-3	-2	-1	0	+1	+2	+3
_____	8. As proof of love	-3	-2	-1	0	+1	+2	+3
_____	9. To lessen boredom	-3	-2	-1	0	+1	+2	+3
_____	10. To meet a duty or obligation	-3	-2	-1	0	+1	+2	+3
_____	11. To release physical tension	-3	-2	-1	0	+1	+2	+3
_____	12. To lessen loneliness	-3	-2	-1	0	+1	+2	+3
_____	13. For the warmth and closeness after sex	-3	-2	-1	0	+1	+2	+3
_____	14. As an experiment	-3	-2	-1	0	+1	+2	+3
_____	15. As an adventure	-3	-2	-1	0	+1	+2	+3

Reaction Questions

1. Do you assume your partner would agree with your reasons for having sex?

2. For which reasons would you definitely not be willing to have sex?

3. List any additional reasons other than those on the previous page for having sex.

Sexual Aversion Scale *

Roger C. Katz, Martin T. Gipson, Annette Kearl, and Melinda Kriskovich

Another sexual dysfunction of note is that of sexual aversion. In this situation a person is capable of functioning sexually but avoids sex for one reason or another. The following scale is designed to measure your sexual aversion. Complete the 30 questions below, using the 4-point scale. This scale will be described more completely in the next research excerpt--"Assessing Sexual Aversion in College Students: The Sexual Aversion Scale."

Items	Not at all like me (1)	A little like me (2)	Somewhat like me (3)	A lot like me (4)
1. I worry a lot about sex.	1	2	3	4
2. I am afraid to engage in sexual intercourse with another person.	1	2	3	4
3. I have avoided sexual relations recently because of my sexual fears.	1	2	3	4
4. The AIDS scare has increased my fear about sex.	1	2	3	4
5. I believe the risks associated with sex are greater than its rewards.	1	2	3	4
6. I worry about being criticized because of my sexual behavior.	1	2	3	4
7. I was sexually molested when I was a child.	1	2	3	4
8. I try to avoid situations where I might get involved sexually.	1	2	3	4
9. I have strong sexual urges that I am unable to express.	1	2	3	4
10. I would like to feel more relaxed in sexual situations.	1	2	3	4
11. The thought of AIDS really scares me.	1	2	3	4
12. I have an abnormal fear of sex.	1	2	3	4
13. I have repeatedly avoided all or almost all genital sexual contact with a sexual partner.	1	2	3	4
14. I'm not afraid of kissing or pettting but intercourse really scares me.	1	2	3	4
15. I worry a lot about catching sexually transmitted diseases.	1	2	3	4
16. I believe my attitudes about sex are abnormal.	1	2	3	4

Items	Not at all like me (1)	A little like me (2)	Somewhat like me (3)	A lot like me (4)
17. When I was a child I was punished because of my sexual behavior.	1	2	3	4
18. The way things are now, I would never engage in sexual intercourse.	1	2	3	4
19. The thought of sex makes me nervous.	1	2	3	4
20. I believe there is no such thing as "safe sex."	1	2	3	4
21. The thought of becoming (or getting someone) pregnant scares me.	1	2	3	4
22. My sex life has always been a source of dissatisfaction.	1	2	3	4
23. I often wonder what other people think of me.	1	2	3	4
24. I would become more sexually active if I knew there was no such thing as a sexually transmitted disease.	1	2	3	4
25. I am more afraid of sex now than I used to be.	1	2	3	4
26. I would like to feel less anxious about my sexual behavior.	1	2	3	4
27. I would go out of my way to avoid being alone with a member of the opposite sex.	1	2	3	4
28. Sex is a chronic source of frustration for me.	1	2	3	4
29. I feel sexually inadequate.	1	2	3	4
30. I would like to get help for a sexual problem.	1	2	3	4

Score the SAS by totaling your overall score (1 point for Column 1, 2 points for Column 2, etc.). You are comparing your score with those of 382 undergraduate students (155 males and 211 females). The average score was 52.61: 53.75 for females, and 50.27 for males. (The Standard Deviation was 11.52).

* Reprinted with permission by Roger Katz, Brunner/Mazel, Inc., 1989.

Research Excerpt

Question: Do college students fear sex? Why?

Assessing Sexual Aversion in College Students: The Sexual Aversion Scale *

Roger C. Katz, Martin T. Gipson, Annette Kearl, and Melinda Kriskovich

The participants were 382 undergraduates who were recruited from various classes at two colleges - a 4-year liberal arts college and a 2-year community college.

Significant gender differences were noted. In general, females reported more fear of sexual intercourse. They worried more about being criticized because of their sexual behavior and were more inclined to avoid situations where they might become sexually involved. Conversely, males tended to perceive themselves as more sexually frustrated, and said they would become more sexually active if they knew they would be immune from sexually transmitted disease.

An inspection of the mean item ratings showed that fear was greatest in response to sexually transmitted diseases (principally AIDS), pregnancy, and negative social evaluation.

These results indicate that sexual fears are widely acknowledged by college students and that some 10% of them may be uncomfortable enough to seek out treatment. An implication is that sexual aversion disorder could become a prevalent problem on college campuses, expecially if predictions about AIDS spreading to the heterosexual population prove correct. If so, there will be an increasing need to develop appropriate interventions to cope with the demand. We must temper this interpretation with the realization that fear expressed as a function of the danger of AIDS is largely real, and that treatment would be appropriate for sexual aversion only where the fear of engaging in sexual activity was not proportional to the actual risk involved. Some assessment of the prevalence of such fear would be possible by asking for information about the relative safety of various "safe sex" practices.

Research Excerpt Reaction Questions

1. Is your score higher or lower that the college average for the Sexual Aversion Scale? Why do you think this is so?

2. Which items for you are the most significant items?

Activities

1. **Enhancing Your Sexuality**

   There are steps a person can take to improve the quality of their sexual relationships. These include using a hand mirror to examine genitals, body relaxation and exploration, masturbation, vibrators, videos, etc. Which of these, that can be done alone, would you be comfortable doing? Which of these that require a partner would you be comfortable doing with your partner? Which would you be least likely to do? Why?

2. **Being Your Own Sex Therapist**

   If you or your partner experience any of the dysfunctions listed in the "Sex Therapy Survey" in this chapter, what modifications might you suggest to help remedy the situation?

3. **Self-Help Books on Sex Therapy**

   The following are a few of the available self-help books on sex therapy. Based on your responses on the "Sex Therapy Survey" in this chapter, choose one of the sexual dysfunctions, read segments concerning that dysfunction from one of these sources, and outline a short treatment protocol for yourself.

   a. Kaplan, *How to Overcome Premature Ejaculation*, 1989
   b. Schnarch, *Passionate Marriage: Love, Sex, and Intimacy in Committed Relationships*, 1998
   c. Rowan, *The Joy of Self-Pleasuring: Why Feel Guilty about Feeling Good?*, 2000
   d. Beck, *Love is Never Enough: How Couples Can Overcome Misunderstandings, Resolve Conflicts, and Solve Relationship Problems Through Cognitive Therapy*, 1989

CHAPTER 14

SEXUALITY IN ILLNESS AND DISABILITY

"The first thing I asked my mom after my auto accident was, 'Will I live?' and the second was, 'Can I have sex?'"

Ellen Stohl, first woman with a disability to pose for *Playboy* magazine

What are your beliefs about sexuality and disability? Many persons might be curious about the sexuality of a chronically ill or disabled person. Bob, a quadriplegic in the documentary film, *Active Partners*, says "I'm a far better lover since my disability than before my disability." What do you think?

Chapter 14 Contents:

A. **Assessing Your Body and Reaction Questions**
B. **Your Sensory Map**
C. **Research Excerpt: "Sexuality and the Chronically Ill Older Adult: A Social Justice Issue" and Reaction Questions**
D. **Activities**
    1. **Interview**
    2. **Films and Disability**
    3. **Television Images of Disability and Chronic Illness**

Assessing Your Body

Your sensuality and sexuality are not focused entirely on your genitals. Your sexuality is the whole you--head to toe, including your brain and how you think about yourself. Erogenous zones are any parts of the body that have nerve endings. Therefore it is important to take the focus away from the genitals and to discover all the other parts with their sensations.

This issue is particularly of importance with persons with disabilities. The following assessment device looks at the whole you and your thinking about your body image, whether able-bodied or disabled. Score yourself according to the following criteria:

Items	Never (0)	Sometimes (1)	Often (2)	Always (3)
1. I feel attractive.	0	1	2	3
2. I am comfortable with my body shape.	0	1	2	3
3. When I get dressed to go out I feel like I look good.	0	1	2	3
4. I like looking in the mirror.	0	1	2	3
5. I'm proud of my appearance in public.	0	1	2	3
6. I think when people look at me that they're thinking I'm attractive.	0	1	2	3
7. I like shopping for clothing and find the experience pleasant.	0	1	2	3
8. I engage in sports and public outdoor activities.	0	1	2	3
9. I wear clothes to accentuate my positive physical attributes.	0	1	2	3
10. I feel good about my body in the presence of someone who I find attractive.	0	1	2	3

Total your score. The possible range is 0-30. A score of 21-30 indicates a positive body image; a score of 0-15 suggests a need to develp a healthier body image.

Reaction Questions

1. What are the body ideals for males and females as shown by the media?

2. When and how are you affected by the body ideals shown in the media, movies, and advertising?

3. Have you ever had an eating disorder? How was it expressed?

4. Is your sexuality affected by your feelings about your body? Explain.

5. Has your health ever interfered with your sense of your own sexuality? Explain.

Your Sensory Map

Below are drawings of the front and back of your body, the right and left sides of your face, and male and female genitalia. Fill in the drawings using the symbols below to indicate your personal sensory map.

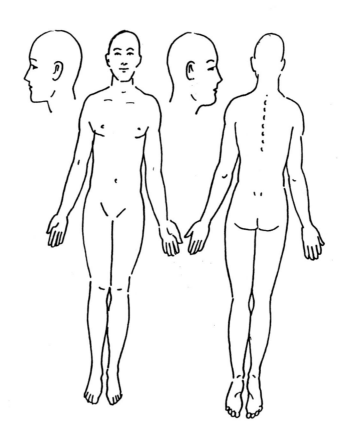

<u>LEGEND:</u>

Pleasant Sensations		Absent or Negative Sensations	
Light Touch	‖‖‖‖‖‖‖‖‖	**Absent Sensation**	☐
Firm Touch	☰	**Painful or Uncomfortable Sensations**	■

Research Excerpt

Question: What assumptions do you make concerning older adults and their sexual expression?

Sexuality and the Chronically Ill Older Adult: A Social Justice Issue*
Verna C. Pangman, R.N., M.Ed., M.N., and Marilyn Seguire, R.N., B.ScN., M.N.

Sexuality can give an embellished meaning to life. Attitudes toward sexuality have generated devaluing reactions from society regarding older adults. These actions have relegated sexuality to be invisible. As the proportion of the older population, relative to the younger generation increases, and as chronic health problems become more prevalent nurses will encounter more elderly people with sexual concerns. Nurses, educated in the field of gerontology and sexuality, are in a favorable position to assess the older adult and to provide health teaching and sexual counseling regarding the sexual concerns of the older adult. Nursing research and policy development are complementary avenues whereby sexuality can be made more visible for the older adult who is experiencing chronic illness. These nursing strategies will facilitate the recognition of the elderly and their rights. These rights need to be respected and exercised to promote social justice in order to enhance their quality of life.

In the literature, sexuality has been described as one of the most natural and basic aspects of life that affects an individual's identity as a human being. Sexuality provides the opportunity to express affection, admiration, and affirmation of one's body and its functionings. It not only encompasses the whole individual, but it serves as a reference frame in relation to others. In addition, sexual health care is an essential component of overall wellness during one's developmental lifespan.

Aging and sexuality are two closely related issues beset by anxiety and myths in our society (Jones, 1994). Because sexuality is so closely identified with youthfulness, the stereotype of sexless older adults who are frail and inactive is a widely held belief. In fact, older adults who are experiencing chronic illness and are disabled find themselves devalued, denied sexual expression, and excluded from meaningful relationships (Tilley, 1996; Kobrin Pitzele, 1995). Society falls short on two counts. First, society fails to recognize the importance of sexuality to the well-being of the elderly. Secondly, society helps to impose barriers which results in the sexuality of older adults being devalued (Ballard, 1995). Such negative reactions have resulted in the sexuality of older adults being rendered invisible. However, during the 1990's a ground swell of transformation of the social reality of oppression towards older adult's sexuality is being slowly realized. For example, in 1992, the United Nations General Assembly declared 1999 the International Year of Older Persons (IYOP) (Government of Canada, 1998), whereby the various sectors in society are encouraged to bring about more intergenerational respect and support for the issues of older adults related to healthy aging. The struggle to make sexuality more visible in the lives of the elderly, who are experiencing chronic illness, is shifting and is reflected in a recognition and an appreciation of older adults across communities in the Western hemisphere.

In the health care sector, nurses educated in the field of gerontology and who work with the older adult are in the position to be considered a primary source to assess the elderly and the perceptions of their families regarding the sexuality of the older adults (Davidson, 1995). Nurses are able to present not only accurate information regarding sexual concerns, but they can provide health teaching and sexual counseling in their practice. As alternative strategies, nurses may consider the importance of conducting nursing research and in developing policies to enhance the visibility of sexuality for the elderly who are experiencing chronic illness (Karlen, 1995). The actualization of these interviews will, hopefully, promote the recognition of older adults and their rights to their sexuality in society. Eckland and McBride (1997) claim that nurses are in a strong position to facilitate the creation of equal opportunities to have the older adults' rights not only respected, but exercised, to promote their quality of life.

In this article a definition of sexuality and sexual health is presented. Second, the invisibility and visibility perspectives of chronically ill older adults' sexuality held by society and health professionals are briefly discussed. Finally, and most importantly, nursing strategies are described in the areas of education, practice, research and policy development that can go far to assist the elderly and their families in dealing with sexuality and sexual concerns. Nurses can promote social justice strongly by raising the level of consciousness regarding sexuality in various sectors of society which can help to dispel the myth that aging renders the chronically ill older adult sexless and worthless.

CONCLUSION

This issue of sexuality and the older adult who is experiencing chronic illness is most important for nurses to consider. Recognizing the older adults' sexuality and sexual concerns is essential in the maintenance of sexual integrity and self-concept. Further, because the Year 1999 was dedicated to the older person, it becomes critical that society embraces older adults' independence, participation, care, self-fulfillment and dignity. Nurses can be instrumental to create changes toward continuing to make sexuality more visible and to claim social justice for the elderly who may still be struggling to be seen and heard.

Research Excerpt Reaction Questions

1. What beneficial role might sexuality play in the self-esteem of chronically ill adults?

2. What myths exist in our society relating to aging, illness, and sexuality?

3. Of what value is naming 1999 the International Year of Older Persons?

4. What particular professional group is thought to be central to the issues of research and practice with elderly populations? Why?

Activities

A. **Interview**

If you have a friend or acquaintance who is disabled or chronically ill, ask them some questions, if they are willing to talk, concerning their knowledge of their specific disability or illness and its impact on their sexuality.

B. **Films and Disability**

Rent one of the following movies: "Coming Home," "The Other Sister," "Scent of a Woman," "The Best Years of Our Lives," "Other Side of the Mountain," "If You Could See What I Hear," "Born on the Fourth of July," "Children of a Lesser God." Observe the person with the disability and describe how they handled their sexual feelings. How did others in the film handle the disability? What was your reaction to the film?

C. **Television Images of Disability and Chronic Illness**

How are men and women with physical limitations or disabilities depicted on television or in the movies? Are they sexual? Give specific examples of TV programs or movies and their presentations of persons with chronic illness or disability.

CHAPTER 15

YOUR BODY AND SOCIAL LEARNING

"Sexuality is not a fact. It is a concept whose meaning is shaped by society and which will continue to change and evolve as the society that has defined it changes and evolves."

King, *Human Sexuality Today*, 2002

You are exposed on a daily basis to messages concerning your body--what it should look like and how it should act. The sources of this information are many and varied--television, advertising, and the internet give messages from afar; your school, home, work, and community give messages "up close and personal." What are the messages you receive? Do these messages lead to comfort, discomfort, or both?

Chapter 15 Contents:

A. "Sexual Self-Image Checklist" and Reaction Questions
B. How Do You Look? and Reaction Questions
C. Research Excerpt: "Gender Differences in Effects of Mood on Body Image" and Reaction Questions
D. Activities
    1. Collection of Ads (Male)
    2. Collection of Ads (Female)
    3. Products for Women in Advertising
    4. Products for Men in Advertising
    5. Menstruation Reactions
    6. Your Partner's Sexual Self-Image

Sexual Self-Image Checklist*
Rita Aero and Elliot Weiner

Your self-image helps to determine your comfort and ease with your sexuality. The greater the comfort the less the likelihood of sexual dysfunction. In the test that begins below, you'll be presented with a list of 100 adjectives.

First go down the list and place an X in the column that reads "As I Am Sexually" each time you come to an adjective that describes how you really are.

Now, without paying attention to the marks you made in the first column, read through the list again. This time place an O in the second column which reads "As I Would Like To Be Sexually" for each adjective that describes that way you would like to be.

Keep in mind that for some of the adjectives both columns will be marked; for others only one will be marked, and some will have no marks next to them.

Remember, read and mark the two columns separately. When you've finished, determine your score.

	(X) As I Am Sexually	(O) As I Would Like To Be Sexually		(X) As I Am Sexually	(O) As I Would Like To Be Sexually
Active			Creative		
Adaptable			Cynical		
Addicted			Daring		
Affectionate			Demanding		
Aggressive			Desirable		
Agreeable			Determined		
Angry			Discreet		
Argumentative			Domineering		
Assertive			Eager		
Athletic			Eccentric		
Attentive			Elegant		
Blunt			Emotional		
Bold			Entertaining		
Boring			Enthusiastic		
Businesslike			Erotic		
Careful			Faithful		
Cautious			Fickle		
Choosy			Flirtatious		
Charming			Forceful		
Competitive			Frustrated		
Compulsive			Fussy		
Confident			Gentle		
Conservative			Habitual		

	(X) As I Am Sexually	(O) As I Would Like To Be Sexually			(X) As I Am Sexually	(O) As I Would Like To Be Sexually
Honest				Persuasive		
Humerous				Playful		
Imaginative				Possessive		
Impulsive				Private		
Indulgent				Relaxed		
Inhibited				Responsive		
Innocent				Romantic		
Insecure				Rushed		
Jealous				Self-conscious		
Judgmental				Sensitive		
Loud				Sensual		
Mischievous				Sentimental		
Modest				Sexy		
Moody				Show-offish		
Mysterious				Shy		
Naive				Spontaneous		
Naughty				Stubborn		
Obedient				Tactful		
Obsessed				Talkative		
Open-minded				Teasing		
Opinionated				Temperamental		
Opportunistic				Timid		
Optimistic				Unselfish		
Out of control				Vengeful		
Patient				Voyeuristic		
Perfectionistic				Vulnerable		
Persistent				Wild		

SCORING: To find your score on the Sexual Self-Image Checklist, go back over the list and give yourself one point for each time the columns *do not* match. *If only one column is marked (with either an X or an O), that's not a match and you score one point.* If there's both an X and an O next to an adjective, that's a match and you don't receive a point; if neither column is marked, that's also a match and doesn't score. Once you've determined how many adjectives on your checklist *don't match*, count the total number and write it in the box below.

Total Score

NORMS TABLE					
	Very Low	Low	Average	High	Very High
MEN	6 and below	7-10	11-23	24-31	32 and above
WOMEN	11 and below	12-16	17-27	28-39	40 and above

In the Norms Table you'll see that there are significant differences between self-image scoring levels for men and women. (Remember that a low score means a low level of discrepancy between how you see your sexual self and how you would like to be). The table shows that women tend to be more unhappy with themselves sexually than men are. Could this be a part of a cultural idea that insists women must strive to be prettier, slimmer, sexier, than they are? Is it easier for men, given their traditional role as the sexual aggressor, to be more at ease with who they are because they feel in more control? We believe the results may indicate this cultural bias.

Low/Very Low Scores: Low scores on the Sexual Self-Image Checklist generally indicate a positive view of who you are sexually. For you, this probably translates into good feelings about yourself, a willingness to take the necessary risks in order to initiate sexual relationships, and the ability to work through the problems that are inevitable in ongoing relationships. For men, a positive sexual self-image is related to a high overall level of sexual satisfaction and to a willingness to move toward commitment in relationships. Women who score in this range generally view themselves as attractive and desirable and report low levels of jealousy in their sexual relationships. A positive self-view, it seems, makes it easier to take sexual risks and to feel able to work out sexual problems should they develop.

A very positive view of yourself sexually can be beneficial as long as you continue to grow and develop. Even a positive self-image has its risks. If you scored well here you must continue to be sensitive to your partner, who may not be as secure as you are. Sometimes, it seems, a high level of confidence in one partner can add to the insecurity of the other, unless effective communication and openness keep the relationship channels clear.

Average Scores: Most healthy people have several qualities that they wish were different about themselves, and that's probably true for you if you scored in the average range. As we discussed earlier, the meaning of discrepancies between who you are and who you would like to be can only be understood by you. You may look at your average score and feel that it's okay because you can't really change who you are. Or you may look at your score and find a challenge; you may see a solid base upon which to build a higher level of sexual self-esteem. Our results say that you'll feel better about your sexual life if you choose the latter.

High/Very High Scores: If you scored in the high or very high range for your own sex, chances are you feel a low level of control in your sexual relationships. High-discrepancy scorers also report a high level of concern about being rejected sexually, as well as a strong fear of commitment in their sexual relationships.

A large gap between how you see yourself and how you would like to be may suggest that you're going through a major change in your sexual life. You may have decided to take a close look at who you are because of events that made you feel the need for sexual change. Or you may be in the process of developing a new sexual personality. Among our test subjects, older men tended to score in the high or very high range. This could be an indicator of the so-called mid-life crisis in men.

If you scored in this range, look back over the list and decide how important each of those discrepancies is in your life. You may feel overwhelmed looking at how far you have to go to become who you want to be, but keep in mind that sexual growth is a lifelong process. Use this information to determine where you want to start. Your sexuality can take a happy leap forward if you'll continue the growth process that you've started by taking this test.

Reaction Questions

1. Did you score as you expected on the Sexual Self-Image Checklist?

2. Choose several qualities from the list that you would like to change. How might you institute a plan to make the necessary changes?

How Do You Look?

In the space provided draw a picture of your body (A) and your ideal body (B).

A. My Body	**B. My Ideal Body**

Reaction Questions

1. What differences do you notice between your body (A) and your ideal body (B)?

2. What parts of your body do you like most?

3. What parts of your body do you like least?

4. What are the sources of your ideal body type? What effect have these sources had on your sense of self?

Research Excerpt

Question: Are happiness and perceived physical attractiveness related?

Gender Differences in Effects of Mood on Body Image*
Nigel Barber

Although a majority of young women in our society accept a slender standard of bodily attractiveness, want to be more slender, and overestimate their body size (Silverstein & Perlick, 1996; Thompson, 1990), a relatively small proportion develops serious eating disorders (approx. 1% for anorexia and 4% for bulimia, Gordon, 1990). Clearly, there must be individual difference factors that constitute risks for developing eating disorders. These may include proneness to depression, perfectionism, genetic vulnerability, and a family environment especially likely to promote weight loss, among other factors (Barber, 1998a). In this study, mood was experimentally manipulated by means of self-descriptive statements to investigate whether the manipulation would alter body image for men or women.

Body image has a complex relationship with weight loss behaviors. Thus, overestimation of body size may stimulate dieting and exercise. This can be understood as one manifestation of adaptive psychological mechanisms that make people conform to the standards of attractiveness of their society (Barber, 1995, 1998a, 1998b, 1998c; Singh, 1993). Inability to attain the prevailing slender standard for women produces an intense negative effect. A person's customary depression can intensify this feeling thereby increasing the motivation to lose weight (Pinchas, Toner, Ali, Garfinkle, & Stuckless, 1999). (For the purposes of this paper, the word "depression" is used as a synonym of low mood [or sadness] without intending to imply that clinical depression is implicated.)

The relevance of low mood to motivation for losing weight is illustrated by experiments in which women were exposed to magazine pictures of women varying in body build (Pinchas, et al., 1999; Stice & Shaw, 1994). Those exposed to slender models produced increased self-rating of depression, stress, and guilt, as well as body dissatisfaction. Paradoxically, Myers and Biocca (1992) found that exposure to slender models in video commercials elevated mood as well as making participants evaluate themselves as more slender, suggesting that the participants may have identified with the slender models in this dramatized depiction. Another relevant piece of evidence is that women (but not men) are sensitive to the emotional character of the instructions in a body estimation procedure and say that they "feel" significantly fatter than they "appear to others" (Thompson, 1990).

Experimental mood induction could contribute to the clarification of the relationships among low mood, body image, and eating disorders. The first report of the effect of experimentally induced mood on body size perception was that of Taylor and Cooper (1991). A negative mood was induced by exposing participants to dismal self-descriptive statements while participants in the "control" condition read cheerful statements about themselves. The mood induction did not affect either perceived body size, or desired body size, as measured using a distorting video procedure although statistical control of desired body size before the mood induction produced a significant effect: low mood made women want to be more slender.

Plies and Florin (1992) reported that experimentally induced mood can affect body image. Moods were induced by asking female participants to ruminate about either a happy or a sad event in their lives and their perceived body width was measured using a distorting video procedure.

The sad mood induction produced modestly larger estimates of body width but the happy induction did not significantly alter body width estimates. This might have been due to the fact that a repeated-measures design was used in which the happy mood induction always followed the sad one.

A study of seven bulimic women and eight controls did not find any significant main effect of a musically induced low mood on body image (Carter, Bulik, Lawson, Sullivan, & Wilson, 1996). The sample size in this study was too small to allow any confidence in the findings.

The role of mood in body self-perception of normal men and women was further investigated in this study, using an experimental manipulation of mood. It was predicted (1) that the induction of a depressed mood would increase women's self-perception of body size but that there would be the opposite effect for men (because most men want to be somewhat heavier than their current size (Abell, & Richards, 1996; Thompson, 1990). Similarly, it was predicted (2) that experimental elevation of mood would cause women to feel (and evaluate themselves as being) more slender and men to feel (and evaluate themselves as being) heavier. Regression analysis was used to enable evaluation of the role of the experimental manipulation with the effects of naturally occurring differences in depression statistically controlled.

It was predicted (3) that people with heavier than average body build would both evaluate themselves as heavier and endorse a heavier body build because this would be consistent with social feedback and would replicate the findings of obesity research (Thompson, 1990). As previous researchers have also reported, it was predicted (4) that women having low mood would endorse a more slender standard of attractiveness than other women (Silverstein & Perlick, 1996) whereas depressed men would endorse a heavier ideal than other men. Because the slender standard prevails when women are entering professions in increasing numbers (Barber, 1999a, 1999b; Silverstein, Perdue, Peterson, Vogel, & Fantini, 1986; Silverstein & Perlick, 1996) and are therefore concerned with educational achievement, it was predicted (5) that GPA would be higher for women (but not for men) who endorsed a slender body ideal.

*Barber, N., "Gender differences in effects of mood on body images" from *Sex Roles*, Vol. 44, Nos. ½, 2001. Reprinted by permission of Kluwer Academic/Plenum Publishers.

Research Excerpt Reaction Questions

1. What percentage of women in our society develop serious eating disorders?

2. What are the differences between men and women in our culture related to their estimation of body size?

3. How are standards of body attractiveness established?

4. Describe the relationship between mood and perception of body attractiveness.

Activities

1. **Collection of Ads (Male)**
   Collect five advertisements from magazines or print that tend to focus on the male "crotch." What is the significance of this in Western advertising?

2. **Collection of Ads (Female)**
   Collect five advertisements from magazines or print that tend to focus on the female breasts. What is the significance of this in Western advertising?

3. **Products for Women in Advertising**
   Observe advertising on television and in the print media. Which advertisements use women to sell their products? What are the messages inherent with the presence of men in some ads and the absence of men in others? Give examples with your interpretations.

4. **Products for Men in Advertising**
   Observe advertising on television and in the print media. Which advertisements use men to sell their products? What are the messages inherent with the presence of men in some ads and the absence of men in others? Give examples with your interpretations.

5. **Menstruation Reactions**
   In our culture how is menstruation discussed? What restrictions are placed on women in our culture during menstruation? What are your thoughts about having intercourse during menstruation?

6. **Your Partner's Sexual Self-Image**
   If you have a regular partner, have your partner take the "Sexual Self-Image Checklist" and discuss together your similarities and differences. What qualities from the list would you both like to change? How would you institute a plan for such a change?

CHAPTER 16

DRUGS AND SEX

"A conservative estimate is that, overall, about half of all cases of diminished desire and arousal and orgasmic difficulties are drug caused."

June Reinisch, *The Kinsey Institute's New Report On Sex,* 1990

You are bombarded on a daily basis with commercial images of drugs, particularly alcohol, and sexuality. The messages seem clear that drugs (alcohol, marijuana, cocaine, etc.) enhance sexuality. The truth, however, is not so simple. What are your beliefs? What is your experience?

Chapter 16 Contents:

Why Do You Drink and Use Drugs?

Small amounts of alcohol lessen inhibitions and enhance your sexuality. On the other hand, using more than small amounts deadens nerve endings and increases the chances that alcohol and drugs will minimize your sensations and increase your incidence of sexual dysfunction.

Respond to the following questions. Be honest with yourself. Are you a candidate for problems based on your responses?

Put a check next to each statement that is true for you <u>some</u> to <u>most</u> of the time.

Do you drink? YES_____ NO_____

When you drink you drink to...

_____ enhance enjoyment of other persons and activities
_____ relax yourself and feel less inhibited
_____ allow yourself to be sensual and sexual
_____ allow yourself to enjoy food more
_____ lessen tensions and anxieties after a day's work
_____ escape problems
_____ cover up any fears or a lack of self-confidence
_____ block out loneliness
_____ block out sexual anxieties

Reaction Questions

1. Do you have any concerns related to your answers to the above questions?

2. What effects have drugs or alcohol had on your sexuality?

3. What is the amount of alcohol for you that is the line between a sex-enhancer and a sex-detractor? Explain.

Research Excerpt

Question: Does drinking have any long-term effect on your sexuality?

Alcohol and Sex *
Nada L. Stotland, MD

Observations concerning the effects of alcohol on sexual performance date back to biblical times, and have been noted in literature and throughout recorded history. Today, physicians often see adolescents, or unsophisticated adults (nearly always male), whose use of alcohol has inhibited their sexual performance.

The paradoxical effect of alcohol - eloquently described in Shakespeare's *Macbeth*: "Drink provokes the desire, but it takes away the performance" - tends to make people feel more relaxed, euphoric and, in being less inhibited, experience heightened desire. But after consuming a significant amount of alcohol, many men discover that they cannot achieve or maintain an erection. They become frightened and anxious, and may carry this uncertainty into subsequent sexual experiences.

Education and reassurance can easily help such men overcome erectile dysfunction, once they understand the acute effects of alcohol consumption, and realize that any resultant sexual dysfunction is probably temporary. It is not clear at this time whether there are analogous effects on women.

Chronic alcoholism presents longer-lasting and complex issues that require an understanding of many other interrelated factors, including the metabolism and effects of alcohol; the genetics, psychology, and epidemiology of alcohol abuse; alcohol's specific sexual and reproductive effects; and the diagnosis and treatment of these effects.

Personality changes associated with alcoholism may have a direct impact on sexual functioning, for the latter is intimately related to the individual's psychological, neurological, and general physical well-being. In the earliest stage, alcoholics become impulsive, insensitive, and thoughtless of their partners. Later on, they become emotionally vulnerable and labile, sometimes appearing to be grandiose and irritable and at other times morose and guilty. In due course, their sexual drive and activity decrease, and they may even become morbidly jealous of their sexual partners. They may be rough with children and lovers, sometimes even violent. After many years of heavy alcohol use, they become disinterested, dull, inhibited, and preoccupied with vague worries and bodily symptoms.

Sexual effects of alcohol on women

Available (although limited) research indicates that alcohol consumption by women who drink only socially produces a decrease in vaginal pulse pressure, but these physiological findings do not correlate with the women's subjective experience. Alcoholic women have been reported to have a low level of sexual activity, to have many sexual partners, and to have a higher incidence of homosexual relationships when compared with nonalcoholic controls.

Alcoholic women's relationships with men tend to be problematic: they are more likely to have intercourse when intoxicated than when sober; they do not experience orgasm; and they report dissatisfaction with their sexual lives. It is therefore difficult to know whether their alcohol abuse is a cause or a result of their sexual and social problems. If these women continue to drink, however, there is little chance of improvement.

Sexual effects of alcohol on men

Acute consumption of large amounts of ethanol as well as its chronic abuse are associated with either complete erectile failure or the inability to maintain a firm erection. After one such episode, the man may become so upset that this anxiety impedes erectile function on his next attempt, either following alcohol consumption or under all circumstances. Moreover, chronic alcohol abuse has a direct adverse effect on the reproductive organs as well as an indirect adverse effect on the hormonal and central nervous systems. Despite cultural beliefs to the contrary, alcohol consumption does not increase sexual arousal or performance. Some men, however, can retain partial or full erectile capacity even when their blood alcohol levels exceed the legal definition of intoxication.

To date, the association between alcohol consumption and rape remains in question. Many convicted rapists had been drinking just prior to committing the act. This finding appears to be inconsistent with documented lower sexual performance under the influence of alcohol, but it may correlate with the increased aggressiveness resulting from acute or chronic alcohol ingestion. Some rapists' difficulties with penetration and ejaculatory control may be related to alcohol.

Unlike most alcoholics, alcoholic rapists who drank before committing a rape have been found to have higher than normal blood testosterone levels. These puzzling findings further underscore the complex relationships among social, psychological, and physiological factors in both alcohol use and sexual behavior.

Research Excerpt Reaction Questions

1. What did Shakespeare mean by the quote, "Drink provokes the desire, but it takes away the performance?"

2. Binge drinking, particularly by college students, is often thought to be harmless. After reading this segment, what are the possible implications for sexual functioning?

3. Some indications exist that alcoholism in women leads to a decrease in vaginal pulse pressure. What could the relationship be between this fact and lack of orgasms in alcoholic women?

4. Why do men in our culture correlate alcohol consumption and sexual performance?

5. What are the media messages that give credence to alcohol consumption and sexual potency?

Case Study: Judy, 19, College Student

Judy is a 19-year-old college student who is attending a state school near her parents' home. She is a terrific student but this was not always the case. During her freshman year she went out and partied almost every night. One night when she was at a party someone asked her if she would like a sip of their drink. She took one huge gulp and almost spit it out. The drink felt warm and salty in her mouth, almost like a gulp of her own saliva. "That was horrible," she told her companion. "What was that?"

"GHB (Gamma Hydroxy Butyrate)," her companion told her.

"That was disgusting."

"How do you feel?"

"I don't know, kind of warm and happy I guess; my skin feels all prickly."

"Good, GHB always gets you in the mood; it makes sex feel great."

"Really? Give me another sip," Judy said grabbing her companion's drink and taking a giant sip followed quickly by another.

"Wow, slow down, if you drink like that you are going to get sick."

"Oh, I'm fine," Judy told her companion. "I'm going to get another beer."

That was the last thing Judy remembered. She woke up in the morning in a strange bed. She realized she was naked and to her horror she was in bed with a guy and another girl who were naked too. She got up and left immediately. Judy felt terrified about what might have happened and she swore to herself she would stop partying and never take another drink from a stranger again.

Today Judy is a dedicated student. She claims that her experience with GHB taught her to be more cautious and more responsible. She also knows she will never do any drugs again, especially if the experience is going to involve sex. Judy feels that if she is going to have sex she wants to be sober and fully coherent so she can be more discerning about her partners and actually enjoy the experience.

REACTION QUESTIONS

1. What rules, if any, do you have about your personal drug use?

2. What advice would you give a freshman student about drug use and sexuality?

Activities

1. **Alcohol Advertising**
   Watch an evening of television and list the alcohol ads that are shown in one three-hour period. What are the messages about alcohol use and sexuality?

2. **Popular Music**
   Choose several popular songs that have a theme of alcohol or drug use. Write out the lyrics. What are the messages about drug use and sexuality? What impact, if any, do you think these lyrics have on young teens and their developing drug use and sexual behavior?

3. **Anti-Drug-Use Advertising**
   Write out the text of two anti-drug-use ads. How effective are these ads? What is the message, if any, about drug use and sexuality?

4. **Movies**
   View two movies with drug use themes e.g., "Traffic," "Blow," "Dazed and Confused." What are the messages about drug use and sexuality?

CHAPTER 17

SEXUALLY TRANSMITTED DISEASES

"Two-thirds of STD cases occur in people under age 25."

Bryan Strong et al., *Human Sexuality,*
Diversity in Contemporary America, 1999

What are your chances of contracting a sexually transmitted disease? Most of you probably feel immune to such misfortunes. You assume that all of your friends and potential partners are "clean." The problem, however, is that you can't tell by looking at a person's face or even their genitals whether or not they might be a carrier. The general rule is, "Be informed and use your head." This is sometimes difficult in the heat of the moment, but an absolute necessity for you if you are sexually active.

Chapter 17 Contents:

Research Excerpt

Question: Is STD really a concern or has it been overrated?

Sexual Behaviors of University Freshmen
and the Implications for Sexuality Education*

Margaret V. Pepe, Ph.D., R.N.; Daniel W. Sanders, Ph.D.;
Cynthia Wolford Symons, D.Ed., CHES

Almost 12 million cases of sexually transmitted disease occur annually, 86% of them in people aged 15 through 29 years (Centers for Disease Control, 1990a). It is estimated that the rate of HIV-related infection is on the rise among college students (Gayle et al., 1990; Tucker & Cho, 1991). Of the 15,917 AIDS cases reported to the Centers for Disease Control thus far, only 604 (approximately 0.4%) have been persons aged 13 to 19 (Centers for Disease Control, 1990b). However, one-fifth of all AIDS cases have been persons aged 20 to 29 (Tucker & Cho, 1991). Due to the long lag period (up to 10 years) between HIV infection and clinical AIDS, many of these persons were probably infected as teenagers (Tucker & Cho, 1991). Current sero-prevalence rates of 8/10,000 for students under age 24 (Gayle et al., 1990) are expected to increase due to such variables as cognitive dissonance, maturation level, and defense mechanisms. In fact, Pestrak and Martin (1985) believe that people in this age group are functioning at a cognitive level that renders them unable to practice "safe sex" techniques. Effective practice of safe sex requires acceptance of one's sexuality and acknowledgment that one is sexually active with the ability to view potential future sexual encounters realistically. This age group also exhibits feelings of immunity to the natural laws by which other people must live their lives (Elkind, 1984). Burke's study (Burke et al., 1990) suggested that the prevalence of HIV infection in university students is much higher than in the teenage applicants for military service. Therefore, until a vaccine or effective treatment becomes available, preventative efforts to counter HIV infection must focus on encouraging changes in risk behaviors with special emphasis on young women of childbearing age (Novick, 1991).

RESULTS

Overall, more than half of students in this sample were sexually active: Caucasian males (66%) and females (60.5%) aged 18.4 years. The women reported fewer partners than their male counterparts (see Figure 1).

Although 71% of the women "always" used some method of birth control, far fewer of the men (54.5%) exhibited this behavior (see Figure 2). In addition, only 13% of the students "sometimes" used birth control, with 11% of the men and 6% of the women stating they "never" used any method.

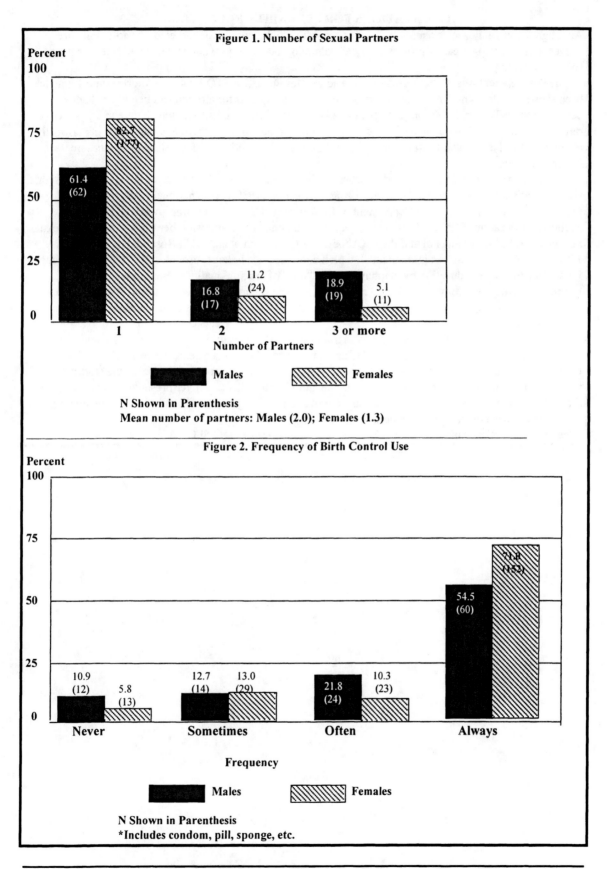

Figure 1. Number of Sexual Partners

Percent

Number of Partners	Males	Females
1	61.4 (62)	82.7 (177)
2	16.8 (17)	11.2 (24)
3 or more	18.9 (19)	5.1 (11)

Number of Partners

■ Males   ▨ Females

N Shown in Parenthesis
Mean number of partners: Males (2.0); Females (1.3)

Figure 2. Frequency of Birth Control Use

Percent

Frequency	Males	Females
Never	10.9 (12)	5.8 (13)
Sometimes	12.7 (14)	13.0 (29)
Often	21.8 (24)	10.3 (23)
Always	54.5 (60)	71.0 (162)

Frequency

■ Males   ▨ Females

N Shown in Parenthesis
*Includes condom, pill, sponge, etc.

IMPLICATIONS FOR SEXUALITY EDUCATORS

Although the impact of intervention will differ according to the population targeted, the following are suggestions regarding areas of professional programming focused on sexual health issues within a post secondary setting.

1. Development of a 30-hour credit course addressing sexuality/STD issues. A shorter time-frame has been shown to affect knowledge, however, more hours are required for attitude and behavior change to occur (Connell, Turner, & Mason, 1985). Fennell (1991) reported student attitude change in a positive direction during a 30-hour course when activities were assigned to make them analyze and think critically about the ethical issues confronting society regarding the AIDS epidemic. Fennell did not measure behavior change.

2. Implementation of the "Sex and Substance Abuse: What Are the Links" module from the Eta Sigma Gamma National Health Science Honorary *Project Direction* (1989). This national peer education program was funded by the U.S. Department of Education and the Fund for Improvement of Post-Secondary Education (FIPSE). Extensive research documents the relationship between young adult sexual behavior and the use of alcohol and drugs (Abbey, 1991; Hingson et al., 1990; Rosenbaum & Kandel, 1990). *Project Direction's* training manual, which addresses this linkage, provides the "how to" approach for student-to-student education by emphasizing the "dos" of making quality presentations as well as learning opportunities appropriate for the classroom, student organization meetings, and student residential settings. The training manual also contains ideas to help generate high levels of student involvement and faculty/administration support.

3. Peer Awareness with Students (PAWS) training groups. This university-funded, volunteer student-governed organization selects salient health-related topics to address each semester (e.g., STDs, date rape). Under the guidance of a faculty advisor, two-day training sessions are conducted to give the students pertinent information on each topic, along with the appropriate skills to deliver presentations requested by the residence hall directors and other campus organizations. The group meets with the faculty adviser approximately two times per month during the academic year.

*Reprinted by permission of the *Journal of Sex Education and Therapy* and AASECT.

Talking About STDs

The time to think about STDs with a new partner is before you have sex. This can be awkward, but practice by yourself or with a friend can make a potentially difficult situation a little easier.

Answer the following questions:

1. List two ways to bring up the subject of STDs and/or AIDS with a new partner. How might you ask whether or not he or she has been exposed or has engaged in any risky behavior?

2. If you had been exposed to an STD or AIDS in the past and might pass it to a new partner, how and when would you tell your partner?

3. How would you bring up the subject of condom use with your partner? How would you convince someone who doesn't want to use a condom to use one?

4. Do you think you would have sex with a partner even if you could not convince them to use a condom? Explain.

Condom Use

Some people don't like to use condoms. Assume you have a partner who has just given you the following reasons for not wanting to use a condom. Write a one-sentence rebuttal to each of the following reasons in order to convince your partner to use a condom.

1. Your partner doesn't like condoms.

2. Your partner doesn't have a condom with him/her.

3. Your partner isn't worried about getting an STD.

4. Your partner doesn't think condoms prevent the spread of HIV.

5. Your partner says he/she is clean.

6. Your partner is ready to conceive a child and you are not.

7. You are afraid your partner would leave you if you suggested using a condom.

8. You are afraid your partner might hurt you if you suggested using a condom.

9. You are too embarrassed to suggest using a condom.

10. Your partner wants to feel physically closer to you.

11. You felt it was your partner's responsibility to use a condom and he/she didn't suggest it.

12. You were too high or drunk to think about using a condom.

Reaction Questions

1. Are any of the above good reasons for not using a condom?

2. What are good reasons, if any, for not using a condom?

STD Assessment

Sexually transmitted diseases are passed from one person to another primarily through genital or oral-genital sexual relations. If any of the following were to happen to you how would you respond? Rank each response in the order in which you might do a particular activity. If you would not consider an activity leave the space blank.

1. If your regular partner told you he or she had been diagnosed with herpes, you would...

    _____ Go to your physician to be tested
    _____ Break up immediately
    _____ Stop having sex forever
    _____ Continue having sex but always use a condom
    _____ Insist your partner go with you to a health professional to get advice on continued sex

2. If you thought you might have gonorrhea or chlamydia, you would...

    _____ Go to your physician to be tested
    _____ Get tested anonymously
    _____ Warn any past partner that they may be carriers of gonorrhea or chlamydia
    _____ Do nothing and hope that the symptoms will disappear

3. You have a partner who has been diagnosed HIV+. You have been together for three years and you both are healthy. What would you do?

    _____ Get tested yourself
    _____ Stop having sex
    _____ Have sex always using a condom
    _____ Break up the relationship
    _____ Encourage your partner to improve their lifestyle

4. Your ex-partner contacted you indicating he or she had just been diagnosed with HPV (Human Papilloma Virus). What would you do?

    _____ If you are asymptomatic, make sure you have protected intercourse each time
    _____ Inform your current partner
    _____ Stop having sex
    _____ Watch for any symptoms and get tested
    _____ If you notice any genital warts get treated
    _____ For women, have regular Pap (pap smear) tests

AIDS Assessment

Answer the following questions as honestly as possible.

1. When was the first time you remember hearing about AIDS?

2. What were your first thoughts about AIDS?

3. When you heard that well-known people were HIV+, what did you think?

4. How has AIDS impacted you life?

5. Have you been tested for HIV? Why or why not?

6. How do you prevent the spread of AIDS?

7. Look at your score on the previous test entitled "What's Your Risk?" Does your decision to be tested agree with your rating? (People with moderate or serious risk should consider testing.)

8. If you had a friend who had had eight partners over the last year and several "one-night stands," would you encourage your friend to be tested? How would you approach your friend and what would you say?

CHAPTER 18

CULTURAL DIFFERENCES IN SEXUAL EXPRESSION

Said one 78-year-old Kenyan Luo gentleman who has had a total of 126 wives, "My most recent marriage is my last. I've retired from marrying. I've fathered 185 children."

Ansentus Ogwela, *Rites of Passage: Videocases of Traditional Africa Peoples,* 2001

The United States is a country full of diversity. It is a unique country in that it is composed of many diverse groups of persons, most all of whom have been immigrants. Look around you. In your neighborhood, in your classroom, how many cultures are represented? Do you assume that all the sexual practices of these different groups are the same? What are the noticeable differences? Are your beliefs and behaviors "right" and those of others "wrong?" How do you make sense of what you see?

Chapter 18 Contents:

Research Excerpt

Question: How do different cultures vary in sexual expression?

Female Circumcision from Africa to the Americas: Slavery to the Present*
Mary Ann Watson, Ph.D.

The Continuing African Diaspora

The so-called rite of passage into womanhood signaled by female circumcision is one of the most problematic and often hotly contended First World/Third World issues today. Estimates from the 1990 U.S. Census posit that there are 7,000 immigrants each year to the United States from regions of the world where female circumcision--excision or infibulation--is commonly practiced (Figures 1.4 and 1.5).

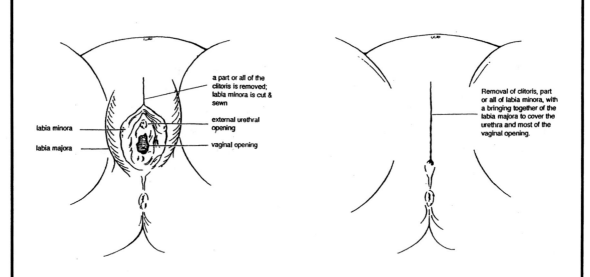

labia minora

labia majora

a part or all of the clitoris is removed; labia minora is cut & sewn

external urethral opening

vaginal opening

Removal of clitoris, part or all of labia minora, with a bringing together of the labia majora to cover the urethra and most of the vaginal opening.

Figure 1.4 Type I Clitoridectomy--Excision   **Figure 1.5 Type II--Infibulation**

Approximately 5,000 of these per year are from areas where infibulation is the norm, i.e. Horn of Africa. Increasing numbers of Western obstetricians and gynecologists have had some exposure to women who have undergone procedures and others have been requested to perform excisions or infibulations on their patients or re-infibulations after childbirth. This pressure on the Western medical community has led to public outcry and attempts to eliminate the procedure in the United States and the world. The effort to ban female genital surgeries in the United States has culminated in the passage of the Federal Prohibition of Female Genital Mutilation Act of 1995, signed into law by President Clinton in 1996. This act prohibits female genital surgeries on anyone below the age of eighteen, unless it is necessary to the woman's health. Practitioners of female genital surgeries are subject to fines or imprisonment for no more than five years or both (Fernandez-Romano, 1999).

In addition, sixteen states have passed legislation prohibiting female circumcision (Figure 1.9).

Figure 1.9 States Where Female Circumcision Has Been Outlawed

All sixteen states criminalize the performer of females circumcision; only six of the sixteen have an educational component to the law, i.e. providing monies for education, prevention, and outreach. Yet, every day in the United States, male neonatal circumcision is practiced and is the most commonly performed surgical procedure in the U.S. (Bond, 1999).

While these bills are touted as representing a serious American response to an international human rights issue affecting women, African women living in this country who are concerned about and connected to the targeted communities have had their voices excluded. Consequently, no serious discussion has occurred over the efficacy of a criminalization approach versus a public health and educational approach similar to the discussion on the topic of AIDS (Gunning, 1999).

According to personal communication with Chief FAMA, an honorary Nigerian chief of the Yoruba, living in San Bernadino, California, and intimately involved in the Nigerian custom as practiced presently in Nigeria and in the U.S. by recent immigrants, "It is true that 90 to 98% of the female population of Nigerian adults in the United States are circumcised. They are circumcised, not mutilated, in accordance with our culture and tradition. Female circumcision is not oppressive to African women." In accordance with the Yoruba tradition, children, male and female alike, are circumcised immediately after birth or within the first month after birth. She claims, "I dare say that female circumcision is not based on gender control or marriageability considerations, but part of Africa's rich, cultural tradition. Those charged with the responsibility are well trained--a midwife professionally trained--who uses tools that are clean and sterilized with a mixture of herbs. Babies heal within seven days." She describes the Yoruba tradition where female and male children are circumcised. "For females, the common practice is that of cutting approximately one-fifth of an inch off the top of the clitoris. For males, the practice is of cutting the prepuce from the glans of the penis. This is done immediately after birth or in the first month of life." She concludes her comments by saying that, "African female circumcision, not mutilation, is a safe, non-gender biased practice" (personal communication, February 25, 2001).

Chief FAMA contends that state laws will not significantly alter the desire of African immigrants to continue their cultural practices. What may change the practice is the desire to be accepted into the new culture of the United States, to avoid being thought of as "backward" or "primitive." Fear of retribution, which Chief FAMA believes was the largest factor in the discontinuation of female circumcision among the African slaves, is not operative among the recent African immigrants to the United States. She believes that another operative factor in the discontinuation of the practice of circumcision during the colonial period was that of the role of religion. As slaves adopted the Christian religion, they participated less and less in their African religious customs. The practice of maintaining privacy within family groups is strongly held among African immigrants to the United States. It is likely, according to Chief FAMA, that the practice will continue in the United States, but these traditions will be preformed in secret.

Other attempts in the past to eradicate female circumcision via the law have generally been unsuccessful. One of the most famous occurred in Kenya where the earliest attempt at legal prohibition of female circumcision dates back to the beginning of the British colonialism. In 1906, the Church of Scotland sought to eliminate female circumcision by having it outlawed. However, native Kenyans perceived this effort as outsider coercion, prompting a renewed attachment to the practice. Performed in secrecy, female circumcision became a symbol of cultural resistance. Instead of fostering any type of reform, the colonizers' law further entrenched the practice in Kenyan culture.

In 1915, the Church of Scotland mission increased its anti-circumcision advocacy by establishing a rule forbidding excision of school children in Kenya. Any boarder who left school to undergo excision was suspended for at least eighteen months. At the time, in response to the above decision, an increased feeling of national loyalty led to the formation of independent churches and schools, so that the Kenyan children could be educated, but also continue the culture's traditions (Sussman, 1998).

Criminalizing, on its surface, seems a justifiable response for practices that are thought to harm or maim another. Nevertheless, the history of criminalizing, particularly of cultural practices, tends to divert the practice underground and therefore lead to more rather than less concerns. Criminalization of such practices is also seen as paternalistic—one society's attempts to elevate their own practices as the correct or moral ones and negate another culture's practices as lesser or immoral. Statutes requiring educational initiatives rather than criminalization initiatives might be the most appropriate compromise.

Conclusions

Various types of female circumcision have been an integral portion of many of the cultural and religious practices in Africa for thousands of years. These practices have taken many forms—a birth practice, a childhood or adolescent rite of passage, a sign of tribal unity, a protection against sexual promiscuity. Each cultural group has its own practices with its own meaning or meanings attached. Therefore, it is inevitable that these practices may continue as the African diaspora occurs. In studying the writings from Herodotus to the present, it becomes clear that the values of the country and the circumstances surrounding the individual as he or she is settled into that country determine which customs will be retained and which will be discontinued. The continuation of female circumcision from Africa is particularly dependent on personal and environmental variables that would discourage or support such a practice. The Americas during the colonial period and the America of today are not supportive of such a practice. There were no laws forbidding female circumcision during the colonial period, but the traumatic, torturous, and humiliating form of the Atlantic passage led to the disruption of the cultural and tribal ties that were central to the practice of circumcision. The African immigrant today comes to an America with many states having laws against female circumcision, but because the laws are so rarely enforced, there is the absence of fear of retribution concerning cultural practices. In many situations today, African immigrants continue an association with other immigrants from their home countries and may continue their practices in secret.

*Reprinted by permission of Mary Ann Watson, Ph.D.

Trends in Western Adult Lifestyles

The following trends have been noticeable in the last twenty-five years in the United States:

A. The average age for first marriage is rising for both men and women.

B. There is more cohabitation without marriage than in the past.

C. Since the early 1970s the percentage of people who have married three or more times has doubled (National Center for Health Statistics).

For each of these trends answer the following questions:

1. What do you believe is the cause(s) of this trend?

A.

B.

C.

2. What is likely to be the impact of this trend in our society?

A.

B.

C.

3. How might this trend be altered?

A.

B.

C.

Traditional versus Modern Marriage

If you prefer marriage, which type would you want? The following is a list of characteristics that define a traditional versus a modern marriage (Knox, 1988).

Traditional Marriage	Modern Marriage
The emphasis is on ritual and traditional roles.	The emphasis is on companionship.
Couples do not live together before marriage.	Couples may live together before marriage.
The wife takes the husband's last name.	The wife may choose to keep her maiden name.
The husband is dominant; the wife is submissive.	Neither spouse is dominant or submissive.
The roles for the husband and the wife are specific and rigid.	Both spouses have flexible roles.
There is one income (the husband's).	There may be two incomes (the couple may share the breadwinning role).
The husband initiates sexual activity; the wife complies.	Either spouse may initiate (or refuse) sex.
The wife takes care of the children.	The parents share child-rearing chores.
Education is considered important for the husband, not for the wife.	Education is considered equally important for both spouses.
The husband's career decides the location of the family residence.	The career of either spouse may determine the location of the family residence.

Reaction Questions

1. Which of the above sounds most suitable for you?

2. Are there some characteristics from your preferred list that are not appealing? Which ones?

3. Do you have family models for the above two types of relationships? Describe.

Activities

1. **Sexual Customs in Other Countries**
    Choose a country with which you are unfamiliar. Do some library research to find one sexual behavior in the country that would be unusual in the United States. How can you explain this behavior in that country? Would this ever be acceptable behavior in the United States? Why or why not?

2. **Sexual Customs in the United States**
    When immigrants enter their new country, they carry with them the customs and values of their native culture. Do some library research to find a sexual custom that, when brought to the US, was considered very inappropriate. How can you explain this clash of beliefs?

3. **Interviews**
    Interview two couples with whom you are familiar--one who has a traditional marriage and one who has a non-traditional marriage. Discuss the strengths and weaknesses of each.

4. **Arranged Marriage**
    Interview someone who has had an arranged marriage. What are the strengths and weaknesses of this arrangement?

CHAPTER 19

SEX AND THE LAW

"Sex is one of the most closely regulated of all human behaviors."

Haas and Haas, *Human Sexuality*, 1993

Sex must be a powerful need to require such stringent regulation. Do you believe such regulation is necessary? How do you differentiate between sexual behavior that is harmful and should be controlled, and sexual behavior that is harmless? Where do you draw the line? Where does your city, county, state, draw the line?

Chapter 19 Contents:

A.   **Sexual Behavior and the Law in the United States**
B.   **Research Excerpt: "Cognitive Distortions Among Child Sexual Offenders" and Reaction Questions**
C.   **Sex For Money Assessment**
D.   **Legal Issues in Obscenity**
E.   **Activities**
    1.   **Regulation of Sexual Behavior**
    2.   **Prostitution Laws**
    3.   **Write Your Own Law**

Sexual Behavior and the Law in the United States *

Look at the map below. Eighteen of the states have prohibitions against many sexual behaviors.

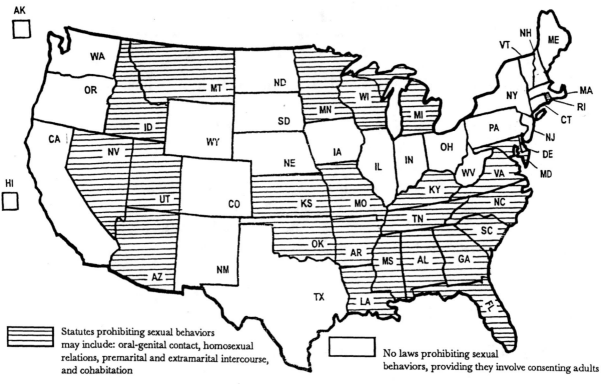

Statutes prohibiting sexual behaviors may include: oral-genital contact, homosexual relations, premarital and extramarital intercourse, and cohabitation

No laws prohibiting sexual behaviors, providing they involve consenting adults

* National Gay and Lesbian Task Force (2000)

Reaction Questions

1. What patterns, if any, do you note in the division of the states that do and do not have adult consensual sex laws?

2. As a society, is there likely to be movement toward more or fewer adult sex laws? Why?

3. Nonmarital cohabitation is forbidden by laws in ten states: Arizona, Florida, Illinois, Michigan, New Mexico, North Carolina, North Dakota, Virginia, and West Virginia. Do you assume this law is enforced in these states? How might that be accomplished?

4. What are the sexual topics that you assume will be legislated in the United States in the future?

Research Excerpt

Question: How do child sexual offenders justify their behavior?

Cognitive Disorders Among Child Sexual Offenders*
Larry Neidigh, Ph.D. and Harry Krop, Ph.D.

The purpose of this study was to initiate a data-based exploration of the specific cognitive distortions and rationalizations that outpatient child sexual offenders utilize with regard to their maladaptive sexual behavior. To this end 101 acknowledged sexual offenders responded to an open-ended questionnaire regarding these factors. The 357 statements generated by the subjects were sorted into equivalent statements, resulting in a list of 38 cognitive distortions and rationalizations. Potential applications of this list for both clinical work and as a base for future empirical investigations are discussed.

Accompanying the dramatic surge in the incidence of reported cases of child sexual abuse (Russell & Mohr-Trainor, 1984), has been an increased need to develop effective treatments for men who sexually abuse children, in the hope that psychotherapy can help them re-direct their sexual desires and behaviors toward age-appropriate adult partners and acquire coping abilities that would prevent them from reoffending.

RESULTS

As a result of [a] card sorting procedure, 357 responses generated by the sexual offenders were reduced to 38 categories containing equivalent statements. Labels for these categories were assigned by selecting verbatim statements from the responses contained in each category. The 38 statements contained in Table 1 represent the categories formed as a result of the card sort, along with the percentage of men in the sample who produced a response indicating that category as one of their cognitive distortions or rationalizations. As can be seen in Table 1, while some items were used by as many as 25% of the respondents, other distortions tend to be quite idiosyncratic and were utilized by as few as 1% of the respondents.

DISCUSSION

The purpose of this study was to examine the nature and content of regressed outpatient sexual offenders' surface level cognitive distortions and rationalizations regarding their abusive sexual behavior. Furthermore, an attempt was made to examine these factors in a more systematic fashion than has been accomplished in the previous literature, which relied primarily on single case studies and unsystematic clinical observations. Although this sample of offenders produced 357 discrete responses to the open-ended questionnaire, a card sorting procedure that reduced the responses to equivalent statements resulted in only 38 separate items. Many of these items are consistent with previous clinical observations (Abel, Becker, & Cunningham, 1984a; Mayer, 1988), other rationalizations tend to be quite specific and idiosyncratic in nature underscoring the importance of uncovering and correcting each offender's specific cognitive content rather than relying on general cognitive disputation strategies (Murphy, 1990) based on general observations from the clinical literature.

With regard to the potential applications of this material, within the context of clinical work this list might be used to familiarize clinicians and workers in the area with the nature and content of regressed outpatient sexual offenders' cognitive distortions and rationalizations. Furthermore, this list might be used to guide clinical inquiry into sexual offenders' cognitive distortions during both assessment and treatment procedures. In this regard, these items could easily be compiled into either a checklist or scale that could be administered in either a self-report or structured interview format. With regard to the potential of using these items for future empirical study, once again the construction of a checklist or scale from these items would seem appropriate. In this regard, these items could easily be placed in the scale format utilized by Glass, Merluzzi, Biever, and Larsen (1982) in their construction of the Social Interaction Self Statement test. The ensuing instrument could then be utilized as an assessment device in studies employing situational competency tests or relapse fantasies to study the characteristics of sexual offenders (Laws, 1989). Likewise, this instrument might be utilized in research employing a known-groups strategy to determine if sexual offenders differ from nonoffenders in their cognitive responses to hypothetical high risk situations involving the potential for sexual abuse.

TABLE 1. Cognitive Distortions of Sexual Offenders and the Percentage of Men Producing Responses Within Each Category

Percentage	Cognitive Distortion
25	She enjoyed it.
25	This won't hurt her or affect her in any way.
21	This is not so bad, it's not really wrong.
20	I was high on drugs or alcohol at the time.
19	I wasn't thinking at all or I wouldn't have done it.
15	No one will ever find out so I won't get caught.
14	She is flirting and teasing me, she wants me to do it.
12	We love each other so this is ok.
10	She didn't say no or tell, so this must be ok with her.
10	There is no force involved, so this must be mutual.
9	She is asleep so she will never know what I am doing.
8	I'm just providing sex education.
7	She is too young to remember this or know what I am doing.
7	I am just curious about her development, this isn't really sexual.
6	She is very mature for her age, she is much more like an adult than a child.
6	Children are supposed to do what I want and serve my needs.
6	This is just a game, like taking a dare to see if I can get away with it.
6	She is sexually active with others.
5	I did it because I was sexually abused as a child.
5	I did it to get revenge on her and/or her mother.
5	I deserve a special treat and she will make me feel better.
4	I am just investigating her previous abuse.
4	I can't control myself so I'm not responsible.
4	We were just playing and it was an accidental touch.
3	We are only touching, this isn't really sex.
3	She said yes to my requests so it is ok.
3	I thought she would like me more if I pleased her.
3	She is not my blood relation so it's not so bad.
2	It's too late to stop now, after all I can't get into any more trouble for one more time.
2	Lots of people do this so it can't be all that bad.
2	I did it to help her grow up and mature.
2	It was my way of punishing and controlling her.
1	I was just testing her to see if she was sexually active.
1	It will be a one time occasion.
1	It was a sin, the devil made me do it.
1	I was impotent and I thought I could regain my potency with her.
1	She is safer against VD than another adult sexual partner would be.
1	If I don't do it someone else will, so it might as well be me.

* Reprinted by permission of the *Journal of Sex Education and Therapy* and AASECT.

Legal Issues in Obscenity

A landmark case in 1957 established the legal basis of obscenity in the United States. ... oth v. United States, the US Supreme Court ruled that portrayal of sexual activity was protect... nder the First Amendment to the Constitution unless its dominant theme dealt with "sex in a ... her appealing to the prurient [base or animalistic] interest."

In a 1973 case, Miller v. California, the US Supreme Court held that obscenity is based on ... three-pronged definition:
  a. whether the average person, applying contemporary community standards, woul... find the work appealing to prurient interests;
  b. whether the work depicts sexual conduct in an offensive way;
  c. whether the work lacks serious literary, artistic, political, or scientific value.

Based on the above listed definitions, how would you define pornography or obscenity? Which of the following would you censor? Explain.

  a. A photo of a two-year-old masturbating himself

  b. A photo of a consenting adult couple having intercourse

  c. A photo of a non-consenting adult couple having intercourse

  d. A photo of a male wearing only a jock strap over an erect penis

  e. A nude photo of a consenting 14-year-old female

  f. An adult couple whipping each other with leather straps

Activities

1. **Regulation of Sexual Behavior**

   Read your local newspaper for one week. List any legal activities in your community related to the regulation or attempted regulation of sexual behavior. What is your opinion on this legislation?

2. **Prostitution Laws**

   Contact your local police office. What are the prostitution laws in your city? Do the laws differ for male and female prostitution? Do you believe that these laws work to prevent prostitution? Why do you believe prostitution continues in the United States and Canada in spite of the fact that it is illegal in most all of the states?

3. **Write Your Own Law**

   Write a brief argument in favor of legalizing prostitution. Write a second brief argument in favor of strengthening laws against prostitution. From these two arguments construct your own city law on prostitution.

CHAPTER 20

COMMERCIAL SEX

"If a man is pictured chopping off a woman's breast, it only gets an 'R' rating; but if, God forbid, a man is pictured kissing a woman's breast, it gets an 'X' rating. Why is violence more acceptable than tenderness?"

Sally Struthers, Actress

Does sex sell? Why do you buy what you buy? You are surrounded daily with media messages designed to persuade you to look, feel, or behave in certain ways. What impact have these messages had on you? What do you do to counter these messages?

Chapter 20 Contents:

A. Research Excerpt: "Sexual Messages on Television: Comparing Findings From Three Studies" and Reaction Questions
B. Popular Culture Evaluation Sheet
C. Breaking the Bonds Questionnaire and Reaction Questions
D. Activities
   1. Daytime Talk Show
   2. Sex Experts
   3. Favorite Television Programs
   4. Media Advertising
   5. Sexual Material in Film

Research Excerpt

Question: What do children and adolescents learn about sexuality from their television viewing?

Sexual Messages on Television: Comparing Findings From Three Studies *
Dale Kunkel, Kirstie M. Cope, and Erica Biely

Television portrayals may contribute to the sexual socialization of children and adolescents, and therefore it is important to examine the patterns of sexual content presented on television. This report presents a summary view across three related studies of sexual messages on television. The content examined ranges from programs most popular with adolescents to a comprehensive, composite week sample of shows aired across the full range of broadcast and cable channels. The results across the three studies identify a number of consistent patterns in television's treatment of sexual content. Talk about sex and sexual behaviors are both found frequently across the television landscape, although talk about sex is more common. Most sexual behaviors tend to be precursory in nature (such as physical flirting and kissing), although intercourse is depicted or strongly implied in roughly one of every eight shows on television. Perhaps most importantly, the studies find that TV rarely presents messages about the risks or responsibilities associated with sexual behavior.

Sexual socialization is influenced by a wide range of sources, including parents, peers, and the mass media (Hyde & DeLameter, 1997). In trying to understand the process by which young people acquire their sexual beliefs, attitudes, and behaviors, the study of media provides information about potential socializing messages that are an important part of everyday life for children and adolescents (Greenberg, Brown, & Buerkel-Rothfuss, 1993). The significance of media content in this realm stems from a number of unique aspects surrounding its role in the lives of youth, including its early accessibility and its almost universal reach across the population.

Electronic media, and television in particular, provide a window to many parts of the world, such as sexually-related behavior, that would otherwise be shielded from young audiences. Long before many parents begin to discuss sex with their children, answers to such questions as "When is it OK to have sex?" and "With whom does one have sexual relations?" are provided by messages delivered on television. These messages are hardly didactic, most often coming in the form of scripts and plots in fictional entertainment programs. Yet the fact that such programs do not intend to teach sexual socialization lessons hardly mitigates the potential influence of their portrayals.

While television is certainly not the only influence on sexual socialization, adolescents often report that they use portrayals in the media to learn sexual and romantic scripts and norms for sexual behavior (Brown, Childers, & Waszak, 1990). Indeed, four out of ten (40%) teens say they have gained ideas for how to talk to their boyfriend or girlfriend about sexual issues directly from media portrayals (Kaiser Family Foundation, 1998).

RESULTS

Talk About Sex
We start our assessment of sexual content by addressing the question of what proportion of television programs contain talk about sex. The data make clear that a majority of programs on television include some such material. The most broad-based sample is found in the V-Chip Study: Composite Week, which includes all programs aired between 7 a.m. and 11 p.m. across both broadcast and cable channels with the exception of news and sports. This study indicates that 57% of programs contain talk about sex, with those shows averaging more than two (2.3) scenes per hour with such content (see Table 2).

Table 2. Frequency and Distribution of Talk About Sex

	Family Hour Study	Teen Study	V-Chip Study: Composite Week	V-Chip Study: Prime-Time
Frequency of Talk About Sex				
Percentage of programs with any talk about sex	59%	67%	57%	67%
Average scenes per hour	n/a	2.8	2.3	2.9
Total number of programs	128	45	840	245
Distribution of Types of Talk About Sex				
Talk about prospective interests	59%	62%	74%	72%
Talk about past sexual experiences	21%	20%	18%	21%
Expert advice/technical info	5%	6%	1%	0%
Other	15%	12%	7%	6%
Number of cases	261	95	2203	722

Although scenes with sexual intercourse represent only a modest proportion of all the sexually-related behaviors shown on television, the presence of intercourse on TV in nonetheless quite substantial. The frequency with which programs included one or more scenes with intercourse depicted or strongly implied held remarkably stable across all four of the data points in the three studies reviewed here, at 12-13% of all shows (see Table 3). In other words, roughly one of every eight shows sampled in each of our studies presented characters engaging in sexual intercourse.

Table 3. Frequency of Sexual Behavior Within Programs

	Family Hour Study	Teen Study	V-Chip Study: Composite Week	V-Chip Study: Prime-Time
Percentage of programs with any sexual behavior	61%	62%	28%[a]	28%[b]
Average scenes per hour with any sexual behavior	n/a	2.2	1.2	1.1
Percentage of programs with sexual intercourse depicted or strongly implied	12%	13%	12%	12%
Total number of programs	128	45	840	245

[a]Family Hour Study and Teen Study included major as well as minor depictions of sexual behavior. The V-Chip Studies reported only major depictions. When minor depictions are included, this statistic increases to 42%. [b] When minor depictions are included, this statistic increases to 44%.

Table 4 presents a summary of our findings on the treatment of risk or responsibility concerns amidst all of the sexual messages found on television. In general, the predominant share of sexual messages on television are conveyed without any element of risk or responsibility concerns. Fewer than one out of every 10 scenes presenting some sexually-related behavior (8% for the Family Hour Study; 3% for the Teen Study) included any reference at all to these issues. The treatment of risk topics was slightly more common in scenes that contained only talk about sex (10% for the Family Hour Study; 14% for the Teen Study), particularly in the programs most popular with teens.

Table 4. Treatment of Sexual Risk or Responsibility Concerns

	Family Hour Study	Teen Study
Percentage of talk-only scenes with risk or responsibility	10%	14%
Total number of talk scenes	182	80
Percentage of behavior scenes with risk or responsibility	8%	3%
Total number of behavior scenes	267	99
Percentage of programs with sexual content that place primary emphasis on risk or responsibility	6%	9%
Total number of programs	128	45

In conclusion, sexual content is a common, if not prevalent, aspect of the overall television landscape. Portrayals of talk about sex, as well as sexually-related behaviors, are a potential source of socialization for most young viewers. Although most sexual behaviors shown on television are relatively modest, intercourse is frequently included. Collectively, these sexual messages provide an opportunity for the television industry to communicate an important and realistic view of the true risks associated with human sexual activity. Our research suggests that this opportunity has not yet been tapped very often by most segments of the industry.

* Reprinted by permission of the *Journal of Sex Research*

Breaking the Bonds Questionnaire

Which of these behaviors would you consider as breaking the bonds of a monogamous relationship?

YES   NO

____ ____ 1. Thinking about an involvement with someone other than your partner.

____ ____ 2. Looking at someone with lust other than your partner.

____ ____ 3. Fairly regular use of pornography.

____ ____ 4. Kissing beyond a peck on the cheek or brush of the lips.

____ ____ 5. Phone sex with a stranger.

____ ____ 6. Internet sex with a stranger.

____ ____ 7. Fantasy sex (no penetration or genital or breast touch) at a fantasy sex establishment.

____ ____ 8. Dinner and drinks with someone whom you find attractive.

____ ____ 9. Kissing and petting with someone other than your partner.

____ ____ 10. Mutual masturbation with someone other than your partner.

____ ____ 11. Oral sex (no genital penetration) with someone other than your partner.

____ ____ 12. A one-night stand with someone not your partner.

____ ____ 13. Consensual sexual intercourse with a person other than one's partner.

Reaction Questions

1. Do you believe that your partner would answer the above questionnaire as you have answered it?

2. Do you believe that there is a significant difference between actual interpersonal sensual or sexual behavior and similar behaviors on the internet? Briefly explain.

Activities

1. **Daytime Talk Show**
   Watch a daytime talk show with a sexual topic and respond using the "Popular Culture Evaluation Sheet."

2. **Sex Experts**
   Watch a daytime talk show which includes a sexuality "expert." What is the role of the sexuality expert? What is the supposed source of their expertise?

3. **Favorite Television Programs**
   Use the "Popular Culture Evaluation Sheet" to evaluate your favorite TV programs. Make a list of three of your favorite TV programs and comment on the portrayal of sexuality in each program.

4. **Media Advertising**
   Look through three popular magazines or watch television advertising for a two-hour period. Collect or observe several ads that are sexually suggestive. Complete the "Popular Culture Evaluation Sheet" for each of the several ads.

5. **Sexual Material in Film**
   Describe your experience with any sexual material in films. What was your response to this material? Is there more or less violence in this material than in TV crime shows? Why might censorship efforts be directed more toward sexually oriented nonviolent material than non-sexual violent material?

CHAPTER 21

SEX EDUCATION

"One reason sex education doesn't succeed better at reducing sexual activity, disease, and pregnancy may be that it is too little, too late."

Strong et al., *Human Sexuality: Diversity in Contemporary America*, 1999

This workbook is an example of planned sex education. Most of your sex education, however, has come from incidental learning. How have these two sources of sex education impacted you? Which has played a larger role? Has this planned format changed your values or behaviors? Complete the two assessment tests in this chapter and compare your scores with the same tests from Chapter 1. What do you find? Has this workbook been an effective sex educator for you?

Chapter 21 Contents:

The Sex Education Survey

Sex education is one of the most controversial of subjects, particularly as it relates to children. What should be taught in the schools? Who should be the sex educator? What subjects should be covered and why?

What are your ideas on the following topics?

1. Should sex education be taught in the schools?

2. At what age would you begin to teach sex education? Why?

3. Should seventh graders be taught about...

    a. contraception?

    b. sexually transmitted diseases?

    c. homosexuality/heterosexuality?

    d. abortion?

    e. premarital and extramarital sex?

    f. sexual anatomy and physiology?

    g. masturbation?

    h. sexual abuse?

    i. menstruation?

    j. loving/caring relationships?

    k. alternatives to intercourse such as oral sex, etc.?

4. Should sex education....

    a. teach moral values?

    b. teach facts that are research-based only?

5. Should school health clinics exist? If so, should they provide access to birth control and contraceptive information? Should they provide free access to condoms?

6. Provide a counter argument to each of the following three arguments opposing sex education in the schools.

    a. Sex education will lead to more promiscuity and an increase in teen pregnancies.

    b. Sex education will undermine the morality on which our country was established.

    c. Sex educators have no right to push their values on others.

Research Excerpt

Question: What is the impact on college students of the use of sexually explicit material (SEM) in the classroom?

Using Sexually Explicit Material in Adult Sex Education: An Eighteen Year Comparative Analysis*

B.R. Simon Rosser, Ph.D., S. Margretta Dwyer, M.A., Eli Coleman, Ph.D., Michael Miner, Ph.D., Michael Metz, Ph.D., Beatrice E. Robinson, Ph.D., and Walter O. Bockting, Drs.

Evaluating 7451 adults' responses to viewing sexually explicit material during Sexual Attitude Reassessment (SAR) seminars held from 1972 to 1991 is the focus of the study. Almost all reported experiencing these media as not harmful, and reported positive responses to the explicit visual material. Evidence of a double standard was also found: namely, while almost all viewed the seminar as not harmful to themselves, a significantly smaller proportion viewed it as not harmful to others. Respondents in the more liberal 1970s were more likely to view the seminar as not harmful than those in the more conservative 1980s. Sexually explicit media were viewed as the most helpful aspect of the seminar by most participants, and judged valuable both in assisting participants explore their issues and concerns, and in helping them clarify their emotional response to aspects of sexuality. The evidence suggests that sexually explicit material is a valuable tool in adult sex education.

The use of sexually explicit media (SEM) in sex education is somewhat controversial. Religious and political movements in the United States are active in attempting to remove sexually explicit material, that is, anything depicting nudity. Court battles have been waged in the 80s and 90s around the issue of SEM, and two U.S. national commissions were set up to address concerns about the effects of exposure to SEM. Davis and Bauserman (1989) concluded that people exposed to SEM can be influenced by the media, but the effects are complex, and there is an interactive function with the predispositions of the person exposed to SEM. Previous research has shown that learning about sexuality is affected by societal attitudes, and by an individual's development, experience, and personal value system (Cohen, Byrne, Hay, & Shmuck, 1994; Fisher, Grenier, Watters, Lamont, Cohen, & Askwith, 1988). Controversy also exists among social scientists regarding the effects of exposure to SEM (Linz, Donnerstein, & Penrod, 1987; Page, 1989) and the policy implications of such research (Byrne & Kelley, 1989; Davis & Bauserman, 1989; Penrod & Linz, 1984; Zillman, 1989). Recently, visual media were demonstrated to decrease homophobia in a college setting (Walters, 1994).

Results

In the 1973-1975 period, of the five types of materials used, SEM received the highest ratings as helpful, with only 1.2% of the same viewing them as harmful (see Table 4).

Table 4. Ratings of the Explicit Media Employed (SAR participants, 1973-1975, *n*=5,125)

Rating as	Sexual Explicit (Movies)		Sexual Nonexplicit (Slides)		Nonsexual Nonexplicit (Music)		Diactic Semiexplicit (Large group)		Discussion Semiexplicit (Small group)	
	n	%	n	%	n	%	n	%	n	%
Helpful	4754	92.8	4170	81.8	4020	78.0	4315	83.8	4663	89.8
Having no effect	308	6.0	939	18.2	1024	19.9	823	16.0	485	9.3
Harmful	63	1.2	34	0.7	107	2.1	12	.2	44	.8

Discussion

Over an 18-year period, over 95% of SAR participants consistently viewed this seminar as not harmful for themselves. Thus, at least when used as part of adult sexual education, SEM is not viewed as harmful to the viewer by almost everyone exposed to it.

Given the composition of SAR participants, this finding is remarkable. The sample composition appears to be weighted conservatively, with a disproportionate number of clergy, physicians, nurses, and other professionals in attendance; the majority of whom attended with their partners and identify themselves as heterosexual. Against the notion of SEM as dangerous, it was almost universally viewed as not harmful, at least in the context of adult sexual education.

Although most also viewed it as not harmful to others, fewer subjects viewed the seminar as not harmful to others than viewed it as not harmful to self. This may indicate the existence of a double standard: that SEM are viewed as not harmful to self, but possibly harmful for others. The small minority who did report it as harmful to themselves appeared equally divided as to whether it would be harmful to others. The subquestions investigated across different time periods all supported the central finding that SEM are not harmful in such settings.

The use of SEM in adult sexual education appears a useful tool to collect information on participants' attitudes to SEM. This study assessed reactions to SEM by participants' reactions to the overall seminar. Given the nature of the seminar and the heavily reliance on SEM in the seminar, the embedded nature of the question was deemed valid, although the methodology is indirect. Future research directions include focusing on aspects of the explicit media rather than using indirect or summary measures. What is clear from these data is that SEM are not judged harmful, and indeed may aid emotional awareness and aid people's understandings of their sexual concerns.

* Reprinted by permission of the *Journal of Sex Education and Therapy* and AASECT.

Reaction Questions

1. What is the typical reaction of young adults to the use of sexually explicit material in the classroom?

2. Comparisons are made between the 1970s and 1980s. What is your belief about the use of such material in the 2000s?

3. What are some of the effects of exposure to sexually explicit material?

4. What percentage of those viewing SEM regarded it as helpful? What percentage regarded it as harmful?

Research Excerpt

Question: What, if any, are the long-term effects of a college human sexuality course?

College Sexuality Education Promotes Future Discussions About Sexuality Between Former Students and Their Children*

Bruce M. King, Ph.D., Linda S. Parisi, B.A., and Katherine R. O'Dwyer, B.A.

Discussion

Numerous studies have found that sex education courses in schools result in substantial gains in knowledge and a more tolerant attitude of others (e.g., DiClimente et al., 1989; Kilmann, Wanlass, Sabalis, &Sullivan, 1981; Kirby, 1985; Story, 1979). Although these are positive accomplishments, results of several studies indicate that school sex education has often not been successful in altering adolescent sexual activity, including high-risk behaviors that can lead to sexually transmitted diseases and/or pregnancy (e.g., Baldwin, Whiteley, & Baldwin, 1990; Dawson, 1986; Eisen & Zellman, 1987; King & Anderson, 1993; Kirby, 1984; Sherr, 1990). In a review of several studies that had found sex education to be ineffective in altering behaviors, Stout and Rivara (1989) concluded that "to place the burden of counteracting the prevailing forces in our society toward premarital sex on our schools alone is both naïve and inappropriate."

Parents are usually considered to be the major conveyors of cultural values, especially for young children. In fact, sexuality education programs are most successful in altering attitudes when parents are involved (Carton & Carton, 1971; The Family Life Education Program Development Project, 1979). Unfortunately, when it comes to the topic of sex, few parents communicate directly with their children (Kisker, 1985; Strouse & Fabes, 1985). For example, of over 20,000 students who have enrolled in the human sexuality course on our campus since 1981, fewer than 10% ever had a single meaningful discussion about sex with their parents (from first-day surveys). This was true of the 102 subjects in the present study as well.

Lack of comfort and/or knowledge are two factors that prevent many parents from discussing sexuality with their children (Casey & Peterson, 1985; Koblinsky & Atkinson, 1982). Even among those parents who would like to talk to their children about sexuality, most plan to delay discussions of important value-laden topics until the early adolescent years (Koblinsky & Atkinson, 1982). By that time, a defensive communication climate has generally developed between parents and their children toward discussing sexuality (Rozema, 1986), so that even adolescents who have had sex education in school are no more likely (than adolescents who have not) to approach their parents about sexuality-related matters (Furstenberg, Moore, & Peterson, 1985).

The results of the present study (Tables 1,2,3) suggest that communication between parents and their children about sexuality may be enhanced by the parents having previously taken sexuality education at the college level. While the control group of parents were continuing the generation-to-generation practice of silence regarding sexuality-related topics, over 85% of the parents who had completed the sexuality course three years previously had begun discussions with their children. Both groups had voluntarily enrolled in a human sexuality course (control group data were obtained on first day of class), so the marked difference cannot easily be attributed to a bias in the selection of samples.

A large majority of the sexuality-educated parents said that they used correct anatomical words for the genitals in discussions with their children, and in the case of parents with adolescent children, had begun discussions about sexual intercourse and reproduction, birth control, sexually transmitted diseases, menstruation, homosexuality, and sexual abuse. Of the surveyed topics, only the subject of masturbation and nocturnal emissions had been omitted by a majority of the sexuality-educated parents. However, even here the results were much better than in the noneducated group.

Enhanced communication about sexuality between parents and their children has been suggested by some to be one of the primary goals of sex education (Alter, 1982; Casey & Peterson, 1985; Kirby, 1984). Although sex education of adolescents may not lead them to discuss sexuality with their own parents (when the parents have established a history of reluctance to do so) (Furstenberg, Moore, & Peterson, 1985), the present results suggest that comprehensive college sexuality education programs will have a beneficial effect on promoting discussions between parents and the next generation of children.

Table 1. Responses by Parents to General Questions Regarding Communication Within the Family About Sexuality

Question/Group	n	Yes	No
Did your parents have meaningful discussions about sexuality with you while you were growing up?			
Completed sexuality education	52	6	46
No sexuality education	50	4	46
Have you ever had discussions about sexuality with your children?*			
Completed sexuality education	52	45	7
No sexuality education	50	9	41

Question/Group			
Do you initiate discussions about sexuality with your children or do you wait for them to ask questions? (Responses only for those who have discussions about sexuality with their children.)			
Completed sexuality education	45	31	14
No sexuality education	9	5	4

*$p<.001$

Table 2. Response by Parents of Children Aged 5-11 Years Old

Question/Group	n	Yes	No
Use of correct anatomical words for genitals**			
Completed sexuality education	32	24	8
No sexuality education	34	6	28
Discussed "where babies come from"**			
Completed sexuality education	32	24	8
No sexuality education	34	5	29
Discussed inappropriate touching by others*			
Completed sexuality education	32	29	3
No sexuality education	34	22	12

*p<.05.
**p<.001

Table 3. Response by Parents of Children aged 12 and Older

Question/Group	n	Yes	No
Use of correct anatomical words for genitals**			
Completed sexuality education	34	28	6
No sexuality education	28	8	20
Discussed menstruation*			
Completed sexuality education	34	30	4
No sexuality education	28	16	12
Discussed masturbation/nocturnal emissions*			
Completed sexuality education	34	14	20
No sexuality education	28	2	26
Discussed sexual intercourse and reproduction**			
Completed sexuality education	34	30	4
No sexuality education	28	4	24
Discussed birth control**			
Completed sexuality education	34	30	4
No sexuality education	28	6	22
Discussed sexually transmitted diseases**			
Completed sexuality education	34	30	4
No sexuality education	28	6	22
Discussed homosexuality**			
Completed sexuality education	34	25	9
No sexuality education	28	5	23
Discussed sexual abuse*			
Completed sexuality education	34	26	8
No sexuality education	28	11	17

*p<.01.
**p<.001.
*Reprinted by permission of the *Journal of Sex Education and Therapy*

Research Excerpt Reaction Questions

1. How is your family response similar to that described in Table 1?

2. React to each of the three responses of parents in Table 2. What would you do in each of these situations with your five to eleven-year-old child?

3. React to each of the eight responses of parents in Table 3. What would you do in each of these situations with your adolescent child?

4. Who are the most successful sex educators for children? Describe briefly.

A Look At Your Sexual Values (Post-Test)

Take a few minutes to complete the following values survey. Circle your response on the 7-point scale below indicating your **intolerance for, neutrality toward, or tolerance for** the behaviors in the column on the left. Your answer does not reflect your personal behaviors, simply your tolerance or intolerance for each specific behavior in general.

Values	Intolerant (disagree with)			Neutral		Tolerant (agree with)	
1. Masturbation	-3	-2	-1	0	+1	+2	+3
2. Sex education in schools for adolescents	-3	-2	-1	0	+1	+2	+3
3. Condom availability in junior high and high schools	-3	-2	-1	0	+1	+2	+3
4. Homosexuality	-3	-2	-1	0	+1	+2	+3
5. Bisexuality	-3	-2	-1	0	+1	+2	+3
6. Teenage sexuality (13-17 years of age)	-3	-2	-1	0	+1	+2	+3
7. Sex with someone you do not love	-3	-2	-1	0	+1	+2	+3
8. Women initiating sex	-3	-2	-1	0	+1	+2	+3
9. Abortions available to anyone who desires to terminate a pregnancy	-3	-2	-1	0	+1	+2	+3
10. Prostitution as a legal behavior	-3	-2	-1	0	+1	+2	+3
11. Explicit magazines being available at all bookstores	-3	-2	-1	0	+1	+2	+3
12. Parents being notified and giving permission for a teen daughter's abortion	-3	-2	-1	0	+1	+2	+3
13. All doctors being HIV tested and all patients notified	-3	-2	-1	0	+1	+2	+3
14. All patients being HIV tested and all doctors notified	-3	-2	-1	0	+1	+2	+3
15. Rights of the biological father to continue an unwanted pregnancy	-3	-2	-1	0	+1	+2	+3
16. Oral sex	-3	-2	-1	0	+1	+2	+3
17. Premarital sex if in love	-3	-2	-1	0	+1	+2	+3
18. Premarital sex if engaged	-3	-2	-1	0	+1	+2	+3
19. Extramarital necking or petting	-3	-2	-1	0	+1	+2	+3
20. Extramarital sex	-3	-2	-1	0	+1	+2	+3

Reaction Questions to "A Look At Your Sexual Values"

Compare your responses on your post-test of values with your pre-test responses (Chapter 1).

1. Are there differences in your level of tolerance from the beginning to the end of the course?

2. To what do you attribute your changes in level of tolerance from the beginning to the end of the course?

3. Are you pleased with your value changes?

4. What additional changes, if any, would you like to make in your future? Why?

A Look At Your Sexual Behaviors (Post-Test)

Take a few minutes to complete the following sexual <u>behaviors</u> survey. Mark on a 5-point scale below the frequency with which you have engaged in this behavior.

Behaviors	Never	Rarely	Some-times	Frequently	Very Often
1. Oral sex	1	2	3	4	5
2. Sex without contraception	1	2	3	4	5
3. Sex with contraception	1	2	3	4	5
4. Use of different positions in sex	1	2	3	4	5
5. Masturbation	1	2	3	4	5
6. Masturbation with a partner	1	2	3	4	5
7. Talk about sex with friends	1	2	3	4	5
8. Talk about sex with partner	1	2	3	4	5
9. Talk about sex with family	1	2	3	4	5
10. Watch sexually explicit movies	1	2	3	4	5
11. Read sexually explicit books or magazines	1	2	3	4	5
12. Abortion	1	2	3	4	5
13. Use sex toys (i.e., vibrators, food)	1	2	3	4	5
14. Sex with more than one partner simultaneously	1	2	3	4	5
15. Have safe sex (when sexual)	1	2	3	4	5
16. Anal sex	1	2	3	4	5
17. Extramarital affairs	1	2	3	4	5
18. Premarital sex	1	2	3	4	5
19. Sex with a partner of the same sex	1	2	3	4	5
20. Using fantasy during sex	1	2	3	4	5

Reaction Questions to "A Look At Your Sexual Behaviors"

Compare your responses on your post-test of behaviors with your pre-test responses (Chapter 1).

1. Are there differences in the frequencies of your behaviors from the beginning to the end of the course?

2. To what do you attribute your changes in behavior from the beginning to the end of the course?

3. Are you pleased with your behavior changes?

4. What additional changes, if any, would you like to make in your future? Why?

REFERENCES

Chapter 1

Abler, R., & Sedlacek, W. (1989). Freshman sexual attitudes and behaviours over a fifteen year period. *Journal of College Student Development, 30,* 201-209.

Allgeier, E., & Allgeier, A. (1984). *Sexual Interactions.* Lexington, Mass. : D.C.Heath.

Alzate, H. (1974). A course in human sexuality in a Columbian medical school. *Journal of Medical Education, 49,* 438-443.

Bernard, H., & Schwartz, A. (1977). Impact of a human sexuality program on sex related knowledge, attitudes, behaviour and guilt on college undergraduates. *Journal of American College Health, 25,* 182-185.

Brecher, E.M., & the Editors of Consumer Reports Books. (1984). *Love, Sex, and Aging.* Boston: Little, Brown.

Carter, J., & Frankel, E. (1983). The effects of a teacher training program on family life and human sexuality on the knowledge and attitudes of public school teachers. *Journal of School Health, 53,* 459-462.

Cerny, J., & Polyson, J. (1984). Changing homonegative attitudes. *Journal of Social and Clinical Psychology, 2,* 366-371.

Davidson, J., & Darling, C. (1988). Changing autoerotic practices among college females: A two-year follow up study. *Adolescence, 23,* 774-792.

Dearth, P., & Cassell, C. (1976). Comparing attitudes of male and female university students before and after a semester course on human sexuality. *Journal of School Health, 46,* 593-598.

Fischer, G. (1986). College student attitudes towards forcible date rape: Changes after taking a human sexuality course. *Journal of Sex Education and Therapy, 12,* 42-46.

Godow, A., & LaFave, F. (1979). The impact of a college course in human sexuality upon sexual attitudes and behavior. *Teaching of Psychology, 6,* 164-167.

Hopson, J.L. (August, 1987). Boys Will Be Boys, Girls Will....Sex and the Spotted Hyena. *Psychology Today,* 60-66.

Kilman, P., Wanlass, R., Sabalis, R., & Sullivan, B. (1981). Sex education: A review of its effects. *Archives of Sexual Behaviour, 10,* 177-205.

Kirby, D. (1980). The effects of a school sex education program: A review of the literature. *The Journal of School Health, 50,* 559-562.

Lance, L. (1975). Human sexuality course socialization: An analysis of changes in sexual attitudes and sexual behaviour. *Journal of Sex Education and Therapy, 1,* 8-14.

Michael, R.T., Gagnon, J.H., Laumann, E.O., & Kolata, G. (1994). *Sex in America: A Definitive Study.* Boston: Little, Brown, & Company.

Pagels, E. (1988). *Adam, Eve, and the Serpent.* New York: Random House.

Patton, W., & Mannison, M. (1993). Effects of a University Subject on Attitudes Toward Human Sexuality. *Journal of Sex Education and Therapy, 19*(2), 93-107.

Redfering, D., & Roberts, R. (1976). Personality correlates and the effects of a human sexuality course on sexual attitudes and information retention of college students. *Journal of Sex Education and Therapy, 2,* 34-39.

Rees, B., & Zimmerman, S. (1974). The effects of formal sex education on the sexual behaviours of college students. *Journal of American College Health Association, 22,* 370-376.

Serdahely, W., & Ziemba, G. (1984). Changing homophobic attitudes through college sexuality education. *Journal of Homosexuality, 10,* 109-116.

Smith, P., Flaherty, C., Webb, L., & Mumford, D. (1984). The long-term effects of human sexuality training programs for public school teachers. *Journal of School Health, 54,* 157-159.

Stevenson, M. (1990). Tolerance for homosexuality and interest in sexuality education. *Journal of Sex Education and Therapy, 16,* 194-197.

Story, M. (1979). A longitudinal study of the effects of a university human sexuality course on sexual attitudes. *Journal of Sex Research, 15,* 184-204.

Strong, B., DeVault, C., Sayad, B., & Yarber, W. (2002). *Human Sexuality, 4th Ed.* New York: McGraw-Hill.

Taylor, M. (1982). A discriminant analysis approach to exploring changes in human sexuality attitudes among university students. *Journal of American College Health, 31,* 124-129.

Wolfe, L. (1981). *The Cosmo Report.* New York: Arbor House.

Woods, N., & Mandetta, A. (1975). Changes in students' knowledge and attitudes following a course in human sexuality. *Journal of Sex Education and Therapy, 2,* 47-49.

Yarber, W., & Anno, T. (1981). Changes in sex guilt, premarital sexual intimacy attitude and sexual behavior during a human sexuality course. *Health Education, 12,* 11-21.

Zuckerman, M., Tushup, R., & Finner, S. (1976). Sexual attitudes and experience: Attitude and personality correlates and changes produced by a course in sexuality. *Journal of Consulting and Clinical Psychology, 44,* 7-19.

Chapter 2

Kinsey, A., Pomeroy, W.B., & Martin, C.E. (1948). *Sexual Behavior in the Human Male.* Philadelphia: W.B. Saunders and Co.

Kinsey, A., Pomeroy, W.B., & Martin, C.E. (1953). *Sexual Behavior in the Human Female.* Philadelphia: W.B. Saunders and Co.

Michael, R.T., Gagnon, J.H., Laumann, E.O., & Kolata, G. (1994). *Sex in America: A Definitive Study.* Boston: Little, Brown, & Company.

Thomas, S.B., & Quinn, S.C. (1991). The Tuskegee Syphilis Study, 1932 to 1972: Implications for HIV Education and AIDS Risk Education in Programs in the Black Community. *American Journal of Public Health, 81,* 1498-1504.

Chapter 3

Conte, J.R., & Fogerty, L.A. (1989). *Attitudes on sexual abuse prevention programs: A national survey of parents.* (Available from Jon Conte, Ph.D., University of Washington, School of Social Work, 4101 15th Avenue NE, JH-30, Seattle, Wash., 98195.)

Dayee, F.S. (1982). *Private zone: A book teaching children sexual assault prevention tools.* Edmonds, Wash.: Chas. Franklin Press.

Ensler, E. (1998). *Vagina Monologues*. New York: Villard.

Gordon, B.N., Schroeder, C.S., & Abrams, J.M. (1990). Age and social-class differences in children's knowledge of sexuality. *Journal of Clinical Child Psychology, 19,* 33-43.

Koblinshky, S., Atkinson, J., & Davis, S. (1980). Sex education with young children. *Young Children, 36,* 21-31.

Miller-Perrin, C. L., & Wurtele, S.K. (1988). The child sexual abuse prevention movement: A critical analysis of primary and secondary approaches. *Clinical Psychology Review, 8,* 313-329.

Schor, D.P., & Sivan, A.B. (1989). Interpreting children's labels for sex-related body parts of anatomically explicit dolls. *Child Abuse & Neglect, 13,* 523-531.

Tharinger, D.J., Krivacska, J.A., Laye-McDonough, M., Jamison, L., Vincent, G.G., & Hedlund, A.D. (1988). Prevention of child sexual abuse: An analysis of issues, educational programs, and research findings. *School Psychology Review, 17,* 614-634.

Wurtele, S.K., Currier, L.L., Gillispie, E.I., & Franklin, C.F. (1991). The efficacy of a parent-implemented program for teaching preschoolers body safety skills. *Behavior Therapy, 22,* 69-83.

Wurtele, S.K., Gillispie, E.I., Currier, L.L., & Franklin, C.F. (1992). A comparison of teachers vs. parents as instructors of a personal safety program for preschoolers. *Child Abuse & Neglect, 16,* 127-137.

Wurtele, S.K., Kast, L.C., & Melzer, A.M. (November/December, 1992). Sexual abuse prevention education for young children: A comparison of teachers and parents as instructors. *Child Abuse and Neglect, 16*(6), 865.

Wurtele, S.K., Kvaternick, M., & Franklin, C.F. (1992). Sexual abuse prevention for preschoolers: A survey of parents' behaviors, attitudes, and beliefs. *Journal of Child Sexual Abuse, 1*(1), 113-128.

Chapter 4

Goldberg, M.S. (September, 1993). Choosing a Contraceptive. *FDA Consumer,* 18-25.

Hatcher, R. (1993). *Contraceptive Technology.* New York: Irvington Publishers.

Hatcher, R.A., Nelson, A.L., Zieman, M., Darney, P.D., Creinin, M.D., & Stosur, H.R. (2001-2002). *A Pocket Guide to Managing Contraception.* Tiger, Georgia: Bridging the Gap Foundation.

McGee, G. (2000). Cloning, Sex, and New Kinds of Families. *The Journal of Sex Research, 37,* 266.

Perlman, S.E., Richmond, D.M., Sabatini, M.M., Krueger, H., & Rudy, S.J. (2001). Contraception: Myths, Facts and Methods. *The Journal of Reproductive Medicine, 46*(2), 169-177.

Pharmacia & Upjohn. (2000). Patient Information About Lunelle Monthly Contraception Injection. Kalamazoo, Michigan: Pharmacia & Upjohn Co.

Strong, B. (1994). *The Resource Book: A Teacher's Tool Kit.* Mountain View, California: Mayfield Publishing Company.

Strong, B., Devault, C., & Sayad, B.W. (1999). *Human Sexuality.* Mountain View, California: Mayfield Publishing Company.

Chapter 5

Beal, E.W., & Hockman, G. (1991). *Adult Children of Divorce*. New York: Delacorte Press.

Calderone, M.S. (1983). Childhood Sexuality: Approaching the Prevention of Sexual Disease. In G. Albee et al., (Eds). *Promoting Sexual Responsibility and Preventing Sexual Problems*. Hanover, N.H.: University Press of New England.

Carrera, M. (1981). *Sex: The Facts, the Acts, and Your Feelings*. New York: Crown.

Chamberlin, R. (1974). Counseling parents about children's sex games. *Medical Aspects of Human Sexuality, 8*(12), 45-56.

Lewis, R.J., & Janda, L.H. (1988). The Relationship Between Adult Sexual Adjustment and Childhood Experiences Regarding Exposure to Nudity, Sleeping in the Parental Bed, and Parental Attitudes Toward Sexuality. *Archives of Sexual Behavior,17*, 349-362.

Myers, T.S. (1990). *How to Keep Control of Your Life After 50: A Guide for Your Legal, Medical, and Financial Well-Being*. Lexington, Mass.: Lexington Books.

Pangman, V.C., & Seguire, M. (2000). Sexuality and the Chronically Ill Older Adult: A Social Justice Issue. *Sexuality and Disability, 18*(1).

Roberts, E.J., Kline, D., & Gagnon, J. (1978). *Family Life and Sexual Learning: Project on Human Sexual Development*. Cambridge, Mass.: Population Education.

Thornburg, H.D. (1981). Adolescent sources of information on sex. *Journal of School Health, 51*, 274-277.

Thornton, A. (1990). The Courtship Process and Adolescent Sexuality. *Journal of Family Issues, 11*, 239-273.

Chapter 6

Allgeier, E.R., & Wiederman, M.W. (1994). How useful is evolutionary psychology for understanding gender differences in human sexuality? *Annual Review Sex Research, 5*, 218-256.

Buss, D.M. (1994). *The evolution of desire: Strategies of human mating*. New York: Basic Books.

Farrell, W. (1993). *The Myth of Male Power*. New York: Simon and Schuster.

Hatfield, E., Sprecher, S., Pillemer, J.T., Greenberger, D., & Wesler, P. (1989). Gender differences in what is desired in the sexual relationship. *Journal of Psychology and Human Sexuality, 1*(2), 39-52.

Keen, S. (1991). *Fire in the Belly*. New York: Bantam.

McGuirl, K.E., & Wiederman, M.W. (2000). Characteristics of the Ideal Sex Partner: Gender Differences and Perceptions of the Preferences of the Other Gender. *Journal of Sex and Marital Therapy, 26*, 153-159.

Purnine, D.M., Carey, A.V., & Jorgensen, R.S. (1994). Gender differences regarding preferences for specific heterosexual practices. *Journal of Sex & Marital Therapy, 20*, 271-287.

Tavris, C. (1992). *Mismeasure of Woman*. New York: Simon and Schuster.

Valois, R.F., & Kammermann, S. (1992). *Your Sexuality: A Self Assessment*. New York: McGraw-Hill.

Wiederman, M.W., & Allgeier, E.R. (1994). Male economic status and gender differences in mate selection preferences: Evolutionary versus sociocultural explanations. In L. Ellis (Ed.). *Social stratification and socioeconomic inequality, Vol.2: Reproductive and interpersonal aspects of dominance and status.* Westport, Conn.: Praeger.

Chapter 7

Bell, A.P. (1973). Homosexualities: Their Range and Character. In J.K. Cole and R. Dienstbier (Eds.). *Nebraska Symposium on Motivation.* Lincoln, Neb.: University of Nebraska Press.

Bell, A.P., & Weinberg, M.S. (1978). *Homosexualities: A Study of Diversity Among Men and Women.* New York: Simon and Schuster.

Bugen, L.A. (1990). *Love and Renewal: A Couple's Guide to Commitment.* Oakland, Calif.: New Harbinger.

Buss, D.M. (1994). *The Evolution of Desire.* New York: Basic Books.

Buss, D.M., & Barnes, M. (1986). Preferences in human mate selection. *Journal of Personality and Social Psychology, 50,* 559-570.

Cunningham, M.R., Roberts, A.R., Barbee, A.P., Druen, P.B. & Wu, C.H. (1995). "Their Ideas of Beauty Are, on the Whole, the Same as Ours": Consistency and Variability in the Cross-Cultural Perception of Female Physical Attractiveness. *Journal of Personality and Social Psychology, 68* (2), 261-279.

Gagnon, J.H. (Eds.). (1977). *Human Sexuality in Today's World.* Boston: Little, Brown, & Company.

Gangestad, S.W., & Simpson, J.A. (1990). Toward an evolutionary history of female sociosexual variation. *Journal of Personality, 58,* 69-96.

Howard, J.A., Blumstein, P., & Schwartz, P. (1987). Social or Evolutionary Theories? Some Observations on Preferences in Human Mate Selection. *Journal of Personality and Social Psychology, 53* (1), 194-200.

Herold, E.S., & Milhausen, R.R. (1999). Dating Preferences of University Women: An Analysis of the Nice Guy Stereotype. *Journal of Sex and Marital Therapy, 25,* 333-343.

Istvan, J., & Griffit, W. (1980). Effects of sexual experience on dating desirability and marriage desirability: An experimental study. *Journal of Marriage and the Family, 42,* 377-385.

Jensen-Campbell, L.A., Graziano, W.G., & West, S.G. (1995). Dominance, prosocial orientation, and female preferences: Do nice guys really finish last? *Journal of Personality and Social Psychology, 68,* 427-440.

Kalof, L. (1995). Sex, power, and dependency: The politics of adolescent sexuality. *Journal of Youth and Adolescence, 24,* 229-249.

Kleinke, C.L., & Staneski, R.A. (1980). First impressions of female bust size. *Journal of Social Psychology, 100,* 123-124.

Kreidman, E. (1991). *Light Her Fire.* New York: Villard.

Livermore, B. (March/April, 1993). The Lessons of Love. *Psychology Today,* 30-39.

Luria, Z., & Rose, M.D. (1979). *The Psychology of Human Sexuality.* New York: Wiley.

Mencken, H.L. (1919). *Prejudices.* New York: Knopf.

O'Sullivan, L.F. (1995). Less is more: The effects of sexual experience on judgments of men's and women's personality characteristics and relationship desirability. *Sex Roles, 33,* 159-181.

Petrie, T.A., Austin, L., Crowley, B.J., Helmcamp, A., Johnson, C.E., Lester, R., Rogers, R., Turner, J., & Walbrick, K. (1996). Sociocultural Expectations of Attractiveness for Males. *Sex Roles, 35*(9/10), 581-602.

Rathus, S.A., & Nevid, J.S. (1992). *Adjustment and Growth: The Challenges of Life, 5ᵗʰ Ed.* Ft. Worth, Texas: Harcourt Brace Jovanovich.

Regan, P.C. (1998). Minimum mate selection standards as a function of perceived mate value, relationship context, and gender. *Journal of Psychology and Human Sexuality, 10*, 53-73.

Regan, P.C., & Berscheid, E. (1997). Gender differences in characteristics desired in a potential sexual and marriage partner. *Journal of Psychology and Human Sexuality, 9*, 25-37.

Sadalla, E.K., Kenrick, D.T., & Venshure, B. (1987). Dominance and heterosexual attraction. *Journal of Personality and Social Psychology, 52*, 730-738.

Simpson, J.A., & Gangestad, S.W. (1992). Sociosexuality and romantic partner choice. *Journal of Personality, 60*, 31-51.

Sprecher, S., Regan, P.C., McKinney, K., Maxwell, K., & Wazienski, R. (1997). Preferred level of sexual experience in a date or mate: The merger of two methodologies. *Journal of Sex Research, 34*, 327-337.

Sprecher, S., Sullivan, Q., & Hatfield, E. (1994). Mate Selection Preferences: Gender Differences Examined in a National Sample. *Journal of Personality and Social Psychology, 66* (6), 1074-1080.

Trapnell, P.D., & Meston, C. M. (August, 1996). Sex and the big five: Nice guys finish last. Poster presented at the American Psychological Association Annual Convention. Toronto, Canada.

Chapter 8

Abbey, A. (1982). Sex differences in attributions for friendly behavior: Do males misperceive females' friendliness? *Journal of Personality and Social Psychology, 42*, 830-838.

Abbey, A. (1987). Misperceptions of friendly behavior as sexual interest: A survey of naturally occurring incidents. *Psychology of Women Quarterly, 11*, 173-194.

Abbey, A. (1991). Misperception as an antecedent of acquaintance rape. In A. Parrot & L. Bechhofer (Eds.). *Acquaintance rape: The hidden crime.* New York: Wiley.

Antioch College. (1990). *Sexual violence and safety.* Yellow Springs, Ohio.

Bart, P.B., & O'Brien, P.H. (1985). *Stopping rape: Successful survival strategies.* Elmsford, NY: Pergamon.

Burt, M.R., & Albin, R.S. (1981). Rape myths, rape definitions, and probability of conviction. *Journal of Applied Social Psychology, 11*, 212-230.

Christopher, F.S., & Frandsen, M.M. (1990). Strategies of influence in sex and dating. *Journal of Social and Personal Relationships, 7*, 89-105.

Crawford, M. (1995). *Talking difference: On gender and language.* Thousand Oaks, Calif.: Sage.

Cupach, W.R., & Metts, S. (1991). Sexuality and communication in close relationships. In K. McKinney & S. Sprecher (Eds.). *Sexuality in close relationships.* Hillsdale, N.J.: Lawrence Erlbaum Associates.

Estrich, S. (1987). *Real rape.* Cambridge, Mass.: Harvard University Press.

Goodman, G., & Esterly, G. (1990). *The Talk Book: The Intimate Science of Communicating in Close Relationships.* New York: Ballantine Books.

Gottman, J., Notarius, C., Gonso, J., & Markman, H. (1976). *A Couple's Guide to Communication.* Champaign, Illinois: Research Press.

Guskin, A.E. (1994). *The Antioch response: Sex, you just don't talk about it.* Yellow Springs, Ohio: Antioch College.

Hickman, S.E., & Muehlenhard, C.L. (1999). "By the Semi-Mystical Appearance of a Condom": How Young Women and Men Communicate Sexual Consent in Heterosexual Situations. *The Journal of Sex Research, 36* (3), 258-272.

Johnson, C.B., Stockdale, M.S., & Saal, F.E. (1991). Persistence of men's misperceptions of friendly cues across a variety of interpersonal encounters. *Psychology of Women Quarterly, 15,* 463-475.

Kleinke, C., Meeker, F.B., & Staneski, R.A. (1986). Preference for Opening Lines: Comparing Ratings by Men and Women. *Sex Roles,5,* 585-600.

Meyer, T.J. (December 5, 1984). "Date rape":A serious campus problem that few talk about. *The Chronicle of Higher Education, 29* (15), 1,2.

Motley, M.T., & Reeder, H.M. (1995). Unwanted escalation of sexual intimacy: Male and female perceptions of connotations and relational consequences of resistance messages. *Communication Monographs, 62,* 355-382.

Muehlenhard, C.L. (1995/1996). The complexities of sexual consent. *SIECUS Report, 24* (2), 4-7.

Muehlenhard, C.L., Powch, I.G., Phelps, J.L., & Giusti, L.M. (1992). Definitions of rape: Scientific and political implications. *Journal of Social Issues, 48* (1), 23-44.

Peplau, L.A., Rubin, Z, & Hill, C.T. (1977). Sexual intimacy in dating relationships. *Journal of Social Issues, 33*(2), 86-109.

Rozema, H. R., & Gray, J. (1994). What's Your Gender Communications Quotient? *Human Sexuality.* Strong & Devault (Eds.). Mountain View, California: Mayfield Publishing Company.

Sanday, P.R. (1996). *A woman scorned: Acquaintance rape on trial.* New York: Doubleday.

Shotland, R.L., & Goodstein, L. (1992). Sexual precedence reduces the perceived legitimacy of sexual refusal: An examination of attributions concerning date rape and consensual sex. *Personality and Social Psychology Bulletin, 19,* 756-764.

Tannen D. (1990). *You Just Don't Understand.* New York: Morrow.

Warshaw, R. (1994). *I never called it rape, 2nd Ed.* New York: Harper & Row.

Chapter 9

Allgeier, A.R., & Allgeier, E.R. (1991). *Sexual Interactions, 3rd Edition.* Lexington, Mass. : Heath.

Atwood, J.D., & Gagnon, J.H. (1987). Masturbatory behavior in college youth. *Journal of Sex Education and Therapy, 13,* 35-42.

Bancroft, J., Sherwin, B.B., Alexander, G.M., Davidson, D.W., & Walker, A. (1991). Oral contraceptives, androgens, and the sexuality of young women. *Archives of Sexual Behavior, 20,* 104-120.

Comfort, A. (1985). *The Joy of Sex: A Gourmet Guide to Lovemaking.* New York: Simon & Schuster.

Davidson, J.K. (1984). Autoeroticism, sexual satisfaction, and sexual adjustment among university females: past and current patterns. *Deviant Behavior, 7,* 13-30.

Davidson, J.K., & Darling, C.A. (1986). The impact of college-level sex education on sexual knowledge, attitudes, and practices: the knowledge/sexual experimentation myth revisited. *Deviant Behavior, 7,* 13-30.

Davidson, J.K., & Darling, C.A. (1989). Self-perceived differences in the female orgasmic response. *Family Practice Research Journal, 8,* 75-84.

Davidson, J.K., & Darling, C.A. (1993). Masturbatory Guilt and Sexual Responsiveness Among Post-College-Age Women: Sexual Satisfaction Revisited. *Journal of Sex and Marital Therapy, 19,* 289-300.

Davidson, J.K., & Moore, N.B. (1992). Masturbation and premarital sexual intercourse among college women: making choices for sexual fulfillment. Paper presented at the meeting of the Society for the Scientific Study of Sex, New Orleans, La.

Gagnon, J. (1985). Attitudes and Responses of Parents to Pre-Adolescent Masturbation. *Archives of Sexual Behavior, 14,* 451-466.

Gerrard, M. (1987). Sex, sex guilt, and contraceptive use revisited: the 1980s. *Journal of Personality and Social Psychology, 52,* 975-980.

Gunderson, M.P., & McCary, J.L. (1979). Sex guilt and religion. *Family Coordinator, 28,* 353-357.

Houck, E.L., & Abramson, P.R. (1986). Masturbatory guilt and the psychological consequences of sexually transmitted diseases among women. *Journal of Research and Personality, 20,* 267-275.

Hsu, B., Kling, A., Kessler, C., Knapke, K., Deifenbach, P., & Elias, J.E. (1994). Gender Differences in Sexual Fantasy and Behavior in a College Population: A Ten-Year Replication. *Journal of Sex and Marital Therapy, 20,* 103-118.

Hulbert, D.F., & Whitaker, K.E. (1991). The role of masturbation in marital and sexual satisfaction: a comparative study of female masturbators and nonmasturbators. *Journal of Sex Education and Therapy, 17,* 272-282.

Jones, J.C., & Barlow, D.H. (1990). Self-reported frequency of sexual urges, fantasies, and masturbatory fantasies in heterosexual males and females. *Archives of Sexual Behavior, 19,* 269-279.

Laws, J.L., & Schwartz, P. (1977). *Sexual scripts: the social constructions of female sexuality.* New York: Dryden.

Lips, H.M. (1993). *Sex and Gender: An Introduction, 2nd Ed.* Mountain View, Calif.: Mayfield.

Mosher, D.L., & Vonderheide, S.G. (1985). Contributions of sex guilt and masturbation guilt to women's contraceptive attitudes and use. *Journal of Sex Research, 21,* 24-39.

Person, E.S., Terestman, N., Myers, W.A., Goldberg, E.L., & Salvadori, C. (1989). Gender Differences in Sexual Behaviors and Fantasies in a College Population. *Journal of Sex and Marital Therapy, 15,* 187-198.

Stewart, F.H., Guest, F.J., Stewart, G.K., & Hatcher, R.A. (1979). *My body, my health: the concerned woman's guide to gynecology.* New York: Wiley.

Stockard, J., & Johnson, M.M. (1992). *Sex and Gender in Society, 2nd Ed.* Englewood Cliffs, N.J.: Prentice-Hall.

Szasz, T. (1990). *Sex By Prescription: The Startling Truth about Today's Sex Therapy.* Syracuse, New York: Syracuse University Press.

Weinberg, M.S., Swensson, R.G., & Hammersmith, S.K. (1983). Sexual autonomy and the status of women: Models of female sexuality in U.S. sex manuals from 1950 to 1980. *Social Problems, 30,* 312-324.

Weiss, D.L., Rabinowitz, B., & Ruckstruhl, M.F. (1992). Individual changes in sexual attitudes and behavior within college-level human sexuality courses. *Journal of Sex Research, 29,* 43-59.

Williams, J.H. (1987). *Psychology of Women: Behavior in a Biosocial Context, 3rd Ed.* New York: Norton.

Chapter 10

Aguero, J.E., Block, L., & Byrne, D. (1984). The relationships among sexual beliefs, attitudes, experience, and homophobia. *Journal of Homosexuality, 10,* 95-107.

Alcalay, R., Sniderman, P.M., Mitchell, J., & Griffin, R. (1990). Ethnic difference in knowledge of AIDS transmission and attitudes towards gays and people with AIDS. *International Quarterly of Community Health Education, 10*(3), 213-222.

Baker, J.G., & Fishbein, H.D. (1998). The development of prejudice towards gays and lesbians by adolescents. *Journal of Homosexuality, 36*(1), 89-100.

Bem, S.L. (1993). On the Inadequacy of Our Sexual Categories: A Personal Perspective. In S. Wilkinson & C. Kitzinger (Eds.). *Heterosexuality: A Feminism and Psychology Reader.* London: Sage.

Berrill, K.T. (1992). Organizing against hate on campus: Strategies for activists. In G.M. Herek & K.T. Berrill (Eds.). *Hate crimes: Confronting violence against lesbians and gay men.* Newbury Park, Calif.: Sage.

Berzon, B. (1988). *Permanent Partners: Building Gay and Lesbian Relationships That Last.* New York: Penguin Books.

Bohan, J.S. (1996). *Psychology and Sexual Orientation: Coming to Terms.* New York: Routledge.

Cotton-Huston, A.L., & Waite, B.M. (2000). Anti-homosexual attitudes in college students: Predictors and classroom interventions. *Journal of Homosexuality, 38*(3), 117-133.

D'Augelli, A.R., & Rose, M.L. (1990). Homophobia in a university community: Attitudes and experiences of heterosexual freshmen. *Journal of College Student Development, 31,* 484-491.

DiClemente, R.J., Boyer, C.B., & Morales, E.S. (1988). Minorities and AIDS: Knowledge, attitudes, and misconceptions among Black and Latino adolescents. *American Journal of Public Health, 78*(1), 55-57.

Duberman, M. (1991). *Cures: A Gay Man's Odyssey.* New York: Dutton.

Elia, J.P. (1993). Homophobia in the high school: A problem in need of a resolution. *The High School Journal,* 177-185.

Faderman, L. (1991). *Real Stories of Lesbian Life in America.* Irvington, NY: Columbia University Press.

Garnets, L., Herek, G.M., & Levy, B. (1993). Violence and victimization of lesbians and gay men: Mental health consequences. In L.D. Garnets & D.C. Kimmel (Eds.). *Psychological perspectives on lesbians and gay male experiences,* 579-597.

Herek, G.M. (1984a). Beyond "homophobia": A social psychological perspective on attitudes toward lesbians and gay men. *Journal of Homosexuality, 10*(1/2), 1-21.

Herek, G.M. (1984b). Attitudes toward lesbians and gay men: A factor analytic study. *Journal of Homosexuality, 10*(1/2), 39-51.

Herek, G.M. (1987). Religious orientation and prejudice: A comparison of racial and sexual attitudes. *Personality and Social Psychology Bulletin, 13*(1), 34-44.

Herek, G.M. (1988). Heterosexuals' attitudes toward lesbians and gay men: Correlates and gender differences. *The Journal of Sex Research, 25*(4), 451-477.

Herek, G.M. (1993a). The context of antigay violence: Notes on cultural and psychological heterosexism. In L.D. Garnets & D.C. Kimmel (Eds.). *Psychological perspectives on lesbians and gay male experiences,* 88-107.

Herek, G.M. (1993b). Documenting prejudice against lesbians and gay men on campus: The Yale sexual orientation survey. *Journal of Homosexuality, 25*(4), 15-28.

Herek, G.M. (1994). Assessing heterosexuals' attitudes toward lesbians and gay men. In B. Greene & G. M. Herek (Eds.). *Lesbian and gay psychology: theory, research, and clinical applications.* Thousand Oaks, Calif.: Sage.

Herek, G.M., & Glunt, E.K. (1991). AIDS-related attitudes in the United States: A preliminary conceptualization. *Journal of Sex Research, 28,* 99-123.

Herek, G.M., & Glunt, E.K. (1993b). Interpersonal contact and heterosexuals' attitudes toward gay men: Results from a national survey. *The Journal of Sex Research, 30*(3), 239-244.

Herek, G.M., & Capitanio, J.P. (1995). Black heterosexuals' attitudes toward lesbians and gay men in the United States. *The Journal of Sex Research, 32*(2), 95-105.

HIV/AIDS among Hispanics in the United States. Retrieved from http://www.cdc.gov/hiv/pubs/facts/hispanic.html. (2001). Centers for Disease Control and Prevention, National Center for HIV, STD, and TB Prevention, Division of HIV/AIDS Prevention.

Irwin, P., & Thompson, N.L. (1978). Acceptance of the rights of homosexuals: A social profile. *Journal of Homosexuality, 3*(2), 107-121.

Kurdek, L.A. (1988). Correlates of negative attitudes toward homosexuals in heterosexual college students. *Sex Roles, 18*(11/12), 727-739.

Levitt, E., & Klassen, A.D. (1974). Public attitudes toward homosexuality: Part of the 1970 national survey by the Institute for Sex Research. *Journal of Homosexuality, 1*(1), 29-43.

Marsiglio, W. (1993). Attitudes toward homosexual activity and gays as friends: A national survey of heterosexual 15- to 19-year-old males. *The Journal of Sex Research, 30*(1), 12-17.

Money, J. (1988). *Gay, Straight, and In-Between.* New York: Oxford University Press.

Montgomery, S.S. (2002). *Assessing Latino(a) and non-Hispanic White College Students' Homophobia.* Unpublished doctoral dissertation, Denver University, Denver, Colorado.

National Gay and Lesbian Task Force. Retrieved January 18, 2002 from http://www.ngltf.org.

Pink Pages. (1999). Distributed by Colorado AIDS Project, Denver, Colorado.

Reiter, L. (1991). Developmental origins of antihomosexual prejudice in heterosexual men and women. *Clinical Social Work Journal, 19*(2), 163-175.

Rosenberg, K.P. (1994). Notes and Comments: Biology and Homosexuality. *Journal of Sex and Marital Therapy, 20,* 147-151.

Chapter 11

American Psychiatric Association. (1994). *Diagnostic and Statistical Manual of Mental Disorders, 4th Edition.* Washington, D.C.: APA.

Bolin, A. (1994). *Third Sex, Third Gender.* In Herdt, G. (Editor). New York: Zone Books.

Bornstein, K. (1994). *Gender Outlaw: On Men, Women and the Rest of Us.* New York: Rutledge.

Boswell, H. (1991). The transgender alternative. *Chrysalis Quarterly, 1.*

Bullough, B., & Bullough, V. (1997). Are Transvestites Necessarily Heterosexual? *Archives of Sexual Behavior, 26* (1), 1-12.

Bullough, V. (1991). Transvestism: A Reexamination. *Journal of Psychology and Human Sexuality, 4,* 53-67.

Coleman, E. (1991). Compulsive sexual behavior: New concepts and treatments. *Journal of Psychology & Human Sexuality, 4,* 37-52.

Cooper, A., Scherer, C.R., Boies, S.C., & Gordon, B.L. (April, 1999). Sexuality on the Internet: From Sexual Exploration to Pathological Expression. *Professional Psychology: Research and Practice, 30*(2), 154-164. Retrieved from *APA Journal* http://www.apa.org/journals/pro/pro302154.html

DeAngelis, T. (2000). Is Internet Addiction Real? *Monitor on Psychology, 31*(4), Retrieved from http://www.apa.org/monitor/apr00/addiction.html

Devor, H. (1989). *Gender Blending: Confronting the Limits of Duality.* Bloomington, Ind.: Indiana University Press.

Leiblum, S.R. (1997). Sex and the net: Clinical implications. *Journal of Sex Education and Therapy, 22,* 21-28.

Money, J. (1983). Pairbonding and Limerence. *International Encyclopedia of Psychiatry, Psychology, Psychoanalysis and Neurology, Progress Volume 1.* (B.B. Wolman, Ed.). New York: Macmillan.

Schaeffer, B. (1991). *Loving Me, Loving You.* New York: Harper Collins.

Schifter, J., & Madrigal, J. (1997). The transvestite's lover; identity and behavior. In Bullough, B., Bullough, V., & Elias, J. (Eds.). *Gender Blending.* Amherst, New York: Prometheus.

Watson, M.A., & Dahms, A. (Producers). (1996). *Videocases in Human Sexuality.* Boston: McGraw-Hill.

Whitam, F.L. (1997). Culturally universal aspects of male homosexual transvestites and transsexuals. In Bullough, B., Bullough, V., & Elias, J. (Eds.). *Gender Blending.* Amherst, New York: Prometheus.

Whitam, F.L., & Mathy, R.M. (1986). *Male Homosexuality in Four Societies: Brazil, Guatemala, the Philippines, and the United States.* New York: Prager.

Young, K.S. (August, 1997). Internet addiction: What makes computer-mediated communication habit forming? Paper presented at the 105th Annual Convention of the American Psychological Association, Chicago.

Zilbergeld, B. (1992). *The New Male Sexuality: The Truth About Men, Sex, and Pleasure.* New York: Bantom Books.

Chapter 12

Beitchman, J.H. (1992). A Review of the Long-Term Effects of Child Sexual Abuse. *Child Abuse and Neglect, 16,* 101-119.

Benson, D. (1992). Acquaintance Rape on Campus: A Literature Review. *Journal of American College Health, 40,* 157-165.

Byers, E.S., & Lewis, K. (1988). Dating couples' disagreements over the desired level of sexual intimacy. *Journal of Sex Research, 24,* 15-29.

Crichton, S. (October 25, 1993). Sexual Correctness: Has It Gone Too Far? *Newsweek,* 52-56.

Muehlenhard, C.L., & Cook, S.W. (1988). Men's self-reports of unwanted sexual activity. *Journal of Sex Research, 24,* 58-72.

O'Sullivan, L.F., & Allgeier, E.R. (1998). Feigning Sexual Desire: Consenting to Unwanted Sexual Activity in Heterosexual Dating Relationships. *Journal of Sex Research, 35*(3), 234-243.

O'Sullivan, L.F., & Byers, E.S. (1996). Gender differences in responses to discrepancies in desired level of sexual intimacy. *Journal of Psychology and Human Sexuality, 8,* 49-67.

Poppen, P.J., & Segal, N.J. (1988). The influence of sex and sex role orientation on sexual coercion. *Sex Roles, 19,* 689-701.

Shotland, R.L., & Goodstein, L. (1992). Sexual precedence reduces the perceived legitimacy of sexual arousal: An examination of attribution concerning date rape and consensual sex. *Personality and Social Psychology Bulletin, 18,* 756-764.

Shotland, R.L., & Hunter, B.A. (1995). Women's "token resistant" and compliant sexual behaviors are related to uncertain sexual intentions and rape. *Personality and Social Psychology Bulletin, 21,* 226-236.

Sprecher, S., Hatfield, E., Cortese, A., Potapova, E., & Levitskaya, A. (1994). Token resistance to sexual intercourse and consent to unwanted sexual intercourse: College students' dating experiences in three countries. *Journal of Sex Research, 31,* 125-132.

Zimmerman, R.S., Sprecher, S., Langer, L.M., & Holloway, C.D. (1995). Adolescents' perceived ability to say "no" to unwanted sex. *Journal of Adolescent Research, 10,* 383-399.

Chapter 13

Barbach, L. (1982). *For Each Other: Sharing Sexual Intimacy.* Garden City, New York: Doubleday.

Beck, A.T. (1988). *Love is Never Enough: How Couples Can Overcome Misunderstandings, Resolve Conflicts, and Solve Relationship Problems Through Cognitive Therapy.* New York: Harper & Row.

Heiman, J., & LoPiccolo, J. (1988). *Becoming Orgasmic: A Sexual Growth Program for Women.* Englewood Cliffs, N.J: Prentice Hall.

Hwang, M.Y. (1999). Silence About Sexual Problems Can Hurt Relationships. *Journal of the American Medical Association, 281* (6), 584.

Kaplan, H.S. (1974). *The New Sex Therapy.* New York: Brunner/Mazel.

Kaplan, H.S. (1979). *Disorders of Desire.* New York: Brunner/Mazel.

Kaplan, H.S. (1989). *How To Overcome Premature Ejaculation.* New York: Brunner/Mazel.

Katz, R.C., Gipson, M.T., Kearl, A., & Kriskovich, M. (1989). Assessing Sexual Aversion in College Students: The Sexual Aversion Scale. *Journal of Sex and Marital Therapy, 15,* 135-140.

Masters, W., & Johnson, V. (1966). *Human Sexual Response.* Boston: Little, Brown.

Rowan, E.L. (2000). *The Joy of Self-Pleasuring: Why Feel Guilty About Feeling Good?* Amherst, New York: Prometheus Books.

Schnarch, D. (1997). *Passionate Marriage: Love, Sex, and Intimacy In Emotionally Committed Relationships.* New York: W.W. Norton.

Zilbergeld, B. (1992). *The New Male Sexuality.* New York: Bantam Books.

Chapter 14

Ballard, E. (1995). Attitudes, myths and realities: Helping family and professional caregivers cope with sexuality in the Alzheimer's patient. *Sexuality and Disability, 13*(3), 255-277.

Davidson, S. (1995). Sexuality in the elderly: What is the health professional role? *Perspectives, 19*(2), 6-8.

Eckland, M., & McBride, K. (1997). Sexual health care: The role of the nurse. *Canadian Nurse, 93*(7), 34-37.

Government of Canada. (1998). *Principles of the national framework on aging.* Ottawa.

Jones, H. (1994). Mores and morals. *Nursing Times,90*(47), 55-99.

Karlen, A., & Moglia, R. (1995). Sexuality, aging and the education of health professionals. *Sexuality and Disability, 13*(3), 191-199.

Kobrin Pitzele, S. (1995). Chronic illness, disability and sexuality in people older than fifty. *Sexuality and Disability, 13*(4), 309-325.

Lemon, M.A. (1993). Sexual Counseling and Spinal Cord Injury. *Sexuality and Disability, 11*, 73-97.

Seftel, A.D., Oates, R.D., & Krane, R.J. (1991). Disturbed Sexual Function in Patients With Spinal Cord Disease. *Neurologic Clinics, 9*, 757-778.

Tilley, C. (1996). Sexuality in women with physical disabilities: A Social justice or health issue? *Sexuality and Disability, 14*(2), 139-151.

Chapter 15

Abell, S.C., & Richards, M.H. (1996). The relationship between body shape satisfaction and self-esteem: An investigation of gender and class differences. *Journal of Youth and Adolescence, 25*, 691-703.

Aero, R., & Weiner, E. (1984). Sexual Self-Image Checklist. *The Love Exam.* New York: Quill Books.

Barber, N. (1995). The evolutionary psychology of physical attractiveness: Sexual selection and human morphology. *Ethology and Sociobiology, 16*, 395-424.

Barber, N. (1998a). The slender ideal and eating disorders: An interdisciplinary "telescope" model. *International Journal of Eating Disorders, 23*, 295-307.

Barber, N. (1998b). Secular changes in standards of bodily attractiveness in women: Tests of a reproductive model. *International Journal of Eating Disorders, 23*, 449-454.

Barber, N. (1998c). Secular changes in standards of bodily attractiveness in women: Different masculine and feminine ideals. *The Journal of Psychology, 132*, 87-94.

Barber, N. (1999a). Reproductive and occupational stereotypes of bodily curvaceousness and weight. *The Journal of Social Psychology, 139*, 247-249.

Barber, N. (1999b). Women's dress fashions as a function of reproductive strategy. *Sex Roles, 40*, 459-471.

Barber, N. (2001). Gender Differences in Effects of Mood on Body Image. *Sex Roles, 44*(1/2), 99-108.

Carter, F.A., Bulik, C.M., Lawson, R.H., Sullivan, P.S., & Wilson, J.S. (1996). Effect of mood and food cues on body image in women with bulimia and controls. *International Journal of Eating Disorders, 20,* 65-76.

Gordon, R.A. (1990). *Anorexia nervosa and bulimia: Anatomy of a social epidemic.* Cambridge, Mass.: Basil Blackwell.

King, B.M. (2002). *Human Sexuality Today, Fourth Edition.* Upper Saddle River, N.J.: Prentice Hall.

Myers, P.N., & Biocca, F.A. (1992). The elastic body image: The effect of television advertising and programming on body image distortions in young women. *Journal of Communications, 42,* 108-133.

Pinchas, L., Toner, B.B., Ali, A., Garfinkel, P.E., & Stuckless, N. (1999). The effects of the ideal of female beauty on mood and body satisfaction. *International Journal of Eating Disorders, 25,* 223-226.

Plies, K., & Floorin, I. (1992). Effects of negative mood induction on the body image of restrained eaters. *Psychology and Health, 7,* 235-242.

Silverstein, P., Perdue, L., Peterson, B., Vogel, L., & Fantini, D.A. (1986). Possible causes of the thin standard of bodily attractiveness for women. *International Journal of Eating Disorders, 5,* 907-916.

Silverstein, P., & Perlick, A. (1996). *The cost of competence.* New York: Oxford University Press.

Singh, D. (1993). Adaptive significance of female physical attractiveness: Role of waist-to-hip ratio. *Journal of Personality and Social Psychology, 65,* 293-307.

Stice, E., & Shaw, H.E. (1994). Adverse effects of the media-portrayed thin ideal on women and linkages to bulimic symptomatology. *Journal of Social and Clinical Psychology, 13,* 288-308.

Taylor, M.J., & Cooper, P.J. (1991). An experimental study of the effect of mood on body size perception. *Behaviour, Research and Therapy, 30,* 53-58.

Thompson, J.K. (1990). Body image disturbance: Assessment and treatment. New York: Pergamon.

Chapter 16

Cottler, L.B., Helzer, J.E., & Tipp, J.E. (September-December, 1990). Lifetime patterns of substance use among general population subjects engaging in high risk sexual behaviors: implications for HIV risk. *American Journal of Drug and Alcohol Abuse, 16* (3-4), 207.

Dyer, J.E. (March, 2000). Evolving abuse of GHB in California: Bodybuilding drug to date-rape drug. *Journal of Toxicology: Clinical Toxicology, 38*(2), 184.

Fetro, J.V., Coyle, K.K., & Pham, P. (January, 2001). Health-risk behaviors among middle school students in a large majority-minority school district. *Journal of School Health, 71* (1), 30.

Grossman, S. (December 22, 1991). Undergraduates Drink Heavily, Survey Discloses. *The New York Times,* 46.

Grunbaum, J. A., Kann, L., Kinchen, S.A., Ross, J.G., Gowda, V.R., Collins, J.L., & Kolbe, L.J. (January, 2000). Youth risk behavior surveillance national alternative high school youth risk behavior survey, Unites States, 1998. *Journal of School Health, 70* (1), 5.

Guerra, L.M., Romano, P.S., Samuels, S.J., & Kass, P.H. (November, 2000). Ethnic differences in adolescent substance initiation sequences. *Archives of Pediatrics & Adolescent Medicine,154* (11), 1089.

Kalichman, S.C., Benotsch, E., Rompa, D., Gore-Felton, C., Austin, J., Luke, W., DiFonzo, K., Buckles, J., Kyomugisha, F., & Simpson, D. (February, 2001). Unwanted sexual experiences and sexual risks in gay and bisexual men: associations among revictimization, substance use, and psychiatric symptoms. *The Journal of Sex Research, 38*(1), 1.

O'Connor, M.L. (March-April, 1998). Adolescents with close family relationships have reduced chances of engaging in risky behaviors. *Family Planning Perspectives, 30(*2), 97.

Reinisch, J.M., & Beasley, R. (1990). *The Kinsey Institute's New Report on Sex.* New York: St. Martin's Press.

Staton, M., Leukefeld, C., Logan, T.K., Zimmerman, R., Lynam, D., Milich, R., Martin, C., McClanahan, K., & Clayton, R. (May, 1999). Risky sex behavior and substance use among young adults. *Health and Social Work, 24* (2), 147.

Sofuoglu, M, Brown, S., Dudish-Poulsen, S, & Hatsukami, D.K. (November, 2000). Individual differences in the subjective response to smoked cocaine in humans. *American Journal of Drug and Alcohol Abuse, 26* (4), 591.

Stotland, N.L. (August, 1989). Alcohol and Sex. *Medical Aspects of Human Sexuality*, 42-49.

Taberner, P.V. (1985). *Aphrodisiacs: The Science and the Myth.* Philadelphia: University of Pennsylvania Press.

Weiss, R.D., & Mirin, S.M. (1987). *Cocaine.* Washington D.C.: American Psychiatric Press.

Chapter 17

Abbey, A. (1991). Acquaintance rape and alcohol consumption on college campuses: How are they linked? *Journal of American College Health, 39,* 165-169.

Aral, S., & Holmes, K.K. (1990). Epidemiology of Sexual Behavior and Sexually Transmitted Diseases. In K.K. Homes et al., (Eds.). *Sexually Transmitted Diseases,2nd Ed.* New York: McGraw-Hill.

Burke, D., Brundage, J., Goldenbaum, M., Gardner, L., Peterson, M., Visintine, R., Redfield, R., & Walter Reed Retrovirus Research Group. (1990). Human immunodeficiency virus infections in teenagers: Seroprevalence among applicants for U.S. military service. The Walter Reed Retrovirus Group. *Journal of the American Medical Association, 263*(15), 2074-2077.

Butcher, A.H., Manning, D.T., & O'Neal, E.C. (1991). HIV-Related Sexual Behaviors of College Students. *Journal of American College Health, 40,* 115-118.

Cates, W.J., & Stone, K.M. (1992). Family Planning, Sexually Transmitted Diseases and Contraceptive Choices: A Literature Update. Part 1. *Family Planning Perspectives, 24,* 75-84.

Centers for Disease Control. (1990a). *Division of STD/HIV Prevention Annual Report, 1989.* Atlanta, Ga: U.S. Department of Health and Human Services.

Centers for Disease Control. (1990b). Progress toward achieving the 1990 objectives for the nation for sexually transmitted diseases. *The Journal of the American Medical Association. Morbidity and Mortality Weekly Report, 263*(8), 1057-1058.

Centers for Disease Control. (1992). *STD Statistics.* Atlanta: U.S. Department of Health and Human Services/Public Health Service.

Connell, D., Turner, R., & Mason, E. (1985). Summary of findings of the school health education evaluation: Health promotion effectiveness, implementation, and costs. *Journal of School Health, 55*(8), 316-321.

Elkind, D. (1984). Teenage thinking: Implications for health care. *Pediatric Nursing, 10,* 383-385.

Fennell, R. (1991). Evaluating the effectiveness of a credit semester course on AIDS among college students. *Journal of Health Education, 22*(1), 35-41.

Gayle, H., Keeling, R., Garcia-Tunon, M., Kilbourne, B., Narkunas, J., Ingram, F., Rogers, M., & Curran, J. (1990). Prevalence of the human immunodeficiency virus among university students. *The New England Journal of Medicine, 323*(22), 1538-1541.

Greenberg, J., Magder, L., & Aral, S. (1992). Age at First Coitus: A Marker for Risky Sexual Behavior in Women. *Sexually Transmitted Diseases, 19,* 331-334.

Hingson, R., Strunin, L., Berlin, B., & Heeren, T. (1990). Belief about AIDS, use of alcohol and drugs, and unprotected sex among Massachusetts' adolescents. *American Journal of Public Health, 80*(3), 295-299.

Joffe, G.P. (1992) Multiple Partners and Partner Choice as Risk Factors for Sexually Transmitted Disease Among Female College Students. *Sexually Transmitted Diseases, 19,* 272-278.

McGregor, J.A., French, J.I., & Spencer, N.E. (1988). Prevention of Sexually Transmitted Diseases in Women. *The Journal of Reproductive Medicine, 33,* 109-118.

Moran, J.S. (1989). The Impact of Sexually Transmitted Diseases on Minority Populations. *Public Health Reports, 104,* 560-564.

Novick, L. (1991). HIV seroprevalence surveys: Impetus for preventive activities. *American Journal of Public Health, 81,* Supplement, 61-64.

Pepe, M.V., Sanders, D.W., & Symons, C.W. (1993). Sexual Behaviors of University Freshmen and the Implications for Sexuality Educators. *Journal of Sex Education and Therapy, 19*(1), 20-30.

Pestrak, V., & Martin, D. (1985). Cognitive development and aspects of adolescent sexuality. *Adolescence, 20,* 981-987.

Project Direction. (1989). *Sex and substance abuse: What are the links?* Module Eta Sigma Gamma Health Science Honorary National Office, Ball State University, Muncie, Indiana. Lindsay, G., Project Director. Funded by U.S. Department of Education, FIPSE.

Rosenbaum, E., & Kandel, D. (1990). Early onset of adolescent sexual behavior and drug involvement. *Journal of Marriage and the Family, 52,* 783-798.

Strong, B., DeVault, C., & Sayad, B.W. (1999). *Human Sexuality: Diversity in Contemporary America.* Mountain View, Cal.: Mayfield Publishing Co.

Tucker, V., & Cho, C. (1991). AIDS and adolescents: How can you help them reduce their risk? *Postgraduate Medicine, 89*(3), 49-53.

Chapter 18

Becerra, R. (1988). The Mexican-American Family. In C. Mindel et al., (Eds.). *Ethnic Families in America: Patterns and Variations.* New York: Elsevier North Holland, Inc.

Belcastro, B. (1985). Sexual Behavior Differences Between Black and White Students. *Journal of Sex Research, 21,* 56-67.

Bond, S.L. (1999). State Laws Criminalizing Female Circumcision: A Violation of the Equal Protection Clause of the Fourteenth Amendment. *John Marshall Law Review, 32,* 353-380.

Bond, S., & Cash, T.F. (1992). Black Beauty - Skin Color and Body Images Among African-American College Women. *Journal of Applied Social Psychology, 22,* 874-888.

Chief FAMA. (April-June, 2000). Female Genital Mutilation. *Odidere Orunmila Gazette, 2*(2), 1-2.

Fernandez-Romano, C. (1999). The Banning of Female Circumcision: Cultural Imperialism or a Triumph for Women's Rights? *Temple International and Comparative Law Journal, 13,*137-161.

Gunning, I.R. (1999). Global Feminism at the Local Level: Criminal and Asylum Laws Regarding Female Genital Surgeries. *Journal of Gender, Race, and Justice, 3,* 45-62.

Mead, M. (1963). *Sex and Temperament in Three Primitive Societies.* New York: William Morrow and Co.

Padilla, E.R., & O'Grady, K.E. (1987). Sexuality Among Mexican Americans: A Case of Sexual Stereotyping. *Journal of Personality and Social Psychology, 52,* 5-10.

Price, J.H., & Miller, P.A. (1984). Sexual Fantasies of Black and White College Students. *Psychological Reports,54,* 1007-1014.

Suggs, D.N., & Miracle, A.W. (Eds.). (1993). *Culture and Human Sexuality.* Pacific Grove, Calif.: Brooks/Cole Publishing Co.

Sussman, E. (1998). Contending With Culture: An Analysis of the Female Genital Mutilation Act of 1996. *Cornell International Law Journal, 31,* 193-250.

Watson, M.A. (2001). Female Circumcision from Africa to the Americas: Slavery to the Present. Paper presented at the 44th Annual Meeting of the African Studies Association, Houston, Texas.

Watson, M.A., & K'okul, R. (Producers). (1999). *Rites of Passage: Videocases of Traditional African Peoples.* Englewood Cliffs, N.J.: Prentice-Hall.

Chapter 19

Abel, G., Becker, J., & Cunningham-Rather, J. (1984). Complications, consent, and cognitions in sex between children and adults. *International Journal of Law and Psychiatry, 7,* 89-103.

Glass, C., Merluzzi, T., Biever, J., & Larsen, K. (1982). Cognitive assessment of social anxiety: Development and validation of a self-statement questionnaire. *Cognitive Therapy and Research, 6,* 37-55.

Jones, F.D., & Koshes, R.J. (1985). Homosexuality and the Military. *American Journal of Psychiatry, 152,* 16-21.

Laws, R. (Ed.). (1989). *Relapse prevention with sex offenders.* New York: The Guilford Press.

Mayer, A. (1988). *Sex offenders.* Holmes Beach, Fla.: Learning Publications.

Murphy, W. (1990). Assessment and modification of cognitive distortions in sex offenders. In W. Marshall, D. Laws, & H. Barbaree (Eds.). *Handbook of sexual assault.* New York: Plenum Press.

National Gay and Lesbian Task Force. Retrieved from http://www.ngltf.org

Neidigh, L., & Krop, H. (1992). Cognitive Distortions Among Child Sexual Offenders. *Journal of Sex Education and Therapy, 18*(3), 208-215.

Rio, L.M. (1991). Psychological and Sociological Research and the Decriminalization or Legalization of Prostitution. *Archives of Sexual Behavior, 20,* 205-218.

Russell, A., & Mohr-Trainor, C. (1984). *Trends in child abuse and neglect: A national perspective.* Denver: American Humane Association.

Chapter 20

Bogaert, A.F., Turkovich, D.A., & Hafer, C.L. (1993). A Content Analysis of *Playboy* Centrefolds from 1953 through 1990: Changes in Explicitness, Objectification, and Model's Age. *Journal of Sex Research, 30,* 135-139.

Brown, J.D., Childers, K.W., & Waszak, C.S. (1990). Television and adolescent sexuality. *Journal of Adolescent Health Care, 11,* 62-70.

Edgley, C. (1989). Commercial Sex: Pornography, Prostitution, and Advertising. In K. McKinney & S. Sprecher (Eds.). *Human Sexuality: The Societal and Interpersonal Context.* Norwood, N.J.: Ablex Publishing Corp.

Greenberg, B.S., Brown, J.D., & Buerkel-Rothfuss, N.L. (1993). *Media, sex, and the adolescent.* New Jersey: Hampton Press.

Hyde, J.S., & DeLameter, J. (1997). *Understanding human sexuality, 6th Edition.* New York: McGraw-Hill.

Kaiser Family Foundation. (1998). *Kaiser Family Foundation and YM Magazine national survey of teens: Teens talk about dating, intimacy, and their sexual experiences.* Menlo Park, Cal.

Kunkel, D., Cope, K.M., & Biely, E. (1999). Sexual Messages on Television: Comparing Findings From Three Studies. *The Journal of Sex Research, 36*(3), 230-236.

Lowry, D., & Towles, D. (1989). Prime Time TV Portrayals of Sex, Contraception, and Venereal Disease. *Journalism Quarterly, 66,* 347-352.

Chapter 21

Alter, J.S. (1982). *Teaching parents to be the primary sexuality educators of their children.* Bethesda, Md.: Math Tech.

Baldwin, J.I., Whiteley, S., & Baldwin, J.D. (1990). Changing AIDS- and fertility-related behavior: The effectiveness of sexual education. *The Journal of Sex Research, 27,* 245-262.

Byrne, D., & Kelley, K. (1989). Basing legislative action on research data: Prejudice, prudence, and empirical limitations. In D. Zillman & J. Bryant (Eds.). *Pornography: Research advances and policy considerations.* Hillsdale, N.J.: Lawrence Erlbaum.

Calderone, M.S., & Johnson, E.W. (1989). *The Family Book About Sexuality.* New York: Harper & Row.

Calderone, M.S., & Ramey, J.W. (1983). *Talking with Your Child About Sex: Questions and Answers for Children from Birth to Puberty.* New York: Random House.

Carton, J., & Carton, J. (1971). Evaluation of a sex education program for children and their parents: Attitude and interactional changes. *The Family Coordinator, 20,* 377-386.

Casey, S., & Peterson, L. (July/August, 1985). Sex education for parents. *Children Today,* 11-15.

Cohen, G., Byrne, C., Hay, J., & Schmuck, M.L. (1994). Assessing the impact of an interdisciplinary workshop in human sexuality. *Journal of Sex Education and Therapy, 20*(1),56-68.

Davis, C., & Bauserman, R. (1989). Exposure to sexually explicit materials: An attitude change perspective. In D. Zillman & J. Bryant (Eds.). *Pornography: Research advances and policy considerations.* Hillsdale, N.J.: Lawrence Erlbaum.

Dawson, D.A. (1986). The effects of sex education on adolescent behavior. *Family Planning Perspectives, 18,* 162-170.

DiClimente, R.J., Ries, C., Stoller, E., Straits, C., Olivia, G., Hasskin, J., & Sutherford, G. (1989). Evaluation of school-based AIDS education curricula in San Francisco. *The Journal of Sex Research, 26,* 188-198.

Eisen, M., & Zellmen, G. (1987). Changes in incidence of sexual intercourse of unmarried teenagers following a community-based sex education program. *The Journal of Sex Research,23,* 527-533.

Family Life Education Program Development Project. (1979). *Family life and sex education: A summary of facts and findings.* Santa Cruz, Calif.

Fisher, W., Grenier, G., Watter, W., Lamont, J., Cohen, M., & Askwith, J. (1988). Students' sexual knowledge, attitudes towards sex, and willingness to treat sexual concerns. *Journal of Medical Education, 63,* 379-385.

Furtensberg, F.F., Moore, K.A., & Peterson, J.L. (1985). Sex education and sexual experiences among adolescents. *American Journal of Public Health, 75,* 1331-1332.

Kilman, P.R., Wanlass, R.L, Sabalis, R.F., & Sullivan, B. (1981). Sex education: A Review of its effects. *Archives of Sexual Behavior, 10,* 177-205.

King, B.M., & Anderson, P.B. (January/February, 1994). A failure of HIV education: Sex can be more important than a long life. *Journal of Health Education, 25,* 13-18.

Kirby, D. (1984). *Sexuality education: An evaluation of programs and their effects.* Santa Cruz, Calif.: Network Publications.

Kirby, D. (1985). Sexuality education: A more realistic view of its effects. *Journal of School Health, 55,* 421-424.

Kisker, E.E. (1985). Teenagers talk about sex, pregnancy, and contraception. *Family Planning Perspectives, 17,* 83-90.

Koblinsky, S., & Atkinson, J. (1982). Parental plans for children's sex education. *Family Relations, 31,* 29-35.

Linz, D., Donnerstein, E., & Penrod, S. (1987). Findings and recommendations of the Attorney General's Commission on Pornography: Do the psychological facts fit the political fury? *American Psychologist, 42,* 946-953.

Page, S. (1989). Misrepresentation of pornography research: Psychology's role. *American Psychologist, 44,* 578-580.

Penrod, S., & Linz, D. (1984). Using psychological research on violent pornography to inform legal change. In N. Malamuch & E. Donnerstein (Eds.). *Pornography and sexual aggression.* New York: Academic Press.

Reinisch, J.M. (1990). *The Kinsey Institute New Report on Sex: What You Must Know to be Sexually Literate.* New York: St. Martin's Press.

Rozema, H.J. (1986). Defensive communication climate as a barrier to sex education in the home. *Family Relations, 35,* 531-537.

Sherr, L. (1990). Fear arousal and AIDS: Do shock tactics work? *AIDS, 4,* 361-364.

Story, M.D. (1979). A longitudinal study of the effects of a university human sexuality course on sexual attitudes. *The Journal of Sex Research, 15,* 184-204.

Stout, J.W., & Rivara, F.P. (1989). Schools and sex education: Does it work? *Pediatrics, 83,* 375-379.

Strouse, J., & Fabes, R.A. (1985). Formal versus informal sources of sex education: Competing forces in the sexual socialization of adolescents. *Adolescence, 20,* 251-262.

Walters, A.S. (1994). Using visual media to reduce homophobia: A classroom demonstration. *Journal of Sex Education and Therapy, 20*(2), 92-100.

Zillman, D. (1989). Effects of prolonged consumption of pornography. In D. Zillman & J. Bryant (Eds.). *Pornography: Research advances and policy considerations.* Hillsdale, N.J.: Lawrence Erlbaum.

GLOSSARY

accumulative: to grow, forming an increasing quantity

actual use failure rate: a measure of how often in one year a birth control method can be expected to fail when human error and technical failure are considered

AIDS: acquired immunodeficiency syndrome; a fatal disease caused by a virus that is transmitted through the exchange of bodily fluids, primarily in sexual activity and intravenous drug use

amniocentesis: a process whereby medical problems with a fetus can be determined, by inserting a needle in the amniotic sac, withdrawing amniotic fluid, and examining fetal cells

anal intercourse: insertion of the penis into the rectum of a partner

androgynous: possessing high frequencies of both masculine and feminine behaviors and traits

anorexia: lack of appetite and inability to eat, often based on abnormal psychological attitudes

antagonist: a drug that counteracts the effects of another drug

aphrodisiacs: food or chemicals to foster sexual arousal; more myth than fact

artificial insemination: injection of the sperm cells of a male into a woman's vagina, with the intentions of conceiving a child

asexuality: a condition characterized by a low interest in sex

autoerotic asphyxiation (asphyxiophilia): arousal from masturbation while hanging oneself; often ends in death

bar girls: prostitutes who hang around in bars soliciting clients

behavior therapy: therapy that uses techniques to change patterns of behavior; often employed in sex therapy

berdache: anthropological term for cross-dressing in other cultures

bestiality: sexual arousal from contact with an animal

birth control: any method or device to prevent pregnancy

bisexual: sexual activity with or attraction to members of both sexes

bondage: a sadomasochistic activity involving physical restraint

bondage and discipline (B and D): sadomasochistic activities involving physical restraint, domination, and humiliation

brothel prostitute: woman who works in a house of prostitution; customers select from among a group of women

call boys: male prostitutes who work on their own through an agency

call girls: prostitutes who arrange for their sexual contacts by telephone

case study: an in-depth look at a particular individual

cervical cap: a birth control device that is shaped like a large thimble and fits over the cervix

cervix: lower neck of the uterus that extends into the back part of the vagina

chlamydia: a common bacterial sexually transmitted disease that can be treated with antibiotics

circumcision: in the male, surgical removal of the foreskin from the penis

clitoridectomy: surgical removal of the clitoris, practiced routinely in some cultures

cohabitation: living together and sharing sex without marrying

coitus: penis in vagina intercourse

coitus interruptus: a method of birth control in which the penis is withdrawn from the vagina prior to ejaculation

coming out: to acknowledge to oneself and others that one is lesbian, gay, or bisexual

concomitant: something occurring with something else

condom: a sheath worn over the penis during intercourse that collects semen and helps prevent disease transmission

contraceptive: a device used to prevent conception

coprophilia: sexual arousal connected to feces

cunnilingus: oral stimulation of the clitoris, vaginal opening, or other parts of the vulva

curvaceous: having curves suggestive of a well-developed female figure

curvilinear: forming or moving in a curved line

cystitis: a nonsexually transmitted infection of the urinary bladder

Depo-Provera: an injectable form of progestin that can prevent pregnancy for three months

desire phase: H.S. Kaplan's term for the psychological interest in sex that precedes a physiological, sexual arousal

diaphragm: a birth control method; a latex rubber cup, filled with spermicide, that covers the cervix

dysfunction: condition in which the body does not function as expected or desired during sex

dyspareunia: persistent genital pain related to sexual activity

ectopic pregnancy: a pregnancy that begins other than in the uterus, usually in the fallopian tube

ejaculation: muscular expulsion of semen from the penis

emission: in males, the release of fluid from the opening of the penis, usually ejaculatory fluid

erogenous zone: any area of the body that is sensitive to sexual arousal

erotica: artistic representations of nudity or sexual activity

escort services: a service in the yellow pages for escorts for persons for various functions, often a front for prostitution

ethnocentrism: a belief in the superiority of one's own group and a tendency to view other groups in terms of one's own culture

exhibitionism: exposing genital to others for sexual pleasure

explicit: fully and clearly expressed

fellatio: oral stimulation of the penis

female condom: a birth control method; a lubricated polyurethane pouch that is inserted into the vagina for intercourse to collect semen and help prevent disease transmission

female sexual arousal disorder: lack of lubrication during arousal and intercourse

fetishism: sexual arousal triggered by objects not usually considered to be sexual, i.e., shoes, underwear

flaccid: the non-erect state of the penis

foreplay: sensual and sexual activities shared in early stages of sexual arousal, prior to intercourse

frequency: rate of occurrence of an event

frotteurism: gaining sexual gratification from pressing or rubbing one's genitals against others, usually in a crowded setting

Gamma Hydroxy Butyrate (GHB): GHB is sometimes characterized as a "date-rape" drug. It is odorless and colorless and has been studied for its ability to induce short-term coma and possible surgical anesthesia. It is not illegal under federal law.

gay: persons who have a predominantly same-gender sexual attraction; more often applied to men

gender dysphoria: a degree of discomfort with one's identity as male or female

gender identity: a person's inner experience of gender

gender role: the outward expression of gender; how masculine or feminine one behaves

gigolo: a male prostitute, usually for wealthy older women

gonorrhea: bacterial STD causing urethral pain and discharge; can be treated with antibiotics

Grafenberg (G-) spot: a vaginal area that some researchers feel is particularly sensitive to sexual stimulation

hallucinations: a sensory experience of something that does not exist outside the mind

herpes: viral STD characterized by painful sores on the sex organs

heterosexual: attractions or activities between males and females

homophobia: negative attitudes and irrational fears relating to gay men and/or lesbians and their lifestyles

homosexual: attraction or activities between members of the same gender

human immunodeficiency virus (HIV): the virus that initially attacks the human immune system, causing HIV disease and eventually AIDS

human papilloma virus (HPV) or genital warts: a viral STD that later increases risks of certain malignancies

hustlers: men who engage in prostitution with male customers

hypoactive sexual desire disorder: loss of interest and pleasure in sexually arousing stimuli

implicit: implied rather than expressly stated

incest: sexual activity between closely related family members

incidence: the rate of occurrence of an event

infantilism: a paraphilia in which arousal occurs while being diapered or treated in a baby-like manner

intrauterine device (IUD): birth control method involving the insertion of a small plastic device into the uterus

in vitro fertilization (IVF): a process whereby the union of the sperm and egg occurs outside the mother's body

klismaphilia: sexual arousal through receiving enemas

lesbian: females who have a predominantly same-gender sexual attraction

lovemap: a formed idea, usually in early childhood, of one's most arousing stimuli

male erectile disorder: difficulty achieving or maintaining an erection with a partner

masochist: a person becoming sexually aroused from experiencing mental or physical pain or humiliation

masturbation: stimulating one's sexual organs for pleasure

monogamous: sharing sexual relations with only one person

natural childbirth: a birthing process that encourages the mother to minimize medical intervention, particularly medications, during childbirth

natural family planning (NFP): a birth control method of scheduling intercourse in which fertile days are identified by the appearance and consistency of cervical mucus

necrophilia: sexual activity with a dead body

neoplasia: the formation and growth of new tissue; tumor growth

Norplant: contraceptive method in which hormone-releasing cylinders are surgically inserted under the skin

orgasm: a rush of pleasurable physical sensation in men and women associated with the release of physical tension

paraphilia: sexual arousal to an object or person apart from the norm

paraplegic: a person paralyzed in the legs, and sometimes pelvic area, as the result of injury to the spinal cord

pedophilia: child sexual abuse

pelvic inflammatory disease (PID): a chronic and painful internal infection associated with occurrences of sexually transmitted diseases or IUD use; may lead to sterility

penile strain gauge: a device placed on the penis to measure changes in size due to sexual arousal

penis: male sexual organ that can become erect when stimulated; it passes urine and sperm to the outside of the body

pimps: men who serve as agents for female prostitutes and live from their earnings

plethysmograph: a laboratory measuring device that charts physiological changes over time by inserting a probe in the vagina to measure lubrication and arousal, or attached to a penile strain gauge to measure penile arousal

polygamy: the practice, in many cultures, of being married to more than one spouse

pornography: photographs, films, or literature intended to be sexually arousing through explicit depiction of sexual activity

premature ejaculation: difficulty men experience in controlling the ejaculatory reflex, resulting in rapid ejaculation

promiscuity: sharing casual sexual activity with many different partners

prurient: characterized by lewdness, baseness, immorality

pubococcygeus (PC) muscle: part of the musculature of the vagina that is involved in orgasm

quadriplegic: a person paralyzed in the upper and lower body as the result of spinal cord injury

rhythm method: a natural method of birth control that depends on awareness of the woman's menstrual and fertility cycle

RU486: a progesterone antagonist used as a postcoital contraceptive

rubber dam/dental dam: a piece of rubber material, such as used in dental work, placed over the genitals during oral sex

sadism: sexual arousal depends on causing mental or physical pain or humiliation

scores: in prostitution, male customers of male prostitutes

sequelae: an abnormal condition resulting from a previous disease

sexual addiction: the inability to regulate one's sexual behavior

sexual aversion disorder: avoidance or fears of sexual expression

sexual harassment: unwanted sexual advances or coercion that can occur in the workplace or other settings

sodomy: general term used legally to describe any type of deviant sexual intercourse, particularly anal sex; these particular laws are often enforced discriminately against particular groups, such as gay males

spermicidal jelly (cream): sperm-killing chemical in a gel base or cream, used with other contraceptives such as diaphragms

sponge: a birth control device; a spongy disk that holds a spermicide and fits over the cervix

statutory rape: a legal term used to indicate sexual activity when one partner is under the age of consent; in most states that age is 18

sterilization: a procedure by which a person is rendered infertile or unable to reproduce

straight: slang term for heterosexual

streetwalkers: prostitutes who solicit customers on the streets

surrogate: substitute, someone taking the place of someone else

syphilis: STD characterized by four stages, beginning with the appearance of a chancre

theoretical failure rate: a measure of how often in a year a birth control method can be expected to fail when used without user error or technical problems

Toxic Shock Syndrome (TSS): a sometimes fatal disease associated with the use of tampons during menstruation

transsexuals: persons who feel as if they should have the body of the opposite sex

transvestite: a person who dresses in, and receives arousal by, clothing of the opposite sex

urophilia: sexual arousal connected with urine or urination

vaginismus: involuntary spasms of the vaginal musculature, making intercourse painful

vasectomy: a surgical cutting and tying of the vas deferens to induce permanent male sterilization

virgin: an individual who has never had sexual intercourse

voyeurism: sexual gratification from viewing others who are nude, or who are engaging in sexual activities

zoophilia: sexual arousal from contact with an animal

NATIONWIDE RESOURCES

AIDS Action Committee
Many links to additional information
about AIDS.
131 Clarendon Street
Boston, MA, 02116
617-437-6200
www.aac.org

AIDS Hotline
Center for Disease Control
Information about the AIDS epidemic.
800-342-AIDS
www.cdc.gov/hiv/pubs/facts.htm

AIDS Law Project
122 Boye Street
Jamaica Plains, MA, 02112
617-522-3003

**American Association for Marriage
and Family Therapy (AAMFT)**
Listing of therapists who specialize in
marriage and family therapy.
1133 15th Street, NW, Suite 300
Washington, DC, 20005-2710
202-452-0109
www.aamft.org

American Cancer Society
Dedicated to helping persons and their
supporters who face cancer by
supporting research, patient services,
early detection, treatment, and
education.
1599 Clifton Rd. NE
Altanta, GA, 80329
800-ACS-2345
www.cancer.org

**American Psychological Association
(APA)**
Professional organization of
psychologists.
750 First Street, NE
Washington, DC, 20002-4242
800-374-2721
www.apa.org

Center for Disease Control (CDC)
National STD Hotline
800-227-8922

Center for Women Policy Studies
Organization dedicated to promote
justice and equality for women.
1211 Connecticut Ave. NW, Suite 312
Washington, DC, 20036
202-872-1770
www.centerwomenpolicy.org/

**Circumcision Information and
Resource Pages**
www.cirp.org/cirp

**Gay and Lesbian Advocates
and Defenders (GLAD)**
Nonprofit, public interest legal
organization to achieve full equality and
justice for lesbian, gay, bisexual, and
HIV or AIDS-affected persons.
294 Washington Street, Suite 301
Boston, MA, 02108
617-426-1350
www.glad.org/

The Kinsey Institute for Research in Sex, Gender, and Reproduction
To promote interdisciplinary research and scholarship in the fields of human sexuality, gender, and reproduction.
Morrison Hall, 313
Indiana University
Bloomington, Indiana, 47405
812-855-7686
www.indiana.edu/~kinsey/

Multi-Focus, Inc.
Films and other visual media for sexuality education.
415-673-5100

National Gay and Lesbian Task Force
Information concerning the gay and lesbian movement at local, state, and national levels.
1700 Kalorama Road, NW
Washington, DC, 20009-2624
202-332-6483
www.ngltf.org/

National Organization for Women (NOW)
Movement dedicated to making legal, political, social, and economic changes in society to eliminate sexism.
733 15th Street, NW, 2nd Floor
Washington, DC, 20005
202-628-8NOW
www.now.org

Planned Parenthood Federation of America
Information on birth control and disease prevention methods. Confidential information and assistance.
810 Seventh Ave.
New York, NY, 10019
212-541-7800
www.plannedparenthood.org/index.html

Project Inform
National nonprofit organization working to provide information on the diagnosis and treatment of AIDS.
205 13th Street, #2001
San Francisco, CA, 94103
800-822-7422
www.projinf.org/

Sex Information and Education Council of the United States (SIECUS)
Nonprofit organization developing and disseminating information promoting comprehensive education about sexuality.
130 W. 42nd Street, Suite 350
New York, NY, 10036
212-819-9770
www.siecus.org/feedback.html

Society for the Scientific Study of Sexuality (SSSS)
Professional organization promoting advancement of research and study of human sexuality.
P.O. Box 416
Allentown, PA, 18105
610-530-2483
www.ssc.wisc.edu/ssss